Ascensions on High in Jewish Mysticism: Pillars, Lines, Ladders

Moshe Idel

 CEU PRESS

Central European University Press
Budapest   New York

Published in 2005 by

CENTRAL EUROPEAN UNIVERSITY PRESS

An imprint of the
Central European University Share Company
Nádor utca 11, H-1051 Budapest, Hungary
Tel: +36-1-327-3138 or 327-3000
Fax: +36-1-327-3183
E-mail: ceupress@ceu.hu
Website: www.ceupress.com

400 West 59th Street, New York NY 10019, USA
Tel: +1-212-547-6932
Fax: +1-212-548-4607
E-mail: mgreenwald@sorosny.org

Published with the support of Pasts, Inc. Center for Historical Studies

ISBN 963 7326 02 2 cloth
ISBN 963 7326 03 0 paperback
ISSN 1786-1438
Pasts Incorporated: CEU Studies in the Humanities

Pasts Incorporated
CEU STUDIES IN THE HUMANITIES

Library of Congress Cataloging-in-Publication Data

Idel, Moshe, 1947–
Ascensions on high in Jewish mysticism : pillars, lines, ladders / by Moshe Idel.
    p. cm.—(Pasts incorporated)
Includes bibliographical references and index.
ISBN 9637326022 (hardbound)—ISBN 9637326030 (pbk.)
1. Cabala—History. 2. Ascension of the soul. 3. Columns—Religious aspects—
Judaism. 4. Mysticism—Judaism. 5. Hasidism. I. Title. II. Series.

BM526.I296 2005
296.7'1—dc22

                    2004028552

Printed in Hungary by
Akadémiai Nyomda, Martonvásár

ASCENSIONS ON HIGH
IN JEWISH MYSTICISM

Pasts Incorporated
CEU Studies in the Humanities

Volume II

Series Editors:
Sorin Antohi and László Kontler

Pasts Incorporated
CEU STUDIES IN THE HUMANITIES

Table of Contents

Preface

When Sorin Antohi kindly invited me to deliver the Ioan P. Culianu lectures at the Central European University in Budapest, the question was not whether or not to accept, but rather what would be the best subject matter. Psychanodia emerged naturally as a topic due to the centrality of this issue in Culianu's opus and because it remains on the margins of the study of Kabbalah and Hasidism. In fact, the first time I came across Culianu's name, I was writing a section of a book in which I addressed the ascent of the soul, and at the last moment, I read his *Psychanodia* and quoted it. In one of his last books, *Out of this World*, he referred to that section of mine, and this instance of inter-quotation prepared the ground for my choice of topic for the lecture series. In fact, chapter four of this book was delivered as a lecture at a conference organized in Paris in 1992 in Culianu's memory, appears here in an expanded version in English, and was translated, in a shorter form, into Romanian several years ago.

There is another dimension implicit in these lectures that goes beyond our common Moldavian background, our common interest in questions concerning experiences of ecstasy and psychanodia, about which we wrote in parallel in the late 1970s and 1980s, and our interest in the theories of Mircea Eliade, another scholar who contributed to some issues discussed in the following pages. The lectures I delivered represent for me a tribute to the memory of a good friend and of someone who dreamed of studying Kabbalah. I imagine that he would have written about these issues had the terror of history and the wickedness of man not forced him to pursue another scholarly and geographical direction. I tried to think in accordance with the categories of his thought and to highlight the potential contributions of his distinctions to a better understanding of some aspects of Jewish mysticism. In a way, I hope that by rethinking some issues as though through his eyes or mind, I may introduce him to scholars who would otherwise miss his thought.

After Culianu's tragic death, I had the pleasure to meet his family in Bucharest: his mother Elena, his sister Tereza and his brother-in-law Dan Petrescu. For them Nene was much more than the academic star abroad, admired now by so many colleagues in Romania and world-wide; his was also and primarily an immense personal loss. I cherished very much the nocturnal discussions in their apartment, during which memories of Ioan mingled with my initiation to the intricacies of post-Ceauşescu Romania and the more recent cultural events in the country. Their hospitality and friendship meant very much to me.

I would like to thank Sorin Antohi for taking the initiative to establish this series of lectures, for arranging their publication, and for the warm friendship and hospitality that both he and Mona extended during my stay in Budapest for the lectures. Without his invitation, this book may never have been written, or alternatively, it would have been much longer and even less accessible than it is now.

Introduction

1. STUDYING RELIGION

There is no single method with which one can comprehensively approach "religion."[1] All methods generate approximations based on insights, on implied psychologies, sometimes even on explicit theologies and ideologies. They assist us in understanding one or more aspects of a complex phenomenon that, in itself, cannot be explained by any single method. "Religion" is a conglomerate of ideas, cosmologies, beliefs, institutions, hierarchies, elites and rites that vary with time and place, even when one "single" religion is concerned. The methodologies available take one or two of these numerous aspects into consideration, reducing religion's complexity to a rather simplistic unity.

The ensuing conclusion is a recommendation for methodological eclecticism. This recommendation is made not only due to the complexity of an evasive phenomenon (itself to a great extent the result of a certain definition) but also as a way to correct the mistakes and misunderstandings at which someone arrived using only one method. At least in principle, the inherent shortcomings of one method may be overcome by resorting to another. Since religion cannot be reified as an entity standing by itself, it would be wise not to subject it to analyses based on a single methodology.

This does not mean that I propose the reduction of religion to disparate and unconnected "moments." But, for example, by emphasizing the differences between elite and popular religion, it may be assumed that specific religious ideas are more dominant in one elite than in another, or than in the masses. Sociological tools—sociology of religion or of knowledge—might help identify the background of the exponents of a certain set of ideas, which then might be compared to the social background of another elite. In both cases, there is nevertheless the need to explore religious ideas, which may lose their original affinity with a certain elite and migrate socially and geographically to other elites in other cultural centers. In such cases, theories on reception, the history of ideas, intellectual history or cultural history might be more helpful in accounting for these developments. Or, to take another example, the emergence of ideas, concepts or beliefs might be investigated as the result of experiences, calling for the use of psychological theories, but attempts to study individuals within their changing environmental circumstances also might help explain these processes. Additionally, cognitive approaches might elucidate the emergence of a particular set of religious ideas, beliefs and rituals from the range of human spiritual possibilities. Religion, however, is also a philosophical system that does not necessarily remain the patrimony of a small number of people or social group. Much of religion is connected to processes of transmission and reception, of adaptation, of inclusion and exclusion that take place within both homogenous and heterogeneous groups. This is the reason why, for example, methods related to oral and written culture, esotericism and exotericism, initiation and social regulation of behavior might be helpful in describing religion as a social phenomenon. Each approach may illumine a moment of religious life, while others remain beyond its scope.

This variety of problems and methods is more pertinent, to be sure, to some forms of religion than to others. Archaic religions, which developed within homogenous groups in isolated geographical and cultural areas, without the complexity introduced by interactions with other religions or cultures and without the specific problems introduced by written transmission and the importance of textuality, may require somewhat less complex tools. This is not because such religions are simpler: some are quite ample bodies of knowledge and deeds. However, fewer dynamic changes and interactions occur under stable circumstances; if limited to a certain geographical area, syncretistic processes that complicate analysis might be less pertinent. So, for example, the conceptual content, history and dissemination of Manichaenism—a world religion that flourished in diverse places, involving interaction and syncretism, and the texts of which are written in a dozen languages (Aramaic, Coptic, Chinese, Turkish, Persian, Greek, Latin, et cetera)—pose problems that are unknown to students of Puritan Protestantism, Mormonism or Quakerism. To put it in more general terms, cosmopolitan religions by the very nature of their expansion and reception are more variegated than and differ sociologically from the religions of specific tribes. The linguistic and historical skills necessary to understand a cosmopolitan religion dramatically diverge from those required for a particularistic one, like Mormonism or the Amish. The complexity of cosmopolitan religions is so great that I wonder to what extent general terms like Judaism, Christianity and Hinduism, used to denote religions that spread to so many regions and interacted with so many cultures, are viable. I wonder if it would not be better to parcel them into smaller segments, like geographical regions, historical periods or specific trends.

These problems, however, touch upon just one set of questions. Others enter the study of religion due to the characteristics of the scholar rather than those of the phenomenon. To define this problem blatantly from the very beginning, scholarship on religion is rarely an innocent and detached enterprise. Individual scholars, and sometimes entire schools of scholars, are entities active in history, space and specific social and political circumstances that affect their approaches and sometimes dictate the direction of research and even its results. This is especially true in extreme cases, such as under communism or other forms of dictatorship. It suffices to compare Henry Corbin's interest in forms of religious syncretism evident in his studies on Sufism and Ismailiyah undertaken during the regime of the Iranian Shah to contemporary Iranian scholarship with its emphasis on puristic Shiite orthodoxy. Even in less extreme cases, scholars operate within a certain society, or tribe, in which taboos exist that do not necessarily depend upon the political regime. Any attempt to question the uniqueness of the Qur'an by a Muslim university scholar, even in a democratic society like Israel, will result in the sharp rejection of that scholar by his Muslim religious group, and this is by no means a theoretical example. Scholarship, especially historical and critical thought, depends upon societal developments that allow the emergence of inner critiques that touch upon even the most sacrosanct values of that society. As such, the evolution of scholarship on religion is strongly situated in freer forms of societies, regimes or religions.

Beyond the various circumstances in which the scholar of religion operates, individual and often idiosyncratic characteristicss must also be taken into consideration. Scholars, even when totally free to select a topic and address it in a non-inhibitive environment, decide which part of the available material they will analyze and which data are most important, relevant or representative. Such selective and subjective decisions are crucial to the nature of the picture produced by scholarship. Even the greatest of scholars identifies a set of questions that reflects his or her basic concerns. The gamut of issues addressed hence is often quite limited, and one can identify many scholars simply by paying attention to the overall agendas of their analyses of certain phenomena or texts.

Though a scholar's repertoire is individually determined, it also may reflect the audience for which the studies are intended. To take a famous example, the Eranos conference organized under the aegis of Carl G. Jung in Ascona included a broad range of excellent scholars dealing with many religions and phenomena. Nevertheless, it would not be an exaggeration to speak of a certain problematic imposed on the participants: myths, symbols and archetypes are issues that appear more frequently in the proceedings than sociological or intellectual–historical topics.[2] This is also the case in the historical–critical school of research of Kabbalah founded by Gershom Scholem, in which problems related to apocalyptic Messianism are more evident than in earlier studies of this mystical lore. Mircea Eliade's school is characterized by its defined set of questions, as are the Cambridge and the Scandinavian schools of myth and ritual. The agendas of individuals and schools are matters not only of the nature of the material but also of specific predilections to certain types of questions.

2. EIGHT APPROACHES TO RELIGION

Here I will attempt to characterize not specific scholars or schools but rather the major concerns that define the particular styles of their scholarship. Or, to rephrase the issue at hand in a more poignant manner, can we identify the major problems that preoccupy scholars of religion? I propose that they may be grouped in eight main categories; for the sake of the discussion that follows, I briefly will enumerate them here.

The first is the theological approach, by which religious texts are analyzed primarily to illuminate the theological aspects upon which other characteristics of religion are organized. Religion is conceived by proponents of this approach to be the mirror by means of which one understands the supreme entity. Or, to put it in different terms, the material under investigation may reflect the idiosyncrasies of a certain religion, experience or group, but it nevertheless reveals something about the nature of the supernal source or sources. This is the approach taken, for example, by one of the towering figures of twentieth-century scholarship on religion, Rudolph Otto. Through analysis of a variety of religious texts, he draws the conclusion that two main theological elements are found in varying proportions in all religions: the rational and what can be called the irrational. Human experiences, reactions to encounters with the transcendental or the immanent divinity, reflect something of the nature of the supreme being. Otto even judges the nature of a certain religion by the balance between the two.[3] This type of theological orientation has had great impact not only on scholars like Friedrich Heiler, but also on perceptions of religion among non-Christian scholars like Scholem and some of his followers.[4]

Another theological orientation is discernible in the erudite studies on mysticism by the Oxford scholar Robert Zaehner. No doubt a great connoisseur of many forms of religion, Zaehner's approach is amazingly orthodox; he assumes that only a Christian type of theology—namely theism—is able to provide a framework for real mystical experiences. He criticizes pantheistic frameworks of Hinduism and Islam and the form of theism that he attributes to Judaism as being unable to provide the conditions for what he considers to be valid mystical experiences.[5] On the opposite conceptual pole of Zaehner is Eliade, who does not subscribe to a theistic religion but rather emphasizes the importance of a cosmic, somehow pantheistic one. Nevertheless, like Zaehner, he passes judgment on religions according to their "cosmicity," an issue to which I shall return later.[6]

A third type of theological orientation is based on the assumption that religious material is deeply concerned with theology, even if the scholar does not seek information about an external entity in religious texts. Thus, a secular scholar may belong to this theological approach due to the centrality of this topic attributed to the systems and texts analyzed. This subcategory shall be explored further later in this essay.

The second major approach is historical, which in its various forms understands religion, like any other type of human activity, as determined by and reflecting the historical circumstances of an individual or a group. Some anthropological and sociological approaches also might be placed in this category.

Next is the psychological approach, by which religious documents are analyzed as reflecting a specific form of psychology, such as psychoanalysis. A reverberation of this approach is feminism, which deals with male repressive psychology as an issue that informs religious discourses. These three major approaches overemphasize a few aspects of the study of religion while minimizing the importance of others.

Quite different is the fourth approach: textual–literary. Developed since the Renaissance to analyze ancient classical texts, it is important to the study of religions that are text oriented. Its philological tools are quintessential for a serious approach to religious texts. The main emphasis is on the linguistic aspects of religious documents, their transmission and their status within the canon of a certain religious structure. Included in this approach are discussions concerning authorship and background, but unlike the historical approach, the resort to historical methods here does not mean that the scholars who adopt these tools are looking for the reflection of some form of external independent history within the texts. Other forms of the textual–literary approach are less historically oriented and emphasize the semantics of religious language or problems of translation.

Many major scholars of religion have adopted a comparative approach, the goal of which, in my way of seeing it, is not to make sporadic references to parallel historical influences, but rather to engage in a sustained effort to compare comprehensive structures found in different forms of religion. This approach is evident in some writings by Otto and Zaehner. Well acquainted with the languages and the texts of more than one religion, both drew comparisons on the basis of philological analysis of texts. Some comparative efforts are found in the writings of Jung, Eliade and Corbin, but their assumptions were based on some form of homogeneity in the notion of religion. In most cases, comparisons are applied with some theological presuppositions in mind, and in one way or another, triumphalism may be discerned.

Quite different is the sixth approach: ritualistic–technical. While religions have important cognitive aspects (beliefs, cosmologies, symbolisms), some place greater emphasis on deeds as quintessential elements. Rituals, pilgrimages, magical practices and mystical techniques may play a more central role in one religion than in another. Religious experiences, therefore, may be induced in some cases by factors related to the cognitive aspects of religion, like an external entity or the impact of theological beliefs, or in other cases by resorting to the bodily exercises prescribed to attain such experiences. In his two main monographs, *Yoga* and *Shamanism*, Eliade contributed much to the analysis of two forms of religiosity that resort, in a dramatic manner, to such techniques. These works represent a major methodological breakthrough in the study of the history of religion by shifting the center of interest from theoretical views and beliefs to modes of achieving religious experiences. The importance of technique is also evident in Ioan P. Culianu's

Eros and Magic, in which the magical techniques are emphasized as central to Giordano Bruno's world view. Ritual also is the subject of studies in the anthropological domain on the one hand and in various forms of myth-and-ritual approaches on the other.[7] Recently, scholars also are utilizing modern developments in medicine in attempts to measure the physiological effects of some deeds on the functioning of the body, especially the brain.[8] From a more analytical point of view, Peter Moore contributed to our understanding of mystical experiences through his interesting observations on the importance of technique.[9] Recently, I elaborated on the need for coherence among techniques, experiences induced by such techniques and theological visions found in certain systems. This is still a novel systemic approach that presupposes some form of organization of the performative, experiential and theological aspects of new structures in an attempt to eliminate discrepancies and allow a smooth relationship among these three elements.[10]

Phenomenological approaches consist of attempts to extrapolate from religious documents the specifically religious categories that organize major religious discourses. Derived to a certain extent from the philosophical approach of Edmund Husserl, particularly the need to bracket one's own presuppositions in order to allow an encounter with the phenomenon, these are the most non-reductionist of approaches, since they do not presuppose that a theological, historical or psychological structure is reflected in the religious documents. The main representative of this school is G. van der Leeuw. To a certain extent, the effort to isolate categories and introduce an approach specific to religion also is found in Eliade's studies. The effort to discern the main categories found in so many religious texts over the centuries might indeed provide a general picture of the evasive concept of religion, but simultaneously might confuse the understanding of any one specific religion. The problem unfolds when the scholar confronts a text, a school or a religion and has to decide what is present and what is absent, what is more important and what is less so, in an effort to define these main categories. Indeed, we may speak of basic forms of order or models found in one religion or another, of appropriations and adaptations, as reflecting the main characteristics of a certain religion, religious movement or school. Moreover, many of the classical phenomenologies of religion problematize deeper analyses of specific texts or phenomena by imposing general categories on the material, which is only rarely submitted to serious analysis. Some phenomenologies may be described as telescopic, since they take general pictures of religion or of some religions and reify what is understood to be their essence.

Last but not least are the cognitive approaches. In contrast to the assumption that religion is a special type of human experience to be analyzed by tools specific to this field, cognitive approaches assume that religion is one of many other human creations, and as such it should be incorporated into the study of human creativity. Though similar to psychoanalytical theories in principle, cognitive theories deal much more with the manner in which the human mind and imagination, or the human soul, operate, emphasizing the systemic nature of human creation. This is the major trend in scholarship related to structuralism, to *imaginaire* and to combinatory developments. The first is represented by the studies of Claude Levi-Strauss, and the second is apparent in the writings of Corbin, whose influence is discernible in the work of Gilbert Durand and his school, including historians like Jacques Le Goff, Jean-Claude Schmidt and Lucian Boia.[11] Most of these scholars are concerned less with ontological structures than with the manner in which humans construct their realities and sometimes their societies. Independent of the *imaginaire* approach and exhibiting some features of structuralism is Culianu's vision of religion—and, in principle, of human creativity—as being based upon different combinations of basic elements. In a way, some Neokantian approaches also may be envisioned as cognitive, as they assume that it is possible to identify categories found in the human mind that condition our understanding of experiences or revelations. Two examples of this category are Otto's famous book *Idea of the Holy* and the numerous studies of Ernst Cassirer and his followers. Both Neokantian thinkers assume that there are cognitive categories that are specific to religion. Last but not least, one of the most interesting controversies, in my opinion, of the last generation between the pure-consciousness approach and what has been called the "constructivist" approach belongs in the cognitive category.[12]

It should be pointed out that we rarely find a case in which a scholar will subscribe solely to one of these methods. With the exception of the founders of each method, other scholars, especially outstanding ones, are less inclined to reduce such complex phenomena to just one of their dimensions. A scholar must understand that adopting a single approach too rigorously may produce simplistic results. Rather, important scholars tend to utilize more than one method in various proportions.

By inspecting the temporal order in which these approaches emerged, we may speak of an evolution from transcendental to immanent forms of explanation. Originating with the theological approach, historical explanations then gave way to sociological and later psychological and cognitive approaches, the most recent being postmodern explanations that place priority on the text over the intentions of the human author. This development from transcendental to immanent, in my opinion, is neither progressive nor regressive.

As mentioned above, I propose a general, loose approach called methodological eclecticism, which resorts to different methodologies when dealing with the various aspects of religion. This proposal does not differ drastically from Wendy Doniger's view of the toolbox that a scholar should bring to his or her analysis of myth or from Culianu's proposal to apply many methodologies to the same phenomenon, given its multidimensional complexity.[13] This is certainly not a new recommendation; many of the scholars mentioned above have utilized such an approach. However, even major scholars like Eliade and Scholem, who played complex games rather than subscribing to a single approach, still explicitly refused to adopt some of the methods described above. Neither, for example, was interested in psychological approaches. Eliade sought grand theories about religion as a universal; Scholem was unconcerned with such generalizations. Eliade underemphasized textual analysis, while Otto and Zaehner were interested in detailed textual analysis and the historical filiation of influences; as comparativists, they never avoided theological questions, but simultaneously were much less concerned with techniques and rituals. Given the fact that they subscribed to one main type of history and to a rather monolithic vision of phenomena, it was hard for them to accept diverse understandings of the same phenomena, which relativizes their history or phenomenology.[14]

Since I am inclined to accept the sensitive—almost postmodern—view of the illustrious historian Marc Bloch, who once asserted that "Le vrai realisme en histoire, c'est de savoir que la réalité humaine est multiple," I cannot work with a monolithic vision of religious phenomena. If this is true for history, it is dramatically more pertinent to the conglomerate of personal and public aspects of religious events and experiences. Given the fact that many Kabbalists operated with concepts of infinity concerning the nature of the Bible and of divinity, a multiplicity of methods would be a fair approach to inquiry into their views.[15]

Even the more modest Midrashic approach, which had a deep impact on subsequent Jewish thought, allowed Jewish mystics to bring together different and even conflicting views concerning the same topic in the same work. This fact invites theories of organization of knowledge that may account for the significance of this phenomenon.

Though I am less enthusiastic about the theological approach, religion deals with the divine, and the different concepts of God should be taken into consideration when offering a more general picture. Moreover, theology is a matter not only of belief but also, in some cases, of informing the nature of the religious experience. In some forms of religion, especially Christianity, the revelation of a certain type of deity is a matter of grace, which means that the technical aspects are less important. In other cases, techniques are used in order to induce such an experience, which can be interpreted as informed by the nature of both the technique and concepts about the divine realm. I propose for the latter example to speak of some forms of consonance or coherence between the details of the technique and the corresponding type of theology.[16] Or, to describe another possible combination of approaches, the ritual–technical might be applied within the confines of a certain religion alone, but the comparative might supply important insights about the different structures of various religions.[17]

To conclude this section, I would say that the development of different approaches certainly is not a matter of evolution. Later approaches do not provide, in my opinion, a better way of understanding, since each method pays attention to an aspect that another ignores. However, accumulatively we may speak of positive development as different approaches unfold collectively or in combination with one another, providing more complex accounts of phenomena that earlier were described in much more simplistic manners.

My proposal is that it is best not to dismiss any of the above approaches out of hand, though one should be aware of the limitations of each. Scholars who are immersed in just one of these methods basically—and quite superficially—tend to dismiss all others. In most cases, the repeated critique of one or more approach stems from an unwillingness or inability to change by learning something new. There is great value in investigating the potential contributions of each approach and utilizing the careful application of such contributions rather than limiting oneself to subscribing to any single method *in toto*.

3. PERSPECTIVISM: AN ADDITIONAL APPROACH

Here I supplement the above proposal for methodological eclecticism with another concept: perspectivism. By this concept I designate the possibility of interrogating a certain religious literature from the perspective of acquaintance with another religious literature. This is neither a matter of comparison between religious figures and systems, as in the case of Otto's monograph on the individual ideas of Eckhart and Shankara, nor a case of historical filiation between two bodies of writing or thought. It is rather an attempt to better understand the logic of systems by comparing substantially different ones and learning about one from the other. Underlying this assumption is the principle that there are manifold scholarly readings of the same religion that may be fruitful—though not always equally so. For example, knowledge of rural religions might raise questions that can be applied to urban religions or vice versa, and religions in which literacy is dominant might be approached from the perspective of a religion dominated by orality. This method might also be applied to different phases of development within the same religion: one phase may be more urban, another more rural; one may be more literate, the other more oral. Or, from a global perspective, a certain religion is not only what its followers accept, believe and perform, but also the way in which it is perceived by outsiders. To adopt the theory of reception, a certain religion is differently understood—and from time to time even sharply misunderstood—from different perspectives. The history of misunderstandings is as important as theories of understanding. Numerous cases of religious anti-Semitism demonstrate that, without taking into account misunderstanding, it is difficult to comprehend fully not only the history of the Jews but also the history of Judaism, as both responded to accusations and adjusted under conditions created by various perspectival (mis)understandings. To take another example, debates about Spinozism shaped not only the history of pre-modern and modern European philosophy, but also the structure of some forms of Judaism, especially in Central Europe, which reacted to Spinozistic challenges. Spinozism encompasses the principles outlined in the specific writings of Barukh—or Benedict—Spinoza as well as the appropriations, misunderstandings and critiques provoked by them. If for Marxists and secular thinkers Spinoza was the precursor of secularism, for others, as we shall see later, he influenced the way in which Kabbalah was perceived, when it was described as expanded

Spinozism. These are rather conflicting views on Spinoza, but both are issued by informed readers of his writings, and both are part of the phenomenon of Spinozism as a whole.

In short, from a scholarly point of view, the complexity of a certain religion or one of its phases or schools is generated not just by the specific contents of its writings or the beliefs and practices of its adherents. Rather, the specificity of a religion is also the result of the particular manner in which it has been understood by outsiders, problematic and distorted as such perceptions may be. To be sure, outside perceptions do not have to be accepted or adopted by insiders; more often, the latter reject the former for good reasons. To be perfectly clear, I do not assume that the inner understanding of one's religion automatically should take into consideration the views of outsiders. However, in seeking a scholarly understanding, the situation is quite different. A serious scholar should be able to approach a topic from different angles, including negative ones, in order to understand the complexity of the phenomenon at hand, which includes its critiques and its distortions. Religion is a part of history in which many factors are active. In principle, each critique and distortion may illumine shadows found in a certain religious literature or structures ignored or suppressed by insiders; they must be examined in order to better understand a given religious phenomenon as it functioned on various historical levels.

Finally, perspectivism may be conceived as part of the need for distanciation from the phenomenon under investigation, a distanciation that is achieved, *inter alia*, by a serious acquaintance with other religious systems and the possibility to address it from the perspective of another culture. However, this distanciation should not mean a total adherence to "alien" structures, as occurs in the application of various forms of psychology or of feminism to Kabbalah, but rather the use of a flexible approach that is capable of modifying both the analysis of Kabbalah and the "method" emerging from acquaintance with and analytical manner applied to different material. As we shall see below, investigating topics related to Jewish mystical literature by means of questions and structures evinced by a rural type of religiosity as analyzed by Eliade strives not to demonstrate that Jewish mysticism is also rural or archaic, but rather to show the differences between religious categories active in Jewish mysticism and Eliade's archaic religion as well as to suggest the need to revise the latter. Viewing a topic from a certain perspective relativizes the way in which the "object" is understood and the very perspective itself. Methods—perspectivism included—are no more absolute than their objects or subjects.

4. KABBALAH AS SYMBOLIC THEOLOGY ACCORDING TO MODERN SCHOLARSHIP

Since the next chapter will deal mainly with topics found in a vast literature designated by the umbrella term "Kabbalah," I will attempt to describe here an approach to Kabbalah adopted by many modern scholars: the theological. Though Scholem and his followers claim that their approach is basically historical, and this is indeed true, another more profound approach nevertheless underlies their investigations of Kabbalistic sources. We shall be concerned with the nature of modern scholarship that, though it does not present the contents of Kabbalah as theological truths, is inclined to emphasize the theological aspects of this lore.

I first turn to a more complex approach to Kabbalah that combines theological and semiotic methods. Johann Reuchlin's widespread description of Kabbalah from the early sixteenth century notes that: "Kabbalah is simply (to use the Pythagorean vocabulary) symbolic theology, where words and letters are coded things, and such things are themselves codes for other things. This drew our attention to the fact that almost all of Pythagoras's system is derived from the Kabbalists, and that similarly he brought to Greece the use of symbols as a means of communication."[18] Writing from the perspective of a theologian who believed that he unearthed an ancient theology found among the Jews, which was then adopted by Pythagoras and subsequently lost, Reuchlin emphasizes both theology and symbolism—an approach used previously by Pythagoreans in the different phases of this lore—which is understandable and consonant to the late fifteenth-century Florentine approach to religious knowledge known as *prisca theologia*. In *De Verbo Mirifico*, Reuchlin resorts to the syntagm *divinitatis symbola*, "the symbols of divinity."[19] Elsewhere he speaks about "the symbolic philosophy of Pythagoras and the wisdom of the Kabbalah."[20] Symbolism is also evident in another important passage: "Kabbalah is a matter of divine revelation handed down to [further] the contemplation of God and the separated forms, contemplations bringing salvation. [Kabbalah] is a symbolic reception."[21]

Eclectic and artificial as their discussions sometimes may be, we may assume that Christian Kabbalists did believe in them *de facto*. It is important to emphasize the centrality of contemplation in Reuchlin's description and the recurrence of this ideal in the manner in which Jewish scholars, especially Scholem and Isaiah Tishby, approached Kabbalah. As I have attempted to show elsewhere, the symbolic interpretation of Kabbalah has remained part and parcel of the modern scholarly approach to this lore under the impact of Reuchlin's book.[22]

Reuchlin's stance had an impact on Scholem's approach before it became a unified scholarly perception of variegated lore. In a letter to Zalman Schocken written in 1937, Scholem wrote: "I arrived at the intention of writing not the history but the metaphysics of the Kabbalah."[23] How did he imagine the path to the "metaphysics of Kabbalah"? In the same letter he wrote that he wanted to decode Kabbalah in order to "penetrate through the symbolic plain and through the wall of history. For the mountain, the corpus of facts, needs no key at all; only the misty wall of history, which hangs around it, must be penetrated. To penetrate it was the task I set for myself."[24] The concept of the key, and of its superfluousity, points to the possibility of having a substantial, definite understanding of Kabbalah.[25]

These plans were more than academic aspirations; it is hard to miss the experiential aspects of the program envisioned by the mature Scholem for his own academic research. Kabbalah is, according to the above discussion, more than a literature important to the understanding of Jewish religion, culture or history; it is a spiritual path for attaining reality by the scholar. It contains facts ("the mountain"), and it has metaphysics. Two main components emerge that are reminiscent of Reuchlin's stance in the above sentences from the epistle: symbolic and ontological. It is important to observe Scholem's resort to the double singular, "metaphysics of Kabbalah": it is not a diversified type of literature but one that consists of a certain type of symbolism that, when decoded correctly, opens the gate to a vision of a non-symbolic reality.

This private plan of research with such a clear personal pursuit in 1937, expressed in a private letter printed more than forty years later, became an academic vision of Kabbalah in 1941: "In Kabbalah [Scholem argues], one is speaking of a reality which cannot be revealed or expressed at all save through the symbolic allusion. A hidden authentic reality, which cannot be expressed in itself and according to its own laws, finds expression in its symbol."[26] According to another revealing statement, "even the names of God are merely symbolic representations of an ultimate reality which is unformed, amorphous."[27] In these two statements, we find an approach to religion that is more consonant with

Otto's concept of numinosity and with other approaches, like that of Ludwig Wittgenstein, which see in religion the "inexpressible."[28] Elsewhere, Scholem describes the Kabbalists as symbolists, who express the ineffable.[29] Though indubitably there are elements in Kabbalistic texts that represent negative theology, like some—though not all—of the discussions regarding the nature of *'Ein Sof*, my assumption is that, by and large, Kabbalists were much less inclined toward negative theology than Scholem's school assumes. In some cases, negative theological language was considered an exoteric strategy hiding an esoteric anthropomorphic propensity, which may be viewed as a sort of positive theology.[30]

To return to Scholem's passage, the assumption of a hidden reality and the importance of the symbol are strongly related. Again, the singular is quite evident: in "Kabbalah" and in "a reality." Similar is Scholem's later stance, celebrating symbolism not only as a very important issue in Kabbalah but also and in fact as the mode of accommodation of Kabbalah as a certain "living center" to various historical circumstances.[31] Here some form of perennial stance is implied: Kabbalah, again in the singular, is altered in accordance with changing circumstances, but the center remains somehow constant.[32] This monochromatic vision of Kabbalah as a spiritual phenomenon and of the ultimate reality as an ontological entity represented by symbols reverberates in the writings of Scholem's followers.[33] Especially pertinent for our point is the following passage, which elaborates a symbolic vision of mysticism as a whole:

[W]hat exactly is this "secret" or "hidden" dimension of language, about whose existence all mystics for all time feel unanimous agreement, from India and the mystics of Islam, right up to the Kabbalists and Jacob Boehme? The answer is, with virtually no trace of hesitation, the following: it is the symbolic nature of language, which defines this dimension. The linguistic theories of mystics frequently diverge when it comes to determining this symbolic nature. But all mystics in quest of the secret of language come to share a common basis, namely the fact that language is used to communicate something which goes way beyond the sphere which allows for expression and formation: the fact also that a certain inexpressible something, which only manifests itself in symbols, resonated in every manner of expression.[34]

In short, the Kabbalists were—like "all mystics," according to Scholem—symbolists. Elsewhere he declares that the Kabbalists were "the main symbolists of rabbinic Judaism. For Kabbalah, Judaism in all its aspects was a system of mystical symbols reflecting the mystery of God and the universe, and the Kabbalists' aim was to discover and invent keys to the understanding of this symbolism."[35]

Again the term "Kabbalah" occurs in the singular, and "the Kabbalists" are described in an unqualified manner. Scholem expresses himself in these quotes as a historian of a specific type of literature reflecting "mysteries" dormant at the core of reality, and one should not confuse, in principle, such a description as being a personal conviction. However, it seems that in some confessions, Scholem reiterates the assumption of a mystery found in reality as part of his own world view.[36] But is not my intention to deal with Scholem's personal theology, an issue that has been addressed elsewhere.[37]

The basis of such an understanding of the affinity between symbols and the symbolized is, ultimately, not only the work of the post-Kantian German thinkers, but also and primarily the negative theology of Neoplatonism, which in addition to Gnosticism were conceived as the formative components of a peculiar blend of theosophy that was embraced by most of the Kabbalists.[38] In fact, Scholem and Tishby regarded the encounter between Neoplatonic negative theology and Gnostic pleroma that contributed the positive aspects of Kabbalistic theology as the very birth of the most dominant aspect of Kabbalah—its theosophy. Thus, not only theological speculations but also the specific Kabbalistic way of prayer have been conceived as the meeting of these two non-Jewish theologies. Dealing with the earliest Kabbalistic texts, Scholem notes that the "gnostic way of seeing things likewise penetrated their [the first historical Kabbalists, Rabbi Jacob ha-Nazir and Rabbi Abraham ben David] prayer mysticism without being able to overcome it entirely."[39] This is an interesting example of the subordination of the performative component—in this case, prayer—to the theological, namely the allegedly Gnostic view of the sefirot. Indeed as Tishby claims, Scholem convincingly demonstrates that:

> As far as the doctrine of the sefirot is concerned, it can be established without a doubt that there is some reflection here of a definite gnostic tendency, and that it did in fact emerge and develop from a historico–literary contact with the remnants of Gnosis, which were

preserved over a period of many generations in certain Jewish circles, until they found their way to early kabbalists, who were deeply affected by them both spiritually and intellectually.[40]

Elsewhere, Scholem discusses the Kabbalah's center of gravity and assumes about the Kabbalists that:

> Their ideas proceed from the concepts and values peculiar to Judaism, that is to say, above all from the belief in the Unity of God and the meaning of His revelation as laid down in the Torah, the sacred law. Jewish mysticism in its various forms represents an attempt to interpret the religious values of Judaism in terms of mystical values. It concentrates upon the idea of the living God who manifests himself in the acts of Creation, Revelation and Redemption. Pushed to its extreme, the mystical meditation on this idea gives birth to the conception of a sphere, a whole realm of divinity, which underlies the world of our sense-data and which is present and active in all that exists.[41]

Indeed, the phenomenology of Kabbalah in these books reflects this general statement. The second chapter in Scholem's *Major Trends* on the book of the Zohar is entitled "The Theosophic Doctrine of the Zohar" and commences with the statement: "the Zohar is chiefly concerned with the object of meditation, i.e., the mysteries of *mundus intelligibilis,*" and the "Zohar represents Jewish theosophy."[42]

In Scholem's last quote and other discussions dealing with contemplation, the issue of meditation gravitates around what is described as an idea. Out of the idea of and belief in divine unity, the idea of divine attributes was born, and according to another of Scholem's texts, the contemplation of divine attributes, which he calls "theosophical contemplation," gave birth to Kabbalistic myths.[43] Scholem sees in contemplation the main type of human attitude toward the divine realm, which is not theurgical, anchored in Halakhic forms of performance. Moreover, this mainly eidetic approach to Kabbalah as interpretation of a theological issue falls short of a vitally mystical experience, and its prevalence in many recent studies demonstrates the tendency to conceive this mystical lore in more theological rather than experiential terms.[44]

Finally, the last quote is based upon a descending vector; the supernal realm reverberates upon the lower worlds and, according to other texts, this reverberation is decoded by fathoming the symbolic valences of reality. Scholem indeed speaks about the mystical interpretation of Jewish values, which is, in my opinion, a better way of understanding Kabbalah than the theosophical one, but this view on the nature of Kabbalistic literature is not widely held. The interpretive approach that generated Kabbalistic theosophy is expressed later in the same book: "the mystical interpretation of the attributes and the unity of God, in the so-called doctrine of the Sefiroth, constituted a problem common to all Kabbalists, while the solution given to it by and in the various schools differ from one another."[45]

Conspicuous in these two last passages is the role played by mental construction, interpretation and meditation, while explicit descriptions of practices or performances are absent in Scholem's analysis of Jewish mysticism. The meditation mentioned by Scholem and the sphere created by the Kabbalists are related to the issue of symbols, and this is the reason why I propose designating Scholem's and his school's approach as pan-symbolic,[46] though I believe that this emphasis is exaggerated.[47] There are some definitions of Kabbalah by Kabbalists that do not address the concept of symbolism at all.[48] However, even when symbols—and this is indeed a matter of definition—are evident, they often are related to the modes of activity that accompany modes of cognition. It is the marginalization of such modes of activity—technical, ritualistic, linguistic—that created an imbalance between the nexus of the theological and the symbolic on the one hand and the ergetic or performative aspects of Kabbalah on the other. I see this imbalance to be the result of the impact of the Christian emphasis on theology and faith as central to understanding religion on Jewish scholars' perception of Jewish mysticism.

An interesting testimony to Scholem's subordination of many important issues in Jewish life to the theological dimension of this religion is found in a passage from the autobiography of one of Scholem's acquaintances; according to George Steiner's *Errata*, "[n]o serious aspect of the Jewish problem, of the history and life of the Jew, can ever be divorced altogether from theosophical–metaphysical sources (how often I heard Gershom Scholem hammer at this nerve). It is, in the final analysis, the theological and the metaphysical which inform the tragic complication of the facts."[49] The context in which this passage occurs deals with discrimination against and oppression of Jews in history.

Nevertheless, I am not sure that this reading of history, which sees the source of theological problems that influenced attitudes on Judaism within the context of the emergence of Christianity and Islam, is the only topic involved in Steiner's reference to Scholem. In any case, it fits what may be described as the theologization of Kabbalah in Scholem's writings and in those of his followers.[50]

Unlike this propensity to Kabbalah as theology, I will try to emphasize in the following chapters some other, and more experiential, aspects of this mystical lore.

NOTES

1. On questions related to the problematics involved in the scholarly concept of religion, see Daniel Dubuisson, *L'Occident et la religion: Mythes, science et idéologie* (Brussels: Editions Complexes, 1998).
2. See Steven Wasserstrom, *Religion after Religion: Gershom Scholem, Mircea Eliade and Henry Corbin at Eranos* (Princeton: Princeton University Press, 2001).
3. For his rather negative attitude toward Islam, see Rudolph Otto, *The Idea of the Holy*, trans. John W. Harvey (Harmondworth: Penguin Books, 1923), p. 107. See also Wasserstrom, *Religion after Religion*, p. 90.
4. This topic deserves a separate study.
5. See, especially, Robert Zaehner, *Hindu and Muslim Mysticism* (New York: Schocken Books, 1972), pp. 2–3 and 86–109. For other examples, see Moshe Idel, introduction to *Enchanted Chains* (forthcoming).
6. See the concluding remarks to this study.
7. See the more recent surveys of this problem found in, for example, William G. Doty, *Mythography: A Study of Myths and Rituals*, 2nd ed. (Tuscaloosa: University of Alabama Press, 2000); Robert Segal, *The Myth and Ritual Theory: An Introduction* (Cambridge: Blackwell, 1998); Bruce Lincoln, *Discourse and the Construction of Society: Comparative Studies of Myth, Ritual, and Classification* (New York: Oxford University Press, 1992); and idem, *Myth, Cosmos, and Society: Indo-European Themes of Creation and Destruction* (Cambridge: Harvard University Press, 1986).
8. See, for example, the numerous studies of Charles Tart, Arthur Deikman and Stanislav Groff.
9. Peter Moore, "Mystical Experience, Mystical Doctrine, Mystical Technique," in *Mysticism and Philosophical Analysis*, ed. Steven T. Katz (New York: Oxford University Press, 1978), pp. 112–14.
10. See the series of lectures delivered at the College de France in February 2001, to be published as Idel, *Enchanted Chains*. For an earlier formulation of this coherence, see idem, "'Unio Mystica' as a Criterion: 'Hegelian' Phenomenologies of Jewish Mysticism," in *Doors of Understanding: Conversa-*

tions in Global Spirituality in Honor of Ewert Cousins, ed. Steven Chase (Quincy: Franciscan Press, 1997), pp. 305–33.

11. On Corbin's work, see chapter 1, n. 109; see also and especially Gilbert Durand's discussion of ascentional symbolism in *Les structures anthropologiques de l'imaginaire* (Paris: Dunod, 1992), pp. 138–62.

12. See Robert K. C. Forman, ed., *The Problem of Pure Consciousness: Mysticism and Philosophy* (New York: Oxford University Press, 1990); and the series of books edited by Steven Katz at Oxford University Press. See also, for example, Moore, "Mystical Experience," pp. 112–14.

13. See, for example, Wendy Doniger, *Women, Androgynes, and Other Mythical Beasts* (Chicago: University of Chicago Press, 1980), pp. 5–7; and the Rumanian version of Ioan Culianu, *Eros and Magic in the Renaissance* (Bucharest: Nemira, 1999), pp. 371–72; as well as Nicu Gavriluta, *Jocurile minţii si lumile multidimensionale* (Iasi: Polirom, 2000), pp. 79–84.

14. See Mircea Eliade, "Methodological Remarks on the Study of Religious Symbolism," in *The History of Religions: Essays in Methodology*, eds. Mircea Eliade and J. M. Kitagawa (Chicago: University of Chicago Press), pp. 86–107.

15. See Moshe Idel, *Absorbing Perfections: Kabbalah and Interpretation* (New Haven: Yale University Press, 2002), pp. 80–110.

16. Ibid.

17. Ibid.

18. See Johann Reuchlin, *On the Art of Kabbalah, De Arte Cabalistica*, trans. M. and S. Goodman (Lincoln: Nebraska University Press, 1993), p. 241. See also S. K. Heninger, Jr., *Touches of Sweet Harmony: Pythagorean Cosmology and Renaissance Poetics* (San Marino, Cal.: Huntington Library, 1974), p. 245.

19. Pistorius, *De Verbo Mirifico*, ed. Johann Reuchlin (Basel, 1587), p. 947.

20. Reuchlin, *On the Art of Kabbalah*, p. 357.

21. Ibid., p. 63. The Latin version is found on p. 62: "Est enim Cabala divinae revelationis, ad salutiferam Dei et formarum separatarum contemplationem traditae, symbolica receptio."

22. See Moshe Idel, "Zur Funktion von Symbolen bei G. G. Scholem," in *Gershom Scholem, Literatur und Retorik*, eds. S. Moses and S. Weigel (Cologne, Weimar, Vienna: Boehlau Verlag, 2000), pp. 51–59. For other influences of the Christian Renaissance understanding of the nature of Kabbalah on modern scholarship, see idem, *Kabbalah: New Perspectives* (New Haven: Yale University Press, 1988), pp. 5–6.

23. David Biale, *Gershom Scholem, Kabbalah and Counter-History* (Cambridge: Harvard University Press, 1979), p. 75.

24. Ibid., p. 31.

25. On the theme of the key in Scholem's writings, see Moshe Idel, "Hieroglyphs, Keys, Enigmas: On G. G. Scholem's Vision of Kabbalah: Between Franz Molitor and Franz Kafka," in *Arche Noah, Die Idee der "Kultur" im deutsch-juedischen Diskurs*, eds. Bernhard Greiner and Christoph Schmidt (Freiburg: Rombach, 2002), pp. 227–48.

26. Gershom Scholem, *On the Possibility of Jewish Mysticism in Our Time and Other Essays*, trans. Jonathan Chipman (Philadelphia: Jewish Publication

Society, 1997), p. 140. See also idem, *On the Kabbalah and Its Symbolism*, trans. R. Manheim (New York: Schocken Books, 1969), pp. 22 and 36.

27. Scholem, *On the Kabbalah*, p. 8.

28. See Otto, *Idea of the Holy*; and Thomas McPherson, "Religion as the Inexpressible," in *New Essays in Philosophical Theology*, eds. Antony Flew and Alastair MacIntyre (London: SCM Press, 1966), pp. 131–42.

29. See Gershom Scholem, *On Jews and Judaism in Crisis*, ed. Werner J. Dannhauser (New York: Schocken Books, 1976), p. 48.

30. See Moshe Idel, "Une figure d'homme au-dessus des sefirot (A propos de la doctrine des 'eclats' de R. David ben Yehouda he-Hassid et ses developpments)," trans. Charles Mopsik, *Pardes* 8 (1988): pp. 131–50.

31. See Scholem, *On Jews and Judaism*, p. 46.

32. On this issue, see also Amos Funkenstein, "Gershom Scholem: Charisma, Kairos and the Messianic Dialectic," *History & Memory* 4 (1992): pp. 123–39.

33. See, for example, Joseph Dan, introduction to *The Early Kabbalah*, trans. Ronald C. Kiener (New York: Paulist Press, 1986), pp. 9–13; and idem, *On Sanctity* (in Hebrew)(Jerusalem: The Magnes Press, 1997), pp. 45–57, 69–70, 383–84, etc.

34. Gershom Scholem, "The Name of God and the Linguistic Theory of Kabbalah," *Diogenes* 79 (1972): p. 60; see also pp. 62, 165 and 193; idem, *On the Kabbalah*, p. 36; idem, *On Jews and Judaism*, p. 48; Isaiah Tishby, *Paths of Faith and Heresy* (in Hebrew) (Ramat Gan: Massada, 1964), pp. 11–22; and Dan, *Early Kabbalah*, p. 13. For more detailed discussions of Scholem's view of the Kabbalistic symbol, see Susan Handelman, *Fragments of Redemption* (Bloomington: Indiana University Press, 1991), pp. 82–84 and 93–114; Idel, *Kabbalah: New Perspectives*, pp. 200–34; idem, "The Function of Symbols," in Reuchlin, *On the Art of Kabbalah*, pp. xv–xvi; and more recently, Andreas Kilcher, *Die Sprachtheorie der Kabbala als Aestetisches Paradigma* (Stuttgart, Weimar: Metzler, 1998), pp. 96–98.

35. Scholem, *On the Kabbalah*, pp. 5–6.

36. See Scholem, *On Jews and Judaism*, pp. 47–48.

37. See Gershon Weiler, "On the Theology of Gershom Scholem" (in Hebrew), *Qeshet* 71 (1976): pp. 121–28; and Biale, *Gershom Scholem*, pp. 142–46.

38. See, for example, Gershom Scholem, *Kabbalah* (Jerusalem: Keter Publishing House, 1974), pp. 45 and 98; and idem, *Origins of the Kabbalah*, ed. R. Z. J. Werblowsky, trans. A. Arkush (Philadelphia: Jewish Publishing Society and Princeton University Press, 1987), p. 98.

39. Scholem, *Origins*, p. 247. See also idem, *Kabbalah*, p. 98. Compare, however, to Scholem, *Origins,* p. 248; and Moshe Idel, "Kabbalistic Prayer in Provence" (in Hebrew), *Tarbiz* 62 (1993): pp. 265–86.

40. Isaiah Tishby, *The Wisdom of the Zohar: An Anthology of Texts*, trans. D. Goldstein (London: Littman Library, 1991), vol. 1, p. 236 (emphases added). *Nota Bene*: Tishby assumes that Kabbalah as such was influenced by Gnostic material. See more on this issue in chapter 3.

41. Gershom Scholem, *Major Trends in Jewish Mysticism* (New York: Schocken Books, 1967), pp. 10–11 (emphases added).
42. Ibid., p. 205. It is no wonder that this is the manner in which other scholars understand the Zohar. See, for example, Antoine Faivre, *Theosophy, Imagination, Tradition: Studies in Western Esotericism* (Albany: State University of New York Press, 2000), pp. 32–33, n. 11. See also ibidem, p. 58.
43. See Scholem, *On the Kabbalah*, p. 99. See also Reuchlin's use of contemplation as central to understanding Kabbalah as different from Rabbinism, and compare to my introduction to Reuchlin's *On the Art of the Kabbalah*, pp. xxi–xxiii.
44. See David Biale, "Jewish Mysticism in the Sixteenth Century," in *An Introduction to the Medieval Mystics of Europe*, ed. Paul Szarmach (Albany: State University of New York Press, 1984), p. 314.
45. Scholem, *Major Trends*, p. 13.
46. See Idel, *Absorbing Perfections*, pp. 279–80. For more on symbolism and Kabbalah, see Boaz Huss, "R. Joseph Gikatilla's Definition of Symbolism and Its Versions in Kabbalistic Literature," in *Rivkah Shatz-Uffenheimer Memorial Volume* (in Hebrew), eds. R. Elior and J. Dan (Jerusalem, 1996), vol. 1, pp. 157–76; and Abraham Elkayam, "Between Referentialism and Performativism: Two Approaches in Understanding the Kabbalistic Symbol" (in Hebrew), *Daat* 24 (1990): pp. 5–40.
47. Idel, *Absorbing Perfections*, pp. 272–313; and idem, *Kabbalah: New Perspectives*, pp. 200–10.
48. See, for example, Moshe Idel, "Defining Kabbalah: The Kabbalah of the Divine Names," in *Mystics of the Book: Themes, Topics, Typology*, ed. R. A. Herrera (New York: Peter Lang, 1993), pp. 106–13.
49. George Steiner, *Errata* (London: Weidenfeld and Nicholson, 1997), p. 57.
50. For more on this issue, see Moshe Idel, "On the Theologization of Kabbalah in Modern Scholarship," in eds. Yossef Schwartz and Volkhard Krech, *Religious Apologetics – Philosophical Argumentation* (Tuebingen: J. C. B. Mohr, 2004), pp. 123–74.

CHAPTER 1:

On Diverse Forms of Living Ascent on High in Jewish Sources

1. INTRODUCTION

The practice of any religion oscillates between the poles of routine ritual and inertial faith on the one hand and ecstatic practices on the other. Differences in the practices of various religions lie not only in the content of beliefs, ritual structures and the details of techniques used to reach extreme experiences, but also in the variety of combinations of and particular emphases on elements found within the wide spectrum of practices. Moving from the pole of inertia to that of ecstasy constitutes an effort to intensify religious life so that contact with the supernal being or beings will be strengthened, increase in frequency or culminate in the identification of some aspect of the mystical being. In most cases, mystics accentuate the importance of their own transformation through such practices. Traits of the human character, human condition or particular individual are viewed as obstacles that should be removed by resorting to special forms of religious practices. The primary intention of such rites, techniques, exercises, methods and processes is to remove sin, corporeality, lust or imagination so that the pure or purified core of the aspirant is then capable of touching or being touched by the divine. Sometimes establishing such contact is a matter not only of overcoming ontic differences between fallen or impure individuals and the supreme and sublime beings, but also of bridging the distance between the mundane place where lower beings live and the realm of the supernal beings. Sometimes the attempt to strengthen contact with the divine is a journey. Other times, special holy persons who have assimilated with the higher being play a pontific role to some extent.

The theme of the ascent to heaven is often mentioned in spiritual biographies of religious *perfecti*: mythical figures in the Mesopotamian religions, the founders of some faiths, Siberian Shamans, apocalyptic figures, Greek medicine men or Jewish *tzaddiqim* (the righteous). Some performed or discussed the possibility of a heavenly tour, a topic that fascinated Ioan P. Culianu. The attribution of such an adventure in some cases is connected to a constitutive experience—the initiation of a new religion or of a new phase in an established one. In more specific terms, the ascent on high is related to events in the lives of the three founders of the monotheistic religions. Access to the divine realm, symbolized by the higher world, was a sign of special distinction, the importance of which was necessary in order to impose a new message, a new interpretation of the old traditions or a radically novel revelation. However, the ways in which such events have been described does not relegate them to what may be defined as psychanodia, namely the ascent of the soul to higher realms. Moses ascended a mountain. Jesus rose *in corpore*, while Paul was taken to the third heaven.[1] Muhammad resorted to a ladder.[2] In those types of mentalities in which the body, the concrete and the spatial structure played a major role, such ascents contributed to the validation of new revelations.

A survey of the history of the ascent to heaven in Judaism, however, reveals a rather interesting difference: in the earliest descriptions, the founding figures, the patriarchs and Moses are never portrayed as ascending to and entering a totally different realm for the sake of a *rendez-vous* with the divine. In the Bible it is God who reveals himself by coming down to the recipients of the divine message rather than by bringing the messenger to his realm in order to receive it. In other words, the biblical apprehension of the revelation is based upon the assumption that man as a psychosomatic entity cannot transcend his mundane situation and penetrate the divine realm, while God is able to adapt himself, and perhaps also his message, to human capacity. While the way down is open, the way up is basically closed. The ascents of Elijah and perhaps of Enoch are presented in the Bible as initiated not by men, but rather by God. In more concrete terms, Moses is portrayed in biblical texts as climbing a mountain in order to receive the Torah, while God, for his part, descends upon the same mountain. The human remains human and is not radically transformed by his reception of the divine message. Man temporarily may touch the divine who descends for the sake of revelation, but this does not indicate an ontic transformation of his personality. Moses remains a man, despite the luminous face he is attributed, and he remains mortal despite his extraordinary experience of direct conversation with and gift of the Torah from God. In other words, the divine theophany—the revelation of the divine personality, especially the divine will—is the constituting moment of biblical Judaism, not an apotheotic experience of an individual mystic. This does not mean that apotheosis or the ascent on high is unknown to biblical Judaism. In fact, the succinct descriptions of the translations of Enoch and Elijah constitute forms of apotheosis, but they remain a tiny minority in the vast biblical literature. My thesis is that one of the major developments in post-biblical Judaism is the continuous growth of the apotheotic vector in the general economy of Judaism, a theophanic religion in its first manifestation, through the emergence and the flowering of some forms of Jewish mysticism.[3]

Judaism, like the two other major monotheistic religions, underwent change over the centuries that introduced new sets of order describing reality, which qualified—sometimes dramatically—older types of order.[4] As such, cases in which ascents of the soul occur do not reflect a simple imitation of the models found in canonical writings but rather are related to major intellectual developments in connection with elite mentalities that place emphasis on more spiritual, mental or mystical forms of elevation. In saying this, I neither judge the validity or superiority of such ascents nor assume an evolution that creates higher forms of religion through transition from the archaic to the mystical. Both are religious modes that are found in all of the three religions mentioned above, and there is no reason to phenomenologically prefer one over another.

The two major twentieth-century Rumanian scholars of religion, Mircea Eliade and Ioan P. Culianu, had many interests in common, and these parallels already have drawn the attention of scholars. What has passed rather unnoticed, however, is the fact that both were concerned particularly with a specific theme in the phenomenology of religion: the flight or the ascent of the soul. In his two major monographs on Yoga and Shamanism, Eliade addresses this topic, which plays an important role in the general economy of his exposition. He not only describes ascents of the soul in themselves but also identifies some forms of convergence among them due to their common ancient sources.[5] Interestingly enough, in these two monographs Eliade does not address the theme of the ascent of the soul in other—namely ancient and late antiquity Near Eastern, Greek and Hellenistic—traditions, which is the scope of Culianu's detailed analyses. In a third study, Eliade addresses the concept of ascension of the soul in ancient religions.[6]

There are few topics that preoccupied Culianu as much as the ascent of the soul. He dedicated three books to this issue: first, the English *Psychanodia*, printed in 1983; then a more complex discussion in the

French book *Experiences de l'extase*, printed in 1984; and finally, *Out of this World*, which appeared posthumously in 1991. It is hardly an exaggeration to state that he started and finished his academic career by dealing with the same topic, though he addressed many other issues in between. In his first two books and in the many articles that preceded them, he dealt primarily with ancient texts and only secondarily with some of their medieval reverberations.

Two related issues illuminate the major shift contributed by Culianu's work in comparison to earlier scholarship. One is historical: the denial of the importance of Iranian sources to later treatments of the ascent of the soul. The other is morphological: the distinction between two main types of discussion of this theme—the Jewish, which deals with ascent into the (three or seven) heavens or palaces, and the Greek or Hellenistic, which addresses the ascent and descent of the soul through planetary worlds.[7] His findings on the bridge for the soul in *IV Ezra* introduced a new strand of historiography on this theme. Culianu traces the Jewish discussion via Arabic sources from the European Middle Ages up to Dante. This penchant for delegating an important role to Jewish post-biblical material in the history of religion is part of a more general development shared by major scholars of Gnosticism, including Culianu himself,[8] and of Christian mysticism, like Culianu's colleague in Chicago, Bernard McGinn.[9] *Out of this World*, however, is much more comprehensive and covers, as its subtitle declares, "Otherworldly Journeys from Gilgamesh to Albert Einstein." Here Culianu gives attention to some later Jewish material.[10] However, the difference between his earlier books and his last is much greater than the expanded scope of material under scrutiny. His final work represents a major methodological shift characteristic of the last years of Culianu's activity and demonstrates a vision of religion that is related more to cognitive studies and to combinatory approaches.[11]

Interestingly enough, in Culianu's earlier two volumes, Eliade's discussions of the ascent of the soul, with which Culianu was well acquainted, play only a marginal role. In his third book, these discussions are almost completely absent, though Eliade is mentioned explicitly in the context of his understanding of the phenomenon of Shamanism.[12] Thus, though both scholars were interested in the same religious theme and in the topic of ecstasy in general, they did not work with the same primary materials, and their analyses did not intersect essentially, but rather quite marginally. Eliade was interested chiefly in techniques of ecstasy, which concern the recurring experiences of living people, while Culianu was interested mainly in the posthumous journey of the soul to the other world.

The main concerns of the many scholars who deal with views of ascent in late antiquity Judaism are phenomena that are specifically characteristic of that period. This is the case in the studies of Culianu as well as Morton Smith, David J. Halperin, Annelies Kuyt, Martha Himmelfarb, James Davila, Elliot R. Wolfson, M. Dean-Otting, Allan Segal, Margaret Barker and, most recently, Israel Knohl.[13] Most of these scholars do not touch upon the vast Jewish material from the medieval period in any significant manner; however, medievalists in the domain of Jewish mysticism have not been attracted by this theme until recently.[14] Even the most important Kabbalistic source—the book of the Zohar, in which there are several discussions of posthumous psychanodia—has not been analyzed from this point of view.

As mentioned above, I propose that the apotheotic vector, which presupposes an ascension on high, gradually gained increasing importance in Jewish mysticism, culminating in eighteenth-century Hasidism. However, it should be emphasized that this vector does not represent a unilinear development. Ascents on high took various forms that, though sometimes related to each other, are phenomenologically different. Thus, bodily apotheosis, to be referred to below also as somanodia, was evident in ancient literatures but became less influential in the Middle Ages. In medieval Jewish literature, types of psychanodia and nousanodia—the ascent of the intellect, or the nous—are by far more frequent. In the following, these different forms will be described and their ascent and decline will be reflected upon as features within more comprehensive cultural and spiritual processes. To be sure, as distinct as these three categories seem to be, they sometimes intersect and complicate simpler descriptions in these literatures. Nevertheless, given the different sources of such descriptions, it is useful to adopt these special terminologies. Using each of these terms is not simply a matter of drawing a specific image or theme from a certain source. As I shall attempt to elaborate in my concluding remarks, I assume that in some religious structures we find forms of *Gestalt*-coherence, which means that several realms of a system—anthropology, theology and eschatology—are understood as having a consonant structure. Again, I propose that the human faculty involved in contact with a supernal power resonates to the very nature of that power. Thus, somanodia, psychanodia and nousanodia are examples not only of ascent terminology but also of broader religious structures.

2. HEIKHALOT LITERATURE: PRECEDENTS AND OFFSHOOTS

The theme of the ascent to the divine realm is well represented in Jewish sources of late antiquity: in inter-testamental Jewish literature, in some rabbinic discussions and in so-called Heikhalot literature, written some time between the third and the eighth centuries.[15] As mentioned above, the material pertinent to this theme has been analyzed time and again by many scholars, including Culianu, and I shall not summarize here the vast literature on the topic. For our discussion it will suffice to mention that this ascent consists of the elevation of some form of body, perhaps similar to an astral body, to the supernal realm; hence, the term psychanodia would be a problematic description of such discussions. In any case, I am not aware of any linguistic terminology that will allow us to assume that those Jewish authors had in mind the ascension of the soul devoid of any form, despite the fact that in Midrashic literature, the soul of man was described as ascending on high every night in order to give an account of his daily deeds and sometimes to draw some form of strength.[16] This nightly ascent of the soul is in no way eschatological, nor does it point to a mystical experience of close contact with the divine essence.

According to Morton Smith, "We can fairly conclude that one or more techniques for ascent into heaven were being used in Palestine in Jesus' day, and that Jesus himself may well have used one."[17] As this scholar indicates, Paul attributed an ascent to Jesus, in which he was brought up to the third heaven, "whether in the body or out of the body."[18] Therefore, the conception of an ascent of the soul to paradise—represented by the phrase "out of the body"—in order to have an ineffable experience even before death is considered by Smith to have been current among Jews of the first century.[19] This obviously represents a concept different from the more widespread belief in the possibility of bodily ascent to heaven, which seems to have been held much earlier. More recently, Margaret Barker pointed out that in the Odes of Solomon, a case of ascent on high that culminated in angelization was attributed to Christ. There, the spirit is described as elevating Jesus:

> Brought me forth before the LORD's face
> And because I was the Son of Man,
> I was named the Light, the Son of God;
> Because I was the most glorious among the glorious ones,
> And the greatest among the great ones
> And he anointed me with his perfection
> And I became one of those who are near him.[20]

Elsewhere in the same book, it is said:

> I went up into the light of truth as into a chariot,
> And the truth led me and caused me to come
> And there was no danger for me because
> I constantly walked with him.[21]

In this context it may be pertinent to mention Rabbi Shimeon bar Yohai's statement, preserved in the Babylonian Talmud, concerning the *benei 'aliyyah*, translated roughly as "those who attended the ascent," which implies that bar Yohai's vision of the few elect in the upper world was the result of a mystical journey.[22]

Apocalyptic literature represents a drastic shift from the dominant biblical point of view. It is the human who takes the initiative for an encounter with the divine, and the divine realm itself—not an elevated mountain—is the scene of the mystical revelation. Apocryphal in its literary genre, this literature propelled a series of figures into celestial zones—"out of this world," to use Culianu's phrase—in order to allow them to return with the credential of having had an interview with the divine monarch. Journeys and books about such journeys have been attributed to Moses, Abraham, Isaiah and Enoch.[23] In some cases, deep transformations of human personality, including some corporeal changes, are evidenced as a result of their visits to the supernal worlds.[24]

This motif—the mythical ascent of man—is preserved and even elaborated upon in Hebrew treatises written after the destruction of the second temple. In these mystical treatises, referred to under the general title of Heikhalot literature, the ascent on high is a major subject. Here, it is the initiative of the mystic that provides the starting point for the mystical journey. As to the goals of these ascents, there are divergences among scholarly interpretations. A more mystical reading of the target views the mystic as experiencing an encounter with God, who is a supernal anthropomorphic entity of immense size.[25] According to other scholarly views, participation in the heavenly liturgy is the goal of the ascent.[26] More recently, some studies place emphasis upon the ascender's ability to magically attain access to the higher world.[27]

In all cases, the protagonists of these heavenly ascents are mainly post-biblical figures, some of which are the founders of the first phase of rabbinic literature, known as Tannaite: Rabbi Akiva ben Joseph, Rabbi Ishmael, Yohanan ben Zakkai, Rabbi Eleazar ben Arakh, Rabbi Nehuniah ben ha-Qanah, Shimeon ben Zoma, Shimeon ben Azzai and Elisha ben Abbuiah. Biblical figures appear from time to time in Heikhalot literature, but they are not the main protagonists. Enoch and Moses are mentioned, but their names surface only rarely in more than one of the writings belonging to this literature.[28]

These Heikhalot writings were composed between the third and eighth centuries. In rabbinic literature of this period, the ascent to heaven plays a much less conspicuous role, though Moses is described both in the Talmud and in some Midrashic discussions as ascending through several heavens in order to receive the Torah.[29] This difference can be explained in at least two different and perhaps complementary ways. First, from the literary point of view, rabbinic literature is more concerned with legalistic and interpretive matters than with mysticism, myth and magic. These topics recur in many places in both the Talmud and Midrash, but they are not the focus of these literary genres. Second, there are proclivities in this literature to suppress centrifugal tendencies in order to cultivate a more worldly religiosity. However, all this said, I wonder if comparison between discussions in rabbinic literature that deal with the question of the ascent on high and such presentations in Heikhalot literature will disclose a vision of this issue that is drastically different. In the Talmud, Moses and four Tannaitic figures are described as ascending on high. It is in this type of literary corpus that a more magical turn is preserved in at least one version of the ascent. The religious capabilities of Rabbi Akiva allowed him to ascend to the divine world, and when the angels attempted to throw him down, God intervened and declared that he was worthy of the magical use of the divine glory—in Hebrew, *lehishtamesh bi-khevodi*.[30] However, in the version found in Heikhalot literature, the same rabbi is described as worthy only of looking at or contemplating the divine glory—*le-histakkel bi-khevodi*.[31] What is the implication of such a difference to the goal of the ascent on high? In my opinion, the rabbinic version of the ascent is concerned with exercising a certain influence—which can be described as magical or theurgical—on the divine glory, while the gazing upon or the contemplation of the glory seems to be the main goal in Heikhalot literature. In this type of mystical literature, awareness of the size of the divine body is a crucial part of soteriological knowledge. I propose that the emphasis upon precise size had certain repercussions on broader religious attitudes in Heikhalot literature. This is why there is no hint of a change in the glory or its being put into the service of man, but rather its static state is contemplated.[32] While rabbinic literature is inclined toward a view that God cannot be seen by mortals, Heikhalot literature subscribes to a much more positive attitude toward the contemplation of the divine.[33]

A third ideal of the ascent, which will concerned us much more thoroughly in the following discussion, is expressed in Heikhalot literature: Rabbi Akiva is described as receiving the revelation of a name while contemplating the vision of the divine chariot.[34] This name enables him and his students to accomplish magical operations, which is hinted at by the verb *mishtammesh*, which means "to use." In this instance, bringing down an occult knowledge that confers extraordinary power is evident. The same is the case in the introduction to a magical treatise named *Shimmushei Torah*. Here, Moses is described as ascending on high and, after a contest with various angels, not only the Torah is revealed to him but also the way to read it as a magical document through the transformation of the common sequel of the canonic text into names that have various magical uses.[35] In other words, magic is revealed to Moses through the divine names that are found in a cryptic manner in the text of the canon. Moreover, Moses is given *segullot*—remedies—as a gift.[36]

Ascending on high and bringing down some form of esoteric knowledge, either in the form of magical names, of remedies or of a magical reading of the Torah, can be understood as a model that I propose calling mystical–magical. The first action—the ascent on high—represents the mystical phase of the model, as it allows the religious *perfectus* contact with the divine or celestial entities. His bringing down of the secret lore, which in many cases has magical qualities, represents the magical aspect of this model. In the ancient literature, this mystical journey takes place either *in corpore* or, as I propose interpreting some of the Heikhalot

discussions, in a sort of astral body.[37] In other words, in Heikhalot literature the concomitant presence of the same person in two places seems
to be a crucial issue. So, for example, Rabbi Nehuniyah ben ha-Qanah
is described as sitting in the special posture of Elijah in the lower world,
surrounded by his disciples, apparently in a lethargic state. At the same
time, he is portrayed as sitting and gazing upon the divine chariot on
high. I would like to emphasize the use of the verb sit—*Yoshev*: the
Rabbi is represented as sitting in two different places at the same time.
This observation of the double presence of the mystic in Heikhalot literature may be a clue to understanding the whole phenomenon of the
ascent to the Merkavah.[38] It is neither an ascent of the soul nor a corporeal ascent; it combines both by the assumption that the spiritual
body of the mystic is the entity that undertakes the celestial journey,
while the corporeal body remains in a special posture in the terrestrial
world. I cannot elaborate here upon the possible implications of such a
proposal for the understanding of Heikhalot literature. For the time
being, it is sufficient to remark that the assumption of a double presence in a Heikhalot text connected to the term *Golem*—which in many
cases since the Middle Ages means "an artificial anthropoid"—may
have something to do with the concept of a spiritual body.

Not only the ideal of the ascent—at least in principle—but also its
techniques persisted as part of the reservoir of Jewish culture. In general, I would say that Scholem's interpretation that the techniques of
Heikhalot literature degenerated into "mere literature" is a curious view
in light of reports of the ascents of souls throughout the nineteenth
century.[39] However, the more dominant method of attaining contact
with divine or semi-divine entities in medieval literature is through
Himmelsreise der Seele. Due to the impact of Greek and Hellenistic psychologies, Jewish authors adopted more spiritual explanations of the
communion of the soul. In lieu of the ascent of the person, the union
or the communion of the soul or the intellect with God or another spiritual supernal entity was conceived as the mystical component of the
mystical–magical model.[40] This is simply a more "spiritualized" version
of the archaic model found in the Heikhalot. In the ninth century, however, the descriptions of the Heikhalot masters were interpreted by
some Babylonian Jewish thinkers belonging to an elite group called
Ge'onim in an interiorized manner, as though indicating inner, rather
than external, experiences. The main text to this effect is the report of
Rav Hai Gaon. In one of his *responsa*, he indicates that:

Many scholars thought that one who is distinguished by many qualities described in the books, when he seeks to behold the Merkavah and the palaces of the angels on high, he must follow a certain procedure. He must fast a number of days and place his head between his knees and whisper many hymns and songs whose texts are known from tradition. Then he perceives within himself and in the chambers [of his heart] as if he saw the seven palaces with his own eyes, and it is as though he entered one palace after another and saw what is there. And there are two *mishnayot*, which the *tannaim* taught regarding this topic, called the *Greater Heykhalot* and the *Lesser Heykhalot*, and this matter is well known and widespread. Regarding these contemplations, the *tanna'* taught: "Four entered Pardes"—those palaces were alluded to by the term *Pardes*, and they were designated by this name.... For God...shows to the righteous, in their interior, the visions of His palaces and the position of His angels.[41]

The spiritual understanding of Rav Hai's view of the ancient mystics drew the attention of Adolph Jellinek, who affirms that Rav Hai was influenced by Sufi mysticism, a statement that indicates that his interpretation of earlier material is based on new spiritual approaches.[42] Scholem's view is that Rav Hai is describing a "mystical ascent." His rendering of "the interiors and the chambers" implies that this phrase was understood to refer to external entities, presumably parts of the supernal palaces.[43] However, this understanding is somewhat problematic; the form *ba-penimi u-va-hedri*, which translates as "within himself and in the chambers," suggests the subject of the verb, *maniah rosho*, thereby referring to the mystic himself. David J. Halperin accepts Scholem's understanding of this passage, although he disagrees with the assumption that it reflects a view occurring in the much earlier treatise, *Heikhalot Zutarti*. He denies the presence of a reference to a celestial journey in this treatise and argues that Rav Hai misunderstood the earlier source, translating the phrase "He thus peers into the inner rooms and chambers" without referring to the possessive form of these nouns. Thus, Halperin's opinion is that Rav Hai's passage indeed reflects a heavenly ascension.[44] Martin Cohen's translation is more adequate: "he gazes within himself." However, his general interpretation is erroneous: Rav Hai did not imply "a mystic communion with God," and his passage does not "have the ring of truth, as well as the support of the gaon's unimpeachable authority."[45]

It is my opinion that Rav Hai Gaon misinterpreted the late antiquity texts by transforming an ecstatic experience that takes place out of the body into an introversive one. The contemplation of the Merkavah is compared here to the entrance into Pardes; both activities are, according to Rav Hai, allegories for the inner experience attained by mystics. The mystical flight of the soul to the Merkavah is interpreted allegorically; the supernal palaces can be gazed upon and contemplated not by referring to an external event, but by concentrating upon one's own "chambers." Thus, the scene of revelation is no longer the supermundane hierarchy of palaces but the human consciousness.[46] Rav Hai Gaon asserts that the mystic may attain visions of palaces and angels, intentionally ignoring the vision of God. It should be mentioned that his father, Rabbi Sherira, refused to endorse the anthropomorphic conception of the Godhead found in the book *Shi`ur Qomah*.[47]

According to a younger contemporary of Rav Hai, Rabbi Nathan of Rome, the Gaon's intention was that the ancient mystics "do not ascend on high, but that they see and envision in the chambers of their heart, like a man who sees and envisions something clearly with his eyes, and they hear and tell and speak by means of a seeing eye, by the divine spirit."[48] Therefore, the earliest interpretation of Rav Hai's view emphasizes inner vision rather than mystical ascent. This type of mystical epistemology is congruent with Rav Hai's view concerning the revelation of the glory of God to the prophets through the "understanding of the heart"—*`ovanta de-libba'*. Far from expounding a mystical ascent of the soul, the Gaon offers instead a radical reinterpretation of ancient Jewish mysticism. In the vein of more rationalistic approaches, he effaces the ecstatic or shamanic aspects of Heikhalot experiences in favor of their psychological interpretation. Though I imagine that this recasting of an earlier religious mentality was motivated by Rav Hai's adherence to rationalist thinking,[49] we cannot ignore the possibility that his psychological perception may bear some affinities to much earlier views of the Merkavah.[50] However, even if such early understandings of Merkavah mysticism indeed existed, they were seemingly marginal in comparison to the bodily and spiritual ascent cultivated by the Heikhalot mystics. This kind of rationalization consistently reveals a reserved attitude toward the object of interpretation; therefore, Rav Hai Gaon seems to have been reacting against a relatively common practice, as we may infer from his remark: "this is a widespread and well-known matter." Even the opening statement of the quotation, although formulated in the past tense, bears evidence of the recognition of the technique by "many scholars."[51] We may conclude on the grounds of Rav Hai's passage that the use of Elijah's posture in order to attain paranormal states of consciousness perceived as visions of the Merkavah was still customary among Jewish mystics, notwithstanding Rav Hai's attempt to attenuate some of its "uncanny" facets.[52] It is plausible that this interpretation, quite incongruent with Heikhalot material, is the result of the impact of the intellectualistic Greek orientation that penetrated the Babylonian regions by the mediation of Arabic thinkers, attenuating the external, more mythical aspects of the journey to the Merkavah. My scheme assumes that the shift from a literal understanding of the ascent and the act of enthronement to an allegorical one is basically medieval, starting with the tenth century, as exemplified by Rav Hai's interpretation of the experience of the Heikhalot.[53] I assume that in some circles the literal understanding of the ascent remained active, while in others, like that of the Gaon, it was internalized.

The most important Jewish thinkers who continued, *mutatis mutandis*, the major tendencies of Heikhalot literature were the so-called Hasidei Ashkenaz. They were a late twelfth- and early thirteenth-century group active mainly in some cities in the Rhineland. These authors reproduced, glossed and perhaps even saved from oblivion some of the earlier Heikhalot texts and used some of their theologoumena in their own writings. However, more concrete instances in which psychanodian legends are related to historical figures were apparent in some regions in France, an area close to the Ashkenazi figures. Rabbi Ezra of Montcontour is described as a prophet who made an ascent on high.[54] Rabbi Moses Botarel, a late medieval Kabbalist, mentions a tradition received from his father, Rabbi Isaac, asserting that: "The soul of the prophet from the city of Montcontour ascended to heaven and heard the living creatures singing before God a certain song; and when he awoke he remembered this song and told his experience as it was, and they wrote down the song."[55]

Therefore, the ascent heavenwards is a technique used to solve a problem. In the first instance, it is a method by which to bring down the song of the angels. In other cases, issues difficult to solve by means of regular speculation, including both halakhic and theological topics, are viewed as questions to be asked of heavenly instances.[56] Rabbi Ezra's particular technique of composing verses by ascending on high and listening to the angelic chorus is not, however, unique. A prominent early medieval *paytan*, Rabbi Eleazar ha-Qalir, is also described as having ascended to heaven and questioning the archangel Michael on the manner in which the angels sing and how their songs are composed. Afterwards, he descended and composed a poem according to the alphabetical order that he learned from the angelic songs.[57] Interestingly enough, Rabbi Eleazar was imagined to ascend to heaven by the use of the divine name, an ascent technique attributed by the famous eleventh-century commentator of the Bible known as Rashi—Rabbi Shlomo Yitzhaqi—to the four sages who entered Pardes.[58] This description of the poet was no doubt an attempt to include Eleazar among the Merkavah mystics. This also seems to be the tendency of another report concerning Rabbi Eleazar: a mid-thirteenth century Italian author, Rabbi Tzedakiah ben Abraham, states in the name of his father, who in turn heard it from his masters, some unnamed Ashkenazic sages, that while Rabbi Eleazar was composing his well-known poem, "The Fourfold Living Creatures," "fire surrounded him."[59] This latter phrase has an obvious connection to the mystical study of sacred texts or discussions of topics particular to the Merkavah tradition.[60] In a third description of Rabbi Eleazar, also from a text of Ashkenazi origin, he is referred to as "the angel of God."[61]

Thus, Rabbi Ezra of Montcontour's study of the celestial academy through the ascent of his soul and transmission of a poem he heard there have close parallels to the practices of a much earlier person, portrayed with the help of motifs connected to Merkavah traditions. Also pertinent to our topic is the following report concerning Rabbi Michael the Angel, a mid-thirteenth-century French figure. He is described as follows:

> [He] asked questions, and his soul ascended to heaven in order to seek [answers to] his doubts. He shut himself in a room for three days and ordered that it not be opened. But the men of his house peered between the gates [!], and they saw that his body was flung down like a stone. And so he laid for three days, shut in and motionless on his bed like a dead man. After three days he came to life and rose to his feet, and from thence on he was called Rabbi Michael the Angel.[62]

Though different from the reports stemming from Heikhalot literature, this description does not leave any doubt that, like the earlier claims of

Jewish mystics, the ascent on high is a matter undertaken by a living person who survives this experience. Unlike their contemporaries in Provence and Catalunia who attributed the experience of prophecy to biblical figures, these two individuals from the Ashkenazi and French regions provide examples of references to historical persons, presumably during their lifetimes, in terms of prophecy. I see no reason on the basis of this passage to surmise the possibility that an astral body made the ascent, despite the fact that a passage dealing with an astral body is known from a text believed to have been written in France in the same period.[63] The term *neshamah*, or "soul," seems to indicate an early instance of psychanodia in the strict sense of the word. Thus, on the one hand, this text reflects a different mentality in comparison to Heikhalot literature because the soul is expressly mentioned. On the other hand, in comparison to the internalized vision in Rav Hai's interpretation where no ascent is mentioned, here it is referred to explicitly. Though there can be no doubt that these two bodies of literature were known to the medieval figures, it seems that they were interested in another understanding of the ascent.

Unlike more mystically oriented descriptions (to be discussed below), however, the soul does not encounter or return to an entity that is its source, or experience some form of lost perfection, but rather is a mode for obtaining hidden information. Hence, this passage is more in line with some ancient apocalyptic materials and with Heikhalot literature than with medieval transformations of psychanodia.

3. NOUSANODIA:
THE NEOARISTOTELIAN SPIRITUALIZATION OF THE ASCENT

The processes of interiorization of mythical modes of thought resorting to new forms of spirituality are part and parcel of many developments in religion.[64] This is also the case with many descriptions of ascents on high and of visions of supernal realms. The adoption of and adaptation from some Greek forms of thought are evident in the elites of the three monotheistic religions. We already have seen above Rav Hai Gaon's rejection of the external elements of the ascent in Heikhalot literature; more dramatic, however, are attempts to reinterpret the biblical descriptions of ascent and descent as references to inner states of consciousness or as metaphorical expressions. This is the general propensity of various Jewish philosophical schools, the major exception being the thought of Rabbi Yehudah ha-Levi. This mode of metaphorical exegesis is applied repeatedly to the Bible and some rabbinic dicta in Maimonides's *Guide of the Perplexed.* The great eagle explains the occurrences of the verb "ascend" in connection to God in the Bible as pointing to "sublimity and greatness."[65] Developing Maimonides's semantic approach, one of his followers, the Kabbalist Rabbi Abraham Abulafia, wrote in one of his commentaries on the secrets of the *Guide:*

> The matter of the name of "ascent" is homonymous, as in their saying, "Moses ascended to God": this concerns the third matter, which is combined with their [allusion] also to the ascent to the tip of the mountain, upon which there descended the "created light." These two matters assist us [in understanding] all similar matters, and they are [the terms] "place" [*maqom*] and "ascent" [*'aliyah*] that, after they come to the matter of "man," the two of them are not impossible by any means; for Moses ascended to the mountain, and he also ascended to the Divine level. That ascent is combined with a revealed matter, and with a matter which is hidden; the revealed [matter] is the ascent of the mountain, and the hidden [aspect] is the level of prophecy.[66]

The hidden sense of the reference to ascent of the mountain is understood as a purely intellectual event that disregards any form of bodily ascent. Elsewhere, Rabbi Abulafia indicates that the human intellectual faculty gradually ascends to the agent intellect "and will unite with it after many hard, strong and mighty exercises, until the particular and personal prophetic [faculty] will turn universal, permanent and everlasting, similar to the essence of its cause, and he and He will become one entity."[67] No spatial adventure is mentioned here besides the opening of the human intellect to the cosmic intellectual presence, thus unifying the two. Ascents or descents found in Rabbi Abulafia's writings are metaphors for intellectual activities. Psychanodia is obliterated; there is no interpretation of Heikhalot discussions as undertaken by Rav Hai Gaon. In lieu of this, we may speak about a figurative nousanodia.

The transition from the sensuous to the intellectual is conceived by Rabbi Abulafia's school as a "natural change"—*sinnuy tiv'iy.* We learn this from a book entitled *Sefer ha-Tzeruf* by an anonymous author connected to Rabbi Abulafia's circle:

Now when the sphere of the intellect is moved by the Agent Intellect and the person begins to enter it and to ascend the sphere which returns, like the image of a ladder, and at the time of the ascent his thoughts shall be really transformed and all the visions shall be changed before him, and there will be nothing left to him of what he had earlier. Therefore, apart from changing his nature and his formation, he is as one who was uprooted from the power of feeling [and was translated to] the power of the intellect.[68]

Unlike Rabbi Abulafia, the anonymous Kabbalist underemphasizes the figurative nature of the term ascent. In this book the phrase "sphere of the intellect" uses a bodily term—sphere—that may indicate an ascent to an entity mediating between the corporeal and the intellectual. In any case, the act of ascension is strongly related to the concept of transformation, which affects the human being who is supposed to operate as an intellectual entity.

In a passage preserved in Rabbi Isaac of Acre's *Me'irat `Einayyim*, there is an extremely interesting discussion cited in the name of Rabbi Nathan, presumably Rabbi Nathan ben Sa`adya:

I heard from the sage Rabbi Nathan an explanation of this name [intellect]: You must know that when the Divine Intellect descends, it reaches the Agent Intellect and is called Agent Intellect; and when the Agent Intellect descends to the Acquired Intellect it is called Acquired Intellect; and when the Acquired Intellect descends to the Passive Intellect, it is called Passive Intellect; and when Passive Intellect descends to the soul which is in man it is called the soul. We therefore find that the Divine Intellect, which is within the human soul, is called the soul. And this is from above to below. And when you examine this matter from below to above, you shall see that when man separates himself from the vanities of this world and cleaves by his thought and soul to the supernal [realms] with great constancy, his soul will be called according to the level among the higher degrees, which he has acquired and attached himself to it. How so? If the soul of the isolated person deserves to apprehend and to cleave to the Passive Intellect, it is called Passive Intellect, as if it is Passive Intellect; and likewise when it ascends further and cleaves to the Acquired Intellect, it becomes the Acquired Intellect; and if it is merited to cleave to the Agent Intellect, then it itself [becomes] Agent Intellect; and if you shall deserve and cleave to the Divine Intellect, happy are you, because you have returned to your source and root, which is called, literally, the Divine Intellect. And that person is called the Man of God, that is to say, a Divine man, creating worlds.[69]

Let us compare the last passage to one that will be adduced later from Rabbi Yehudah Albotini, a Kabbalist who was heavily influenced by Rabbi Nathan's book. Both resort to the cleaving of thought and soul, and both conceive the culmination of the ascent with the acquisition of magical capacities. Both combine Neoaristotelian and Neoplatonic terminology. And, what is more pertinent to our discussion, both describe a rather easy transition from the lower human capacity to the highest spiritual level of the divine world. In other words, Rabbi Albotini's passage offers a synthesis of theories found in the writings of Rabbi Abulafia and two of his followers, who belong to what I call the Eastern group of his disciples. Similarly, we read in the mid-fourteenth-century Byzantine writings of Rabbi Elnathan ben Moses Qalqish, a prolific author influenced by ecstatic Kabbalah, that:

> This is the distinguished level of the man of God, and this is the daily and light intellect, the light of which is above the heads of the creatures inscribed as in the vision, "and upon the image on the throne was an image like that of a man," to whom he cleaved and by whom he ascended. And the prophets who came after him prophesied by means of the Unclear mirror, and that is the imagination of night-time, [which is] dark, like the light of the sun upon the moon, to receive light from the sparks, and from the flame of his warmth to warm from its extreme cold, like the warmth of the heart which is extreme in its simplicity, to extinguish the extreme cold of the spleen.[70]

There can be no doubt that the human intellect, described as hovering over or surrounding the head of man and constituting his real "image," is described here as the vehicle for man's ascent on high. This is no doubt a metaphorical ascent, but nevertheless the concept of ascension is explicit.

These are just a few examples of cases of *ascensio mentis* in ecstatic

Kabbalah, which can easily be multiplied. As we shall see below in the work of some of the followers of Rabbi Abulafia, there are also examples of psychanodia that betray the impact of Neoplatonism.

4. NEOPLATONIC CASES OF PSYCHANODIA

In Heikhalot literature it seems that the main protagonist of the ascent is not the soul, but rather some form of spiritual body. As seen above, it is only later in the Middle Ages that the term "soul" occurs in an ascensional context. In most cases, this is part of an ascensional approach that sees the soul as the main protagonist of the upward journey, demonstrating the impact of Neoplatonism.[71] Explicit mention of the soul, though not in a literal sense, is found in a highly influential text by Plotin. Following is a translation of this passage as mediated by the *Theology of Aristotle* by Rabbi Shem Tov ibn Falaquera, a Jewish philosopher active in the second half of the thirteenth century in Spain:

> Aristotle has said: Sometimes I become as if self-centered and remove my body and I was as if I am a spiritual substance without a body. And I have seen the beauty and the splendor and I become amazed and astonished. [Then] I knew that I am part of the parts of the supernal world, the perfect and the sublime, and I am an active being [or animal]. When this has become certain to me, I ascended in my thought from this world to the Divine Cause [*ha-ʿIllah ha-ʾElohit*] and I was there as if I were situated within it and united in it and united with it, and I was higher than the entire intellectual world and I was seeing myself as if I am standing within the world of the divine intellect I was as if I was united within it and united with it, as if I am standing in this supreme and divine state.[72]

The language of ascent is quite obvious, despite the fact that, conceptually speaking, nothing similar to psychanodia or nousanodia is surmised by the Neoplatonic author. This is the reason why the expression "as if" occurs six times. We may assume that here there is an interiorization of a psychanodian vision found in Hellenistic sources, understood now as an inner flight.[73] However, in some reverberations of Neoplatonism, an ascent of the soul to the supernal soul becomes nevertheless obvious. In a passage authored by the early thirteenth-century Kabbalist, Rabbi Ezra of Gerona, such a process is well illustrated:

[T]he righteous causes his unblemished and pure soul to ascend [until she—the human soul—reaches] the supernal holy soul [and] she unites with her [the supernal soul] and knows future things. And this is the manner [in which] the prophet acted, as the evil inclination did not have any dominion over him, to separate him from the Supernal Soul. Thus, the soul of the prophet is united with the Supernal Soul in a complete union.[74]

The righteous, acting in the present, and the prophets, who are ideals relevant to the glorious past, use the same comic–psychological structure: naturally, when the soul is unblemished and unstained by sin, it can ascend to the source, and by doing so, it can know the future. Ascent is therefore part of a more complex process that involves a more practical implication in both the righteous and the prophet.

A mixture of psychanodia and nousanodia is found in an influential anonymous Kabbalistic writing composed in the early fourteenth century in Catalunia. Again, the soul of the righteous is the main subject of the ascent: "The soul of the righteous one will ascend—while he is yet alive—higher and higher, to the place where the souls of the righteous [enjoy their] delight, [an event] that is [called] 'the cleaving of the mind.' The body will [then] remain motionless, as it is said: 'But you that cleave unto the Lord your God are alive every one of you this day.'"[75] Interestingly enough, the adherence or the union is the main purpose of the ascent in these cases, and the mystics are called by the name "righteous"—Tzaddiqim—a term that does not play a significant role in Heikhalot literature. It recurs elsewhere, however, in Rabbi Ezra's writing; this Kabbalist uses the term to describe those who perform an operation in the divine world—namely those who first adhered to the supernal realm and then acted thereupon.[76]

The philosophical terminology of these two quotes is obvious. In the case of Rabbi Ezra, the Neoplatonic terminology of two souls is explicit. In the second quote, the cleaving to the place of supernal thought is mentioned. In any case, neither firmaments, palaces, rings or thrones nor angelic structures that played such a crucial role in Heikhalot and other late antiquity types of Jewish literature occur in these cases of ascensio. The role of the cosmic pillar, a topic that will be addressed later, is also absent here.

Now I turn to a passage found in an anonymous Kabbalistic treatise belonging to what is known as the circle of the `Yuun book:

And this attribute [*Middah*] was transmitted to Enoch, son of Jared, and he kept it, and would attempt to know the Creator, blessed be He, with the same attribute. And when he adhered to it, his soul longed to attract the abundance of the upper [spheres] from the [sefirah of] wisdom, until his soul ascended to and was bound by the [sefirah of] discernment, and the two of them became as one thing. This is the meaning of what is written, "And Enoch walked with God." And it is written in the *Alpha Beta of Rabbi Akiva* that he transformed his flesh into fiery torches and he became as if he were one of the spiritual beings.[77]

This is an important example for the attenuation of the mythical ascent from Heikhalot literature by a more unitive description that puts the soul at the center of the experience. The soul's adherence to and union with the third sefirah, that of Binah, which is considered in many early Kabbalistic texts to be the source of the soul, is conceived to be the "real" meaning of Enoch's ascent. Though bodily transformation is mentioned at the end of the excerpt, the reference to *Alpha Beta of Rabbi Akiva* serves as a proof text for expounding upon the medieval theory of mystical union.

Now let us examine the evidence found in the Zohar in a passage from *Midrash ha-Ne'elam* on the Song of Songs:

When the Holy One, blessed be He, created Adam, He placed him in the Garden of Eden, in a garment of glory, out of the light of the Garden of Eden.... And those garments left him.... And the luminous soul ascended...and he remained bereft of all...and that luminosity of the supernal soul which left him ascended upwards, and it was stored in a certain treasury, that is the body, up to the time that he begat sons, and Enoch came into the world. Since Enoch came, the supernal light of the holy soul descended into him, and Enoch was enwrapped in the supernal soul which had left Adam.[78]

Unlike the Neoplatonic use of the term "supernal soul" to indicate the cosmic or universal soul, as seen above and as shall be seen again below, the Zoharic passage deals with the superior part of the human soul. Adam's soul is understood Neoplatonically—that is, as an entity that descended from a higher sphere of reality and returns thereto—but this is a soul preserved for the few, and as such, Enoch merits it. In a way, the soul that deserted the sinful Adam is also a light that descends upon meritorious individuals.

The spiritual shift from the individual to the universal soul is exemplified in Rabbi Nathan ben Sa`adya's book *Sha`arei Tzedeq*. In one case, Moses is described as having "been transformed into a universal [being] after being a particular, central point. And this is the matter of the lower man that ascended and became 'the man who is on the throne,' by the virtue of the power of the Name."[79] This description is reminiscent of many Neoplatonically-oriented transformations of the particular soul into the universal soul, a phenomenon I propose calling universalization. This form of expression, which may or may not represent an experience that is different from others described as involving cleaving and union, already had a history in Jewish mysticism, and Rabbi Nathan's *Sha`arei Tzedeq* is one link in a longer chain of tradition. Indeed, some lines further, our author refers explicitly to the "soul of all."[80] Moses's transformation was accomplished by means of a name—in Hebrew, *ha-shem*, which stands for the Tetragrammaton and the consonants of which are identical to a permutation of those of Mosheh. Therefore, resorting to the Kabbalistic technique based on names used by the author, Moses was able to become a supernal man. The above transformation from the particular to the general is found elsewhere in the group of Rabbi Abulafia's followers related to *Sha`arei Tzedeq*. Rabbi Isaac of Acre mentions that "the Nought, that encompasses everything" and the "soul should cleave to Nought and become universal and comprehensive after being particular because of her palace when she was imprisoned in it, [she] will become universal, in the secret of the essence of the secret of her place from which she was hewn."[81]

This common language of universalization does not mean, to be sure, that the earlier text authored by Rabbi Nathan had an impact on Rabbi Isaac, who was acquainted with at least some concepts found in the book. Nevertheless, for an examination of unitive imagery, this neglected passage is of great importance since it includes a syntagm that is reminiscent of much later Hasidic discussions of union with the divine nought—*le-hidabbeq be-'ayin*.[82] Earlier in his treatise, Rabbi Nathan reports on a conversation between God and Moses, who is told by the divine voice that he cannot contemplate the divine glory, despite the fact that he "ascended to the rank of the supernal man, who is the Living."[83] These phrases unequivocally indicate an expansion of the lower man, more precisely of his soul, its ascension to its supernal source and its transformation into that source. The Neoplatonic assumption that there is only one soul, particularized by matter into individual souls without fragmenting that of the universal, underpins the above discussions.[84] It should be emphasized that, though the vision in the biblical proof text is that of an *anthropos*, the interpretation offered by Rabbi Nathan speaks solely of the transformation of the soul. The ascent of the soul gained impetus from sixteenth-century Safedian Kabbalah onwards. Its main hero, the famous Ashkenazi Rabbi Isaac Luria (1538–1572), is reported in a hagiographic book as one:

> ...whose soul ascended nightly to the heavens, and whom the attending angels came to accompany to the celestial academy. They asked him: "To which academy do you wish to go?" Sometimes he said that he wished to visit the Academy of Rabbi Simeon bar Yohai, or the Academy of Rabbi Akiva or that of Rabbi Eliezer the Great or those of other Tannaim and Amoraim, or of the prophets. And to whichever of those academies he wished to go, the angels would take him. The next day, he would disclose to the sages what he received in that academy.[85]

This passage describes one of two ways in which the mystic may acquire the supernal secrets of the Kabbalah: he may either ascend to study the Torah together with ancient figures, as above, or be taught by Elijah and others who descend to reveal Kabbalistic secrets, as we read in other texts that describe the manner in which Rabbi Luria obtained his knowledge.[86] The frequency of heavenly ascent is indeed remarkable: each and every night, Rabbi Luria visited one of the celestial academies, and thereafter transmitted the teachings to his students. This perception of Rabbi Luria is no doubt closely connected to the huge amount of Kabbalistic material that emerged from him and that produced the extensive Lurianic literature. It should be emphasized that the description of Rabbi Luria, unlike any of the other masters to which ascension of the soul has been attributed, mentions nighttime explicitly as the only occasion on which such ascents take place.

Let me address now a passage preserved by the main disciple of Rabbi Luria. In the fourth part of his *Sha`arei Qedushah*, Rabbi Hayyim Vital quotes passages dealing with *hitbodedut*—mental concentration or solitude—that are not present in any other Kabbalistic source. So, for example, in a manner reminiscent of Rabbi Abulafia's recommendations for solitude, Rabbi Vital's source recommends that one:

> Meditate in a secluded house as above, and wrap yourself in a *tallit*, and sit and close your eyes and remove yourself from the material world, as if your soul had left your body, and ascended into the heavens. And after this divestment, read one *mishnah*, whichever one you wish, many times, time after time, and intend that your soul commune with the soul of the *Tanna'* mentioned in that *mishnah*.[87]

From some points of view, this text combines ecstatic Kabbalah with practices of reciting the Mishnah found among sixteenth-century Safedian Kabbalists.[88] In his mystical diary, Rabbi Vital reported the dream of one of his acquaintances, Rabbi Isaac Alatif, concerning himself, which he described as follows:

> Once I fainted deeply for an hour, and a huge number of old men and many women came to watch me, and the house was completely full of them, and they all were worried for me. Afterwards the swoon passed and I opened my eyes and said: "Know that just now my soul ascended to the Seat of Glory and they sent my soul back to this world, in order to preach before you and lead you in the way of repentance and charity."[89]

It may be assumed that the ascent of the soul to the seat of glory has a certain mystical implication, perhaps an attempt to contemplate God, such as Rabbi Vital attempted according to one of his dreams.[90]

The concept of ascension is important in eighteenth-century Hasidism, as we shall see in greater detail in chapter four, where some of the discussion will address the Neoplatonic concept. Here I would like to draw attention to just one case, which reverberates with many followers of the master who formulated it, the Great Maggid of Medzirech. In a manner reminiscent of Rabbi Nathan ben Sa'adya Harar's discussion of the two halves in a passage found in his *Sha'arei Tzedeq*, Rabbi Dov Baer of Medziretch interprets the biblical verse "Make thee two trumpets" as follows:

[T]wo halves of forms, as it is written "on the throne, a likeness in the appearance of a man above upon it," as man [that is, *ʾADaM*] is but *D* and *M*, and the speech dwells upon him. And when he unites with God, who is the Alpha of the world, he becomes *ʾADaM*.... And man must separate himself from any corporeal thing, to such an extent that he will ascend through all the worlds and be in union with God, until [his] existence will be annihilated, and then he will be called *ʾADaM*.[91]

The Maggid bases his homily on the verse: "Make thee two trumpets of silver, of a whole piece shall thou make them." [92] The Hebrew word for trumpets—*Hatzotzerot*—is interpreted as *Hatzi-Tzurah*—namely "half of the form," which together, since they are two halves, create a perfect form. Here, we may see this process as the completion of a perfect structure by the ascent of one of its halves. No hierarchy is implied here, but rather direct contact between man and God in a manner reminiscent of Rabbi Nathan's point of view.

5. THE ASCENT THROUGH THE TEN SEFIROT

Ascents on high are more meaningful when detailed hierarchies are involved. This is obvious in the theosophical–theurgical Kabbalah, where the system of ten sefirot constitutes a median structure between infinity—*ʾEin Sof*—and the created world. To be sure, the understanding of these powers varies from Kabbalist to Kabbalist, and I use here a simplistic description, which is much more salient for the later, sixteenth-century understanding of Kabbalah.[93] As instruments of the divine power, which is also immanent within them, the sefirot were and still are involved in sustaining and governing the created world. In a way, they play a role reminiscent of the celestial bodies in medieval astronomy and astrology. However, while celestial bodies often assumed negative valences, as Culianu points out, sefirotic powers were conceived of in a much more positive light.[94] There are many forms of upward processes, however, that involve the ascension of both the lower sefirot, who draw on and suck influx from the higher sefirot, and the human intention or soul.[95] This type of ascent is exemplified in an influential passage by Rabbi Moses Cordovero describing the nature of Kabbalistic prayer:

The man whom his Creator has bestowed with the grace of entering the innerness of occult lore and knows and understands that by reciting *Barekh `Aleinu* and *Refa'enu* the intention is to draw down the blessing and the influx by each and every blessing to a certain *sefirah*, and the blessing of *Refa'enu* to a certain *sefirah*, as it is known to us. Behold, this man is worshiping the Holy One, blessed be He and his *Shekhinah*, as a son and as a servant standing before his master, by means of a perfect worship, out of love, without deriving any benefit or reward because of that worship...because the wise man by the quality of his [mystical] intention when he intends during his prayer, his soul will be elevated by his [spiritual] arousal from one degree to another, from one entity to another until she arrives and is welcome and comes in the presence of the Creator, and cleaves to her source, to the source of life; and then a great influx will be emanated upon her from there, and he will become a vessel [*keli*] and a place and foundation for [that] influx, and from him it [the influx] will be distributed to all the world as it is written in the *Zohar*, pericope Terumah, until the *Shekhinah* will cleave to him... and you will be a seat to Her and [then] the influx will descend onto you...because you are in lieu of the great pipe instead of the *Tzaddiq*, the foundation of the world.[96]

The Kabbalist is supposed to ascend daily through the sefirotic realm in order to adhere to the supernal source, from which he demands that the influx be drawn down. Ascent in this case is not only a matter of individual attainment but also part of a wider and more complex model—the mystical–magical, which has already been addressed above. However, what is much less clear is what exactly ascends on high: the intention—some form of noetic process focusing upon the content of the divine map while praying—or some form of energy that is acquired through concentration during prayer. What is important in this passage is the fact that the ascent is no longer a rare experience attributed only to a small elite group but rather is a matter of daily experience that is accessible to every Kabbalist. The ascendant Kabbalist is not only capable of triggering the descent of the influx but also becomes a pipeline for its transmission to the mundane world.

The ascent from one degree to another, which is found before Rabbi Cordovero, became a standard expression for ascent in the supernal world, and it recurs in many texts, especially in Hasidism. It also occurs in an explicit discussion of the ascent through the sefirot attributed to an influential messianic figure, Sabbatai Tzevi, by a Yemenite apocalypse, which stems from a rather early period of the Sabbatean movement. In a passage printed and previously analyzed by Gershom Scholem, the Messiah is described as ascending from "one degree to another, [all] the degrees of the seven sefirot from Gedullah to Malkhut...after two years he ascends to the degree that his mother is there."[97] The sequence of the sefirot is not clear at all: Gedullah in classical descriptions stands for the fifth sefirot, the sefirah of Hesed, while Malkhut is a much lower one. Thus it is hard to understand how movement from the former to the latter can be considered an ascent. It is even harder to characterize the nature of this ascent: which human faculty is utilized, what is meant by the length of time needed to reach the highest attainment, and who the "mother" is. Scholem has correctly interpreted this text as referring to the third sefirah, which is commonly symbolized as the mother. He even proposes, on the basis of this passage, that a mystical event occurred in the spiritual life of Tzevi in 1650, and again, he correctly intuited that the meaning of this attainment would be the understanding of the "secret of the Divinity."[98] What Scholem does not specify is the nature of this secret. On the basis of the above quotes as well as others to be adduced below, I suggest that this secret should be understood not just as reaching the third sefirah; rather, this sefirah itself may be the very secret of the divinity, the most intimate secret of Sabbatean theology, as proposed by Tzevi himself.[99] In any case, elsewhere in the same epistle, the nest of the bird, the mystical place of the Messiah, is none other than the third sefirah.[100] Thus, the axis of the sefirot also constitutes the vertical ladder that is climbed by the mystic when he progresses in both understanding and in discovering experientially the higher levels of the divine structure. I have great doubt, however, that the above text reflects an experience or a statement stemming from Tzevi himself. It seems that the ascensional language related to the sefirot more aptly reflects the views of the anonymous Sabbatean author of the so-called Yemenite apocalypse rather than that of the Messiah, whose views were closer to Rabbi Abulafia's stance. In any case, it should be pointed out that the issue of ascent is related not only to founders of religions, as mentioned at the beginning of this chapter, but also to Messianic figures like Jesus. As we shall see, the ascent occurs in connection to the Messiah in the book of the Zohar and in relation to the activity of the Besht in his encounter with the Messiah.[101]

Eighteenth-century Hasidism is even more concerned with ascension. In a passage written by an important Ukrainian author, Rabbi Menahem Nahum of Chernobyl, we find a stance that may reflect a view of the founder of Hasidism, the Besht:[102]

> By means of the Torah, the union between the bridegroom and the bride, the Assembly of Israel and the Holy One, blessed be He, takes place... And just as the bridegroom and the bride will delight in joy, so the Holy One, blessed be He, and the Assembly of Israel are [enjoying] "like the joy of the bridegroom for/on his bride".... He compared us to a bridegroom and a bride, since the permanent delight is not a delight, only the union of the bridegroom and the bride, which is a new union, because they did not previously have an intercourse. So has someone to unify the Holy One, blessed be He, a new union every day, as if this day it has been given, as the sages, blessed be their memory, said: "Let the words of the Torah be new, et cetera." And the reason is that the Holy One, blessed be He, is renewing every day the creation of the world and the Torah is called "creation of the world" because by means of it [the Torah] all the worlds have been created, as it is well known. And God is continuously innovating and there is no one [single] day that is similar to the other one, and every day there is a new adherence and coming closer to the Torah, since the day has been created by it in a manner different from "yesterday that passed." This is the reason why Israel is called a virgin...because every day its youth is renewed and the union of that day never existed [beforehand] since the creation of the world, and from this point of view it is called a virgin. Whoever is worshiping in such a manner is called the walker from one degree to another always and from one aspect to another aspect, and he unifies every day a new union... And the Torah is called an aspect of the fiancée that is an aspect of the bride, so that always a new union will be achieved as at the time of the wedding. This is the meaning of [the story about] Moses that he was studying and forgetting, namely that he is forgetting the delight, because "a permanent delight is not delight," until the Torah has been given to him as a bride to a bridegroom. This means that he received the power to go every

day from one degree to another, and every new degree and ascent was for him an aspect of a bride, a new union, and this is the great delight like that of the bridegroom and the bride.[103]

Unlike the daily ascent on the sefirotic axis, as we saw in Rabbi Cordovero's passage, here the ascent is not connected explicitly to an articulated hierarchy, but such progress is assumed. Moreover, again unlike the Safedian Kabbalist, the Hasidic master does not mention the expert—the Kabbalist—in matters of esotericism, but Jews in general. It seems that the importance of the process is so great that attainment is underemphasized; rather, the event of gradual ascent from one degree to another is the purpose of the exercise. The Hasidic master recommends an ascent for the sake of the pleasure of doing so.

6. "As If" and Imaginary Ascents

The language "as if" is obvious in the passage by Plotin adduced above and in its numerous reverberations in medieval material. It may be concluded, therefore, that ascent language is figurative, but it does not indicate an imaginary process that resorts to a specific spiritual faculty like the imagination. Following are some examples in which Kabbalists used "as if" to describe their ascents on high.[104] Found as early as the classic book of Neoplatonism, its occurrence is part of Hellenistic thought attenuated by the earlier somanodia phenomena. In a book by Rabbi Yehudah Albotini, an early sixteenth-century author belonging to ecstatic Kabbalah and active in Jerusalem, the "as if" language is quite obvious. Departing from Rabbi Abraham Abulafia's discourse, which does not resort to the word *ke-'Illu*—translated as "as if"—to describe a figurative ascent, he suggests to the Kabbalist that:

> ...he should prepare his true thought [*mahshavto*] to visualize in his heart and mind as if he sits on high, in the heavens of heavens, in front of the Holy One, blessed be He, within the splendor and the radiance of His Shekhinah. And it is as if he sees the Holy One. blessed be He, sitting as a king.... And he should ascend and link and cleave his soul and thought [*mahshavto*] then from one rank to another insofar as spiritual issues are concerned [and] as far as his power affords, to cause her to cleave and to cause her to ascend on high, higher than the world of the spheres, and the world of the sep-

arate intellects and to the supernal and hidden world of emanation, so as to be then as if it is an intellect *in actu* and it has no sense for the *sensibilia* because it [already] exited from the human dominion and entered then into the divine dominion, and he said [commanded] and his will is done.[105]

We witness again a combination of nousanodia and psychanodia in the same passage. Not only are the soul and the intellect mentioned, but I also assume that the two organs—the heart and the mind—indicate a dual understanding of the ascension. However, the language of ascent is much more concrete here, as an entire hierarchy of worlds is explicitly mentioned. Steeped as he was in the language of Neoaristotelianism, as mediated by Maimonides and Rabbi Abulafia, Rabbi Albotini describes the result of ascent as the actualization of the intellect. The theosophical structure of the ten sefirot, therefore, is conceived not only as the place from which the soul descended and to which it should return, but also as the locus of the actualization of the intellect.

The introvertive experience that calls for the "as if" language recurs in a text by Rabbi Hayyim Vital that describes the technical preparations necessary for the imaginary ascent:

Behold, when someone prepares himself to cleave to the supernal root, he will be able to cleave to it. However, despite the fact that he is worthy to achieve this [achievement] he should divest his soul in a complete manner, and separate it from all matters of matter, and then you should be able to cleave to her spiritual root. And, behold, the issue of divestment that is found written in all the books dealing with issues of prophecy and divine spirit, a real divestment that the soul exits from his body really, as it happens in sleep, because if it is so this is not a prophecy but a dream like all the dreams. However, the dwelling of the Holy Spirit upon man takes place while his soul is within him, in a state of awakenedess, and she will not exit from him. But the matter of divestment is that he should remove all his thoughts whatsoever, and the imaginative power...will cease to imagine and think and ruminate about any matters of this world as if his soul exited from it. Then the imaginative power transforms his thought so as to imagine and conceptualize, as if he ascends to the supernal worlds, to the roots of his soul that are there, from one [root] to another, until the concept of his imagination [*Tziyyur dimy-*

ono] arrives to his supernal source... All this is the divestment of the power of imagination from all the thoughts of matter in a complete manner.[106]

Elsewhere in the same book we read that one should:

> ...remove his thoughts from all matters of this world, as if his soul had departed from him, like a person from whom the soul departed and who feels nothing.... And he should imagine that his soul has departed and ascended, and he should envision the upper worlds, as though he stands in them. And if he performed some unification— he should think about it, to bring down by this light and abundance into all the worlds, and he should intend to receive also his portion at the end. And he should concentrate in his thought, as though the spirit had rested upon him, until he awakens somewhat...and after a few days he should return to meditate in the same manner, until he merits that the spirit rest upon him.[107]

Dealing with Rabbi Vital's mystical thought, R. J. Z. Werblowsky duly points out that the imaginary nature of the references to the ascent diminish its ecstatic nature. He attributes this attenuation to Maimonides's theory of imagination that detracts from the importance of the ascent in favor of the language "as if."[108] There can be no doubt that Rabbi Vital was indeed acquainted with Maimonides, and there is no historical problem in assuming such an influence. On the one hand, as seen above, the language "as if" in the specific context of ascents on high is found in some texts before Rabbi Vital, and on the other, those mystics drawing more directly from Maimonides, like Rabbi Abulafia, did not use this language in order to describe their ascents. Thus, it would be much more pertinent to attribute the occurrence of this language to the Neoplatonic influence.

Rabbi Vital combines this language with a certain theory of imagination that is not, however, entirely Aristotelian. His approach to this faculty is much more positive than that of Maimonides, possibly due to the impact of a theory found in the Middle Ages in Sufi and Kabbalistic texts regarding the world of imagination. Due to the influence of some forms of Sufism, the role of the imaginary faculty is highlighted. Events are described as taking place in the imagination and in a place described as the "world of images," *`alam al-mithal*—in Hebrew, *`olam ha-*

demut, and translated by Henry Corbin in Latin as *mundus imaginalis*.[109] One of the few Kabbalists to adopt this vision of imagination was Rabbi Nathan of Sa'adyah Harar, who has been mentioned above.[110] Rabbi Vital, however, was acquainted with theories concerning the visualization of letters of divine names in different colors—letters that were imagined to ascend to the sefirotic realm. In a text presumably written some time in the fourteenth century in Spain, we read that:

> ...when you shall think upon something which points to the [sefirah of] *Keter* and pronounce it with your mouth, you shall direct [your thought] to and visualize the name YHWH between your eyes with this vocalization, which is the *Qammaz* [vowel pronounced as a long a] under all the consonants, its visualization being white as snow. And he [!] will direct [your thought] so that the letters will move and fly in the air, and the whole secret is hinted at in the verse, "I have set the Divine Name always before me."[111]

According to this passage, the colored letters visualized are meant to ascend. Thus, human imagination is ontologically creative, its products being able to ascend to the supernal realm of the Merkavah. Following this trend in theosophical–theurgical Kabbalah, Rabbi Hayyim Vital adduces elsewhere in his *Sha'arei Qedushah* a text ending with the ascent of thought to the highest firmament, the 'Aravot, where "he shall visualize that above the firmament of 'Aravot there is a very great white curtain, upon which the Tetragrammaton is inscribed in [color] white as snow, in Assyrian writing in a certain color."[112] The issue is quite obvious here: the Kabbalist does not see what is inscribed objectively on the firmament but imagines what is written there. The ascent is therefore some form of induced imaginary vision of ascent and contemplation.

7. ASCENSION AND ANGELIZATION

In some cases of late antiquity Christianity the ascension is connected to forms of transformation that culminate in the phenomena of angelization, apotheosis or theosis.[113] In a hierarchical society, the very act of ascending means acquiring a higher status and coming closer to entities that are more sublime, powerful, knowledgeable or even divine. Processes of angelization are reported in the Odes of Solomon adduced above, particularly in Enoch's case, according to the different versions of books dealing with this figure. However, as previously noted, examples of an ascent of some form of bodily entity are few in the Middle Ages. The emphasis is on phenomena that may be described as psychanodia and nousanodia. However, in some cases it is assumed that not only the soul or the intellect but also some other aspect of the human psyche might ascend. Nevertheless, even instances in which the ascent of the soul is expressly mentioned, as is the case for Rabbi Michael from France, one nevertheless may acquire the attribute "angel."

The human intention—known in Hebrew as *kavvanah*—is sometimes understood as ascending on high as part of the theurgical effort to impact processes taking place within the divine sphere. So, for example, we read about "those who abandon the affairs of this world and pay no regard to this world at all, as though they were not corporeal beings, but all their intent and purpose is fixed on their creator alone, as in the case of Elijah and Enoch, who lived on forever in body and soul, after having attained union of their souls with the Great Name."[114]

In addition to the process of angelization attributed to Enoch, it is the figure of Elijah who assumes the role of an angel-like entity, who ascends on high and continues to reveal himself at various occasions by descending to this world. So, for example, in a late fifteenth-century Kabbalistic book written in Spain, we read:

When he [Elijah] has ascended on high, he has acquired the power of spirituality as an angel indeed, to ascend and to become [afterwards] corporeal and descend to this lower world where you are existing. This in order to perform miracles or to disclose My power and My dynamis in the world. And he [Elijah] is causing the descent of My power in the world, forcefully and compelling, from My great name, that is an integral part of him. And because of this great secret he did not have the taste of death, so that he will be able to cause the descent of My power and disclose My secret by the power of My precious names. And he is called "The bird of heaven will bring the voice" and no one should have any doubt of it. He was revealing himself to the ancient pious one, factually in a spiritual body, which was enclosed and embodied in matter, and they were speaking with him, by the virtue of their piety, and he was revealing himself *in corpore et in spiritu.* This is the reason why those dreaming a dream are causing the descent of My power, by his mediation, within you, without speech and voice, and this is the secret of [the

verse] "for this is your wisdom and your understanding in the sight
of the nations." And My power is bound to him and he is bound to
your souls and discloses to you the secrets of My Torah, without
speech. And a time will come, very soon, that he will reveal himself
to you *in corpore et in spiritu* and this will be a sign for the coming of
the Messiah. And by his descending to earth together with him then
will he reveal *in corpore et in spiritu*, and many other will see him.[115]

Thus, though Elijah's ascent is an apotheosis, his descent is not a return of the deified person to a human existence, but in fact a case of
theophany, since the divine power descends with him. It is in this literary body of Kabbalistic writing, which fiercely opposes both Greek and
Jewish philosophy, that a more concrete vision of the ascent and descent may be found.[116] On the other hand, what is conspicuous in this
passage is the continuum among the divine, the angelic and the human.
The ascent is a motion taking place between planes of existence that
are not separated by ontic gaps but that are different forms of manifestations of a Protean and more comprehensive being.[117]

8. Astral Psychanodia in Jewish Sources

As pointed out by Culianu, the rather widespread ascent of the soul
through the seven planets found in Hellenistic and early Christian
sources was alien to late antiquity Jewish sources, which provide a
separate and independent model of psychanodia.[118] I believe that this
phenomenological remark is an important insight and holds not only
for the ancient Jewish texts but also for vast majority of medieval and
premodern Jewish texts. Despite the impact of astrology and of hermetic sources on various Jewish literatures, discussions of the ascent
through the planetary system are few and explicitly literary; in fact, I
am aware of only two examples. Rabbi Abraham ibn Ezra, the influential twelfth-century thinker, produced a literary composition entitled
Hay ben Meqitz under the influence of Avicenna.[119] Another composition was authored by Rabbi Abraham Yagel, a Kabbalist in the second
half of the sixteenth century, that is entitled *Gei Hizzayon*, which follows Italian models.[120] It should be mentioned, however, that unlike
late antiquity cases of psychanodia in which some negative aspects are
attributed to the planets, in these two Jewish sources, as well as in
Avicenna, this is not so.

9. Concluding Remarks

It may be said that the heavenly journey depicted as an act of leaving the body in order to explore the higher realms and then returning to it, as found in Heikhalot literature, is missing in the vast Kabbalistic literature written on the Iberian Peninsula. In lieu of this, as we shall see in chapter three, we have the elaboration of a tradition of the ascent of dead souls—post-mortem—on a cosmic pillar, from the lower to the higher paradise.

Whether the astral body is involved or not, ascents of the soul as part of an initiated endeavor do not occur in Spanish Jewish literature known as Kabbalah; Heikhalot literature had no impact. Here, we may find many instances of ascent and adhesion of the human soul, thought or intellect to higher spiritual entities, be they God, the agent intellect or the cosmic soul. Such forms of ascent are influenced by Neoaristotelian and Neoplatonic sources as mediated by Arabic, Jewish and—more rarely—Christian philosophical writings that address the ideal of cleaving to the source of the human's spiritual faculties. At least within the topic of the spiritual ascent, a major shift in the phenomenology of Jewish mysticism can be discerned. While the bodily forms of ascent of mortals are dominant in late antiquity Jewish mysticism, such phenomena remain on the margin of its medieval forms and lingered only in instances in which Greek–Hellenistic theories were not influential. In all other cases—the vast majority of Jewish mysticism—Greek–Hellenistic theories prevailed and obliterated earlier forms of Jewish ascent. These forms remained active in one way or another *in corpora* that were much less interested in noetic processes, like the posthumous ascents in the book of the Zohar that will be analyzed in chapter three and in some Hasidic cases that will be discussed in chapter four. Though the theme of ascent on high remained in medieval European literature, as is evident from Dante's *Divina Commedia* and other cases mentioned in section eight, they are literary, not experiential, treatments. In the mystical literature of Muslims, Christians and Jews in the Middle Ages, the ascent lost most of the centrality it had in late antiquity due to the accumulative impact of the noetic valences of both Neoplatonism and Neoaristotelianism. It is only in the posthumous journey of the soul that the ascent remained important in the three monotheistic religions in the Middle Ages.[121]

To return to Culianu's distinction between ancient Jewish ascents through the heavens and Greek ascents involving a system of planets or spheres, both forms were marginalized in most medieval forms of Kabbalah. Other Greek and Hellenistic theories of psychanodia and nousanodia were adopted and transformed the late antiquity Jewish form of ascent via the heavens. Helpful as Culianu's distinction is for the period he investigated—namely late antiquity—it becomes less relevant for other periods in Jewish mysticism. Nevertheless—and this should be emphasized—there was a reticence in Jewish sources to adopt celestial spheres and planets as ladders for the ascent of the soul.

NOTES

1. See Pierre Benoit, "L'ascension," *Revue Biblique* LVI (1940): pp. 161–203; Morton Smith, "Ascents to Heavens and the Beginning of Christianity," *Eranos Jahrbuch* 50 (1981): pp. 403–29; and James D. Tabor, *Things Unutterable: Paul's Ascent to Paradise in its Greco-Roman, Judaic, and Early Christian Contexts* (New York: University Press of America, 1986). For Patristic discussions, see Felix Asiedu, "The Song of Songs and the ascent of the soul: Ambrose, Augustine, and the language of mysticism," *Vigiliae Christianae* 55:3 (2001): pp. 299–317.

2. See Geo Widengren, *Muhammad, the Apostle of God, and His Ascension* (Wiesbaden: Lundequistska bokhandeln Uppsala, 1955), pp. 96–114 and 220–26; Shmuel Tamari, *Iconotextual Studies in the Muslim Vision of Paradise* (Ramat Gan: Bar Ilan University; and Wiesbaden: Harrassowitz, 1999), pp. 72–75; David J. Halperin, "Hekhalot and Mi'raj: Observations on the Heavenly Journey in Judaism and Islam," in *Death, Ecstasy, and Other Worldly Journeys*, eds., J. J. Collins and Michael Fishbane (Albany: State University of New York Press, 1995), pp. 269–88; B. Schrieke, "Die Himmelsreise Muhammeds," *Der Islam* VI (1916): pp. 1–30; Joseph Horovitz, "Muhammeds Himmelfahrt," *Der Islam* IX (1919): pp. 159–83; and R. Hartmann, "Die Himmelsreise Muhammeds und ihre Bedeutung in der Religion des Islam," *Vortrage der Bibliothek Warburg, 1928–1929* (Leipzig-Berlin: 1930), pp. 42–65. For mystical interpretations of the ascension in Islam see, for example, R. A. Nicholson, "An Early Arabic Version of the Mi'raj of Abdi Yazid al-Bistami," *Islamica* (1926): pp. 402–16; James Winston Morris, "The Spiritual Ascension: Ibn 'Arabi and the Mi'raj," *JAOS* 107:4 (1987): pp. 629–52; idem, 108:1 (1988): pp. 63–77. For philosophical interpretations of the ascent of the soul in Islam, see chapter 5.

3. For a short survey of the importance of theophany and apotheosis in the history of Jewish mysticism, see, for example, Moshe Idel, "Metatron: Some Remarks on Myth in Jewish Mysticism" (in Hebrew), in *Myth in Judaism*, ed. H. Pedaya (Beer Sheva: University of Ben Gurion Press, 1996), pp. 29–44; and idem, *BEN: Sonship and Jewish Mysticism* (forthcoming).

4. See Moshe Idel, "On Some Forms of Order in Kabbalah," *Daat* 50–52 (2003): pp. xxxi–lviii.

5. See Mircea Eliade, *Yoga, Immortality and Freedom* (Princeton: Princeton University Press, 1971), pp. 311–41.

6. Mircea Eliade, *Myths, Dreams, and Mysteries* (New York: Harper Torchbooks, 1960), pp. 99–122.

7. Chapter II in Ioan P. Couliano, *Psychanodia I: A Survey of the Evidence Concerning the Ascension of the Soul and Its Relevance* (Leiden: Brill, 1983); and idem, *Experiences de l'extase: Extase, ascension et recit visionaire de l'Hellenisme au Moyen Age* (Paris: Payot, 1984), pp. 79–92. See also idem, "Ascension," *Encyclopedia of Religion*, ed. Mircea Eliade (1987), vol. I, pp. 435–440; and the description of Culianu's views by Eduard Iricinschi in *Ioan Petru Culianu, Cult, magie, erezii*, ed. Sorin Antohi (Iasi: Polirom, 2003), pp. 244–48. For a substantial contribution to Culianu's thesis, see the study of Adela Yarbro Collins, "The Seven Heavens in Jewish and Christian Apocalypses," in her *Cosmology and Eschatology in Jewish and Christian Apocalypticism* (Leiden: Brill, 1996), pp. 21–54.

8. See Ioan P. Couliano, *The Tree of Gnosis*, trans. Hillary Wiener and Ioan P. Couliano (San Francisco: Harper, 1992), pp. 42–43. See also Michel Tardieu and J. D. Dubois, *Introduction a la litterature gnostique* (Paris: Cerf/CNRS, 1986), p. 33.

9. Bernard McGinn, *The Foundations of Mysticism* (New York: Crossroad, 1991), pp. 9–22.

10. Ioan P. Couliano, *Out of this World: Otherworldly Journeys from Gilgamesh to Albert Einstein* (Boston and London: Shambhala, 1991), pp. 181–87.

11. For the source of combinatory proclivities in the late Culianu, see Moshe Idel's preface to Nicu Gavriluta, *Culianu: Joculire mintii si lumile multidimensionale* (Iasi: Polirom, 2000), pp. 16–17.

12. Couliano, *Out of this World*, p. 38.

13. See, for example, Annelies Kuyt, *The "Descent" to the Chariot* (Tubingen: J. C. B. Mohr, 1995). For Elliot R. Wolfson's treatment, see *Through a Speculum that Shines: Vision and Imagination in Medieval Jewish Mysticism* (Princeton: Princeton University Press, 1994), pp. 74–124, especially pp. 108–19; and idem, "*Yeridah la-Merkavah*: Typology of Ecstasy and as Enthronement in Ancient Jewish Mysticism," in *Mystics of the Book: Themes, Topics, and Typologies*, ed. R. A. Herrera (New York: Peter Lang, 1993), pp. 13–44. For Israel Knohl's work on this topic, see *The Messiah before Jesus: The Suffering Servant of the Dead Sea Scrolls*, trans. David Maisel (Berkeley and Los Angeles: University of California Press, 2000).

14. See Alexander Altmann, "The Ladder of Ascension," *Studies in Mysticism and Religion Presented to Gershom G. Scholem* (Jerusalem: The Magnes Press, 1967), pp. 1–32; Moshe Idel, *Kabbalah: New Perspectives* (New Haven: Yale University Press, 1988), pp. 88–96; and Elliot R. Wolfson, "Weeping, Death and Spiritual Ascent in Sixteenth-Century Jewish Mysticism," in Collins and Fishbane, *Death, Ecstasy*, pp. 207–43.

15. See, especially, Martha Himmelfarb, *Ascent to Heaven in Jewish and Christian Apocalypses* (New York: Oxford University Press, 1993); Peter

Schaefer, *Hekhalot Studien* (Tuebingen: J. C. B. Mohr, 1988), pp. 234–49 and 285–89; David J. Halperin, "Ascension or invasion: Implications of the heavenly journey in ancient Judaism," *Religion* 18:1 (1988): pp. 47–67; idem, "Heavenly ascension in ancient Judaism: The nature of the experience," *SBLSP* 26 (1987): pp. 218–32; and idem, *Faces of the Chariot* (Tuebingen: J. C. B. Mohr, 1987).

16. *Genesis Rabba'* 14:9 in *Midrash bereshit Rabba*, eds. J. Theodor and C. Albeck (Jerusalem: Wahrman Books, 1965), vol. I, pp. 133–34.

17. Morton Smith, "Ascents to Heavens and the Beginning of Christianity," *Eranos Jahrbuch* 50 (1981): p. 415. See also idem, *Clement of Alexandria and a Secret Gospel of Mark* (Cambridge: Harvard University Press, 1973), pp. 237–49; and idem, *Jesus the Magician* (New York: 1981), pp. 124–25.

18. Smith, *Clement of Alexandria*, pp. 426–28. The quote is II Corinthians 12:3. On this text, see Peter Schaefer's article, "New Testament and Hekhalot Literature: The Journey into Heaven in Paul and in Merkavah Mysticism," *Journal of Jewish Studies* 35 (1984): pp. 19–35. Schaefer did not consider the possibility that Smith's, or his predecessors', reading of Paul's statements related to Jesus himself.

19. See Tabor, *Things Unutterable*; Gershom Scholem, *Jewish Gnosticism, Merkabah Mysticism and Talmudic Tradition* (New York: Jewish Theological Seminary, 1960), p. 18; Smith, *Clement of Alexandria*, pp. 238–43; and Ithamar Gruenwald, "Knowledge and Vision," *Israel Oriental Studies* 3 (1973): p. 106.

20. *Ode* 36.3, 4 and 6, in *The Old Testament Pseudepigrapha*, ed. J.H. Charlesworth (New York: Doubleday, 1985), vol. II, pp. 765–66; Margaret Barker, "The Secret Tradition," *The Journal of Higher Criticism* 2:1 (1995): pp. 31–67. I assume that this text is the source of, or at least a parallel to the views found in, the Gnostic *Apocalypse of Zostrianos* VIII.1, where an ascent on high is described that culminates with becoming one of the glories. This view is found also in the Slavonic Book of Enoch. See Madeleine Scopello, "The Apocalypse of Zostrianos (Nag Hamadi VIII.I) and the Book of the Secrets of Enoch," *Vigiliae Christianae* 34 (1980): pp. 376–78. See also Frederik H. Borsch, *The Son of Man in Myth and History* (London: SCM Press, 1967), pp. 195–96.

21. *Ode* 38.1 and 5, in Charlesworth, *Old Testament Pseudepigrapha*, vol. II, p. 766. "Truth" is to be interpreted here as the name of a hypostasis or an angel. In ancient Jewish literature, truth points in some cases to God. See Moshe Idel, "Golems and God: Mimesis and Confrontation," in *Mythen der Kreativitaet*, eds. Refika Sarionder and Annette Deschner (Frankfurt am Main: Lembeck, 2003), p. 242; and idem, *Golem: Jewish Magical and Mystical Traditions on the Artificial Anthropoid* (Albany: State University of New York Press, 1990), pp. 306–08. *Nota Bene*: The chariot here is a means for ascent, not an object of contemplation, as is the case in Heikhalot literature.

22. *Sukkah*, fol. 45a. On this statement and the parallels adduced by the author, see Aharon Kaminka, "Die Mystischen Ideen des R. Simon b. Johai," *HUCA* X (1935): p. 165.

23. See Martha Himmelfarb, "Heavenly Ascent and the Relationship of the Apocalypses and Hekhalot Literature," *HUCA* LIV (1988): pp. 73–100.

24. See Moshe Idel, "Enoch is Metatron," *Immanuel* 24/25 (1990): pp. 220–40; C. R. A. Morray-Jones, "Transformational Mysticism in the Apocalyptic-Merkavah Tradition," *Journal of Jewish Studies* 43 (1992): p. 17.

25. On the gigantic dimension of divinity designated as *Shi`ur Qomah*, see Martin S. Cohen, *The Shiur Qomah: Liturgy and Theurgy in Pre-Kabbalistic Jewish Mysticism* (Lanham: Scholars Press, 1983).

26. Schaefer, *Hekhalot Studien*, p. 286. On transformation of the person in this literature, see Daphna V. Arbel, "'Understanding of the Heart,' Spiritual Transformation and Divine Revelations in the Heikhalot and Merkavah Literature," *Jewish Studies Quarterly* 6 (1999): pp. 320–44.

27. Schaefer, *Hekhalot Studien*, pp. 277–95.

28. See the lengthy discussions on Moses's role in Heikhalot texts in Halperin, *Faces of the Chariot*, pp. 289–322, 335–36 and 420–26. See also the texts of Heikhalot literature and the short discussion in Michael D. Swartz, *Scholastic Magic: Ritual and Revelation in Early Jewish Mysticism* (Princeton: Princeton University Press, 1996), pp. 115–18, 166, 171 and 212.

29. See especially *BT, Sabbath*, fol. 88b. See also Moshe Idel, "The Concept of the Torah in Heikhalot Literature and Its Metamorphoses in Kabbalah" (in Hebrew), *Jerusalem Studies in Jewish Thought* 1 (1981): pp. 25–32.

30. See *BT, Hagigah*, fol. 15b. In several early and late Midrashic cases, expressions similar to this one are found; they deserve separate treatment.

31. Rachel Elior, ed., *Heikhalot Zutarti* (Jerusalem: Institute for Jewish Studies, Hebrew University, 1982), p. 23.

32. See Idel, *Kabbalah: New Perspectives*, pp. 157–58.

33. See Nathaniel Deutsch, *The Gnostic Imagination: Gnosticism, Mandaeism, and Merkabah Mysticism* (Leiden: Brill, 1995), pp. 135–50.

34. Elior, *Heikhalot Zutarti*, p. 22; Peter Schaefer, ed., *Synopse zur Hekhalot-Literatur* (Tuebingen: J. C. B. Mohr, 1981), pp. 143–44.

35. Idel, "Concept of the Torah," pp. 27–29.

36. See J. D. Eisenstein, ed., *'Otzar ha-Midrashim*, 2 vols. (New York; Reznik and Co., 1915), p. 307. Compare to Idel, "Concept of the Torah," pp. 27–29; and Halperin, *Faces of the Chariot*, pp. 289–319. For more on this issue, see discussion of the revelation received by the Besht in chapter 4.

37. See Idel, *Golem*, pp. 285–86.

38. See the texts printed in Schafer, *Synopse*, pp. 59–60, par. 119–21; and Gottfried Reeg, *Die Geschichte von den Zehn Martyrern* (Tuebingen: J. C. B. Mohr, 1985), p. 90, par. 40. This passage also is translated into German on pp. 82–83. In most of the manuscripts of this text, the passage on the miraculous exchange between the Rabbi and a Caesar are missing. On the interchanges between the images of two persons in the ancient period, see Ithamar Gruenwald, *Apocalyptic and Merkavah Mysticism* (Leiden: Brill, 1980), p. 157, n. 28; and Peter Schaefer, *Uebersetzung der Heikhalot-Literatur* (Tuebingen: J. C. B. Mohr, 1987), vol. 2, pp. 43–51.

39. See Gershom Scholem, *Major Trends in Jewish Mysticism* (New York: Schocken Books, 1967), p. 51.

40. See Gershom Scholem, *Kabbalah* (Jerusalem: Keter Publishing House, 1974), pp. 45–145; and section 5 below.

41. Bejamin Levin, ed., *'Otzar ha-Geonim* (Jerusalem, 1932), on *Hagigah*, part of Teshuvot, pp. 14–15. I have partially followed the translation of the first half of the quotation given in Scholem, *Major Trends*, p. 49. See also Wolfson, *Through a Speculum*, pp. 144–50. "Qualities" here is the translation of *Middot*, a recurring term in Heikhalot literature, the meaning of which changes from context to context. For more on the technique described in this passage, see Idel, *Kabbalah: New Perspectives*, p. 91; and Paul Fenton, "La 'tête entre les genoux': Contribution à l'étude d'une posture méditative dans la mystique juive et islamique," *Revue d'Histoire et de Philosophie Religieuses* 72:4 (1992): pp. 413–26.

42. See Adolph Jellinek, *Beitraege zur Geschichte der Kabbala* (Leipzig: C. L. Friotzsche, 1852), part 2, pp. 15–16, n. 22.

43. Scholem, *Major Trends*, pp. 49–50.

44. See David J. Halperin, "A New Edition of the Heikhalot Literature," *Journal of American Oriental Society* 104:3(1984): pp. 544, 547 and 550–51. See also idem, *The Merkabah in Rabbinic Literature* (New Haven: American Oriental Society, 1980), pp. 3, 89 and 177.

45. See Cohen, *Shi`ur Qomah*, pp. 5–6.

46. See Idel, *Kabbalah: New Perspectives*, pp. 90–91; Wolfson, *Through a Speculum*, pp. 110–11, 146–48; Himmelfarb, *Ascent to Heaven*, pp. 109 and 148, n. 53; and Ron P. Margolin, *The Interiorization of Religious Life and Thought at the Beginning of Hasidism: Its Sources and Epistemological Basis* (in Hebrew) (Ph.D. diss., The Hebrew University, Jerusalem, 1999), pp. 176ff, 196–201.

47. See Levin, *'Otzar ha-Geonim*, Hagigah, pp. 11–12.

48. A. Kohut, ed., `Arukh ha-Shalem* (Vienna: Grab, 1878), vol. I, p. 14, under the word *'avnei shayish tahor*; and Assi Farber-Ginat, "Inquiries in *Shi`ur Qomah*" (in Hebrew), *Massu'ot: Studies in Kabbalistic Literature and Jewish Philosophy in Memory of Prof. Ephraim Gottlieb*, eds. Michal Oron and Amos Goldreich (Jerusalem: Mossad Bialik, 1994), p. 374, n. 70.

49. See E. E. Urbach, ed., *R. Abraham ben Azriel, `Arugat ha-Bosem* (Jerusalem: Mekize Nirdamim, 1947), vol. 1, p. 198, n. 2 and pp. 199–200. See also p. 202 for the phrase *ba-sekhel libam*, "the intellect of their heart"; and David Halperin, "Origen, Ezekiel's Merkavah, and the Ascension of Moses," *Church History* 50 (1981): pp. 263 and 273–74. The occurrence of the phrases *cordis oculis* in Origen or *binat levavkhem* in Hebrew texts may evidence a psychological interpretation of the vision of the Merkavah in ancient Jewish sources; see also Halperin, *Merkabah*, pp. 174–75; Wolfson, *Through a Speculum*, pp. 147–48; and Adena Tanenbaum, *The Contemplative Soul: Hebrew Poetry and Philosophical Theory in Medieval Spain* (Leiden: Brill, 2002), pp. 77–79 and 190.

50. See Scholem, *Major Trends*, p. 29, where he refers to Macarius the Egyptian, who in the fourth century interpreted the vision of Ezekiel as a vision of "the secret of the soul."

51. See also Rav Hai's reservations concerning mystical and magical practices connected with the divine names: Levin, *'Otzar ha-Geonim*, Hagigah, pp. 16–24; and Colette Sirat, *Les teories des visions surnaturelles dans la pensee juive du Moyen Age* (Leiden: Brill, 1962), pp. 33–35.

52. See especially Rav Hai's view in Levin, *'Otzar ha-Geonim*, on *Hagigah*, p. 15, that inner visions are miraculous events granted by God to the righteous. This attitude is an obvious attempt to discredit the efficacy of mystical techniques.

53. See Idel, *Kabbalah: New Perspectives*, pp. 90–91. For another stance that emphasizes the importance of a docetistic reading of many rabbinic sources, see Wolfson, *Through a Speculum*, pp. 33–51.

54. See Gershom Scholem, "On the Prophecy of Rabbi Ezra of Moncontour" (in Hebrew), *Tarbiz* 2 (1931): p. 244.

55. This poem, consisting of three verses, was printed in Hebrew by Naftali Fried, *Tarbiz* 2 (1931): p. 514. Unfortunately, Botarel is an unreliable witness, and his testimonies in general are suspect of fabrication. Here, however, the testimony is corroborated by other material.

56. See Israel Ta-Shma, "*She'elot ve-Teshuvot me-ha-Shamayim*: The Collection and the Additions" (in Hebrew), *Tarbiz* 87 (1988): pp. 51–66. See also the passage above by Rabbi Ezra of Montcontour.

57. See Rabbi Naftali Zevi Hirsch Treves, *Commentary on the Siddur* (Thiengen, 1560), fol. 40, Ib.

58. On *Hagigah*, fol. 15b.

59. Samuel K. Mirsky, ed., *Shibbolei ha-Leqet* (New York: Sura, 1966), vol. I, no. 28, p. 46; and R. Simhah of Vitry, *Mahzor Vitri*, ed. S. Horowitz (Nurenberg: Bulka, 1923), p. 364. Compare also to Mirsky, *Shibbolei ha-Leqet*, p. 176. The Rabbi Eleazar's poem is printed in Daniel Goldschmidt, *Mahzor to Rosh ha-Shanah* (Jerusalem: Koren, 1970), p. 216. Its content is, significantly enough, closely related to Ezekiel's vision.

60. See E. E. Urbach, "The Traditions of Merkabah Mysticism in the Tannaitic Period" (in Hebrew), in *Studies in Mysticism and Religion Presented to Gershom G. Scholem* (in Hebrew) (Jerusalem: The Magnes Press, 1967), pp. 4–10.

61. Rabbi Moshe of Taku, *Ketav Tammim*, printed in *'Otzar Nehmad*, IV (1863), p. 85.

62. See Rabbi Abraham of Torrutiel's supplements to *Sefer ha-Kabbalah of R. Abraham ben David*, reprinted in *Two Chronicles from the Generation of the Spanish Exile*, intro. by A. David (Jerusalem: Merkaz Zalman Shazar, 1979), p. 28. Compare to the description of the *incantatores* discussed in chapter 4, section 3 below. For a somewhat earlier description of ascent, see Rabbi Nehemiah ben Shlomo the Prophet's *Commentary on Seventy Names of Metatron*, stemming from late twelfth- or early thirteenth-century Ashkenazi circles. Enoch is described as someone who ascended to the firmament; the terminology used implies that he did so by himself: *'alah la-raqi'a*. He also is described as becoming an angel and at the same time as "the brother of God"—a clear case of apotheosis. See *Sefer ha-Hesheq*, ed. Y. M. Epstein (Lemberg: Kugel, Levin & Co., 1865), fol. 4b.

63. See Idel, *Golem*, pp. 86–91.

64. For an important survey of these processes in Judaism, see Margolin, *Interiorization of Religious Life*.

65. See Maimonides, *The Guide of the Perplexed*, trans. Shlomo Pines (Chicago: Chicago University Press, 1963), I:10, pp. 35–37.

66. *Hayyei ha-Nefesh*, Ms. Munchen 408, fols. 7b–8a. The first quote is Exodus 19:3. For the mountain as a metaphor for the human intellect in Rabbi Abulafia, see Moshe Idel, *The Mystical Experience in Abraham Abulafia*, trans. Jonathan Chipman (Albany: State University of New York Press, 1988), pp. 102–03 and 156–57, n. 128. On the term "place," see Maimonides, *Guide of the Perplexed*, I:8, pp. 33–34. On the interiorization of the term "place" in Jewish mysticism, see Margolin, *Interiorization of Religious Life*, pp. 129–31.

67. Ms. Paris BN 774, fol. 155a. On the concept of universalization, see Moshe Idel, "Universalization and Integration: Two Conceptions of Mystical Union in Jewish Mysticism," in *Mystical Union and Monotheistic Faith: An Ecumenical Dialogue*, eds. M. Idel and B. McGinn (New York: MacMillan, 1989), pp. 27–58. On immortality as deification, see W. R. Inge, *Christian Mysticism* (London, 1925), pp. 357–58. Rabbi Abulafia's stance would confirm Inge's category of deification through transformation. See ibid., p. 365; and idem, *Mysticism in Religion* (Chicago: University of Chicago Press, 1948), p. 46.

68. Ms. New York JTS 1887, fol. 105b. "Sphere of the intellect" is translated from *galgal ha-sekhel*. This phrase corresponds to the view of the Empireum in the Middle Ages. On this issue, see Adena Tenenbaum, "Nine Spheres or Ten?" *Journal of Jewish Studies* 47 (1996): pp. 294–310.

69. Rabbi Isaac of Acre, *Me'irat 'Einayyim*, ed. Amos Goldreich (Jerusalem: Hebrew University, 1984), p. 222; this passage was reprinted from Ms. Munchen 17 in Appendix II of J. Hercz, *Drei Abhandlungen u"ber die Conjunction des separaten Intellects mit dem Menschen* (Berlin: Hermann, 1869), p. 22. In Hercz's view, this text reflects the impact of Averroes's theory of the intellect. The passage was translated into French by Vajda, who contends that it was influenced by the psychological doctrine of Ibn Bajja; see Vajda, *Recherches*, p. 379, n. 3; and Micheline Chaze, "Quelques aspects du thème de l'ascension de l'âme dans la Kabbale du XIIIe siècle," *Revue des etudes juives*, vol. 156, 1–2 (1997), pp. 107–111.

The term "Divine Intellect" also appears in the early works of Rabbi Joseph Gikatilla and Rabbi Abraham Abulafia as well as in Rabbi Nathan ben Sa'adya's *Sha'arei Tzedeq*. For more on this issue, see Moshe Idel, *Studies in Ecstatic Kabbalah* (Albany: State University of New York Press, 1988), p. 151, n. 62.

Rabbi Jacob ben Sheshet, a Geronese Kabbalist of the mid-thirteenth century, formulated the view that an entity that cleaves to another entity is called by the name of the latter. See chapter II in Georges Vajda, ed., *Recherches sur la philosophie et la Kabbale dans la pense juive du Moyen Age* (Paris: Mouton, 1962), p. 76. On the impact of this stand on a contemporary Kabbalist, see Efrayyim Gottlieb, *The Kabbalah in the Writings of Rabbi*

Bahya ben Asher (in Hebrew) (Jerusalem: Reuven Mass, 1970), pp. 115–16; and Rabbi Joseph Angelet, *Sefer Quppat ha-Rokhlim*, Ms. Oxford-Bodleiana 1618, fol. 70ab.

On the source and root of the soul, see also Natan ben Sa`adyah Har'ar, *Le Porte della Giustizia*, ed. Moshe Idel, trans. Maurizio Mottolese (Milan: Adelphi, 2001), p. 453. On the magical implications of the mystical attainment, see Idel, *Golem*, pp. 106–07.

70. *Sefer 'Even Sappir*, Ms. Paris BN 727, fol. 28b. The quote in this passage is Ezekiel 1:26. The Kabbalist also mentions in this context a translucent mirror as an allegory for either the human-actualized intellect or the cosmic agent intellect; the unclear mirror in the passage is the human imagination. See the Talmudic sources adduced and discussed in Wolfson, *Through a Speculum*, pp. 147–48. In "the prophets who came after him," "him" refers to Moses.

71. On this issue in medieval Judaism, see Alexander Altmann and Samuel M. Stern, *Isaac Israeli: A Neoplatonic Philosopher of the Early Tenth Century* (Oxford: Oxford University Press, 1958), pp. 189–95; and Tanenbaum, *Contemplative Soul*, pp. 40–42.

72. Ludwig Venetianer, ed., *Sefer ha-Ma`alot* (Berlin: Verlag von S. Calvary & Co., 1894), p. 22. "Aristotle" at the beginning of this passage is, in fact, Plotin. For the appropriation of the "as if" language for ascent in Kabbalistic texts, see section 6 in this chapter. See also Gershom Scholem, *On the Mystical Shape of the Godhead* (New York: The Schocken Books, 1991), pp. 257–58; idem, *Major Trends*, p. 203; and Moshe Idel, *Messianic Mystics* (New Haven: Yale University Press, 1998), p. 52. On the impact of this work on thirteenth-century Jewish thought, see Alexander Altmann, "The Delphic Maxim in Medieval Islam and Judaism," in *Von der Mittelalterlichen zur Modernen Aufklaerung: Studien zur Juedischen Geistgeschichte* (Tuebingen: J.C.B. Mohr, 1987), pp. 26–28; Altmann and Stern, *Isaac Israeli*, pp. 191–92; Moshe Idel, "Types of Redemptive Activity in the Middle Ages," *Messianism and Eschatology: A Collection of Essays* (in Hebrew), ed. Zvi Baras (Jerusalem: The Shazar Center, 1983), pp. 256–57, n. 20; Paul B. Fenton (Ynnon), "Shem Tov Ibn Falaquera and the *Theology of Aristotle*" (in Hebrew), *Daat* 29 (1992): pp. 27–40; idem, "The Arabic and Hebrew Versions of the *Theology of Aristotle*," in *Pseudo-Aristotle in the Middle Ages*, Warburg Institute Surveys and Texts, ed. J. Kraye (London: Warburg Institute, 1996), vol. 11, pp. 241–64.

73. For more on Plotin, see chapter 5. See also Margolin, *Interiorization of Religious Life*, pp. 113–15.

74. See Scholem, *Elements*, p. 194. Though this text is anonymous in all manuscripts in which it is extant, Scholem seems to be correct in his attribution of the text to Rabbi Ezra.

For more on the union of the righteous and the supernal, see Rabbi Abraham ibn Ezra's *Commentary on Psalms* 139:18. In a passage by an influential nineteenth-century master, Rabbi Qalonimus Qalman Epstein of Cracow, we find a similar stance attributed to the righteous: "It is known and I have indeed seen some great *tzaddiqim* who had attached themselves to the supernal worlds, and they divested themselves of the garment of their corporeality, so that the *Shekhinah* dwelled upon them and spoke from within their throats, and their mouths spoke prophecy and future things. And these *tzadiqqim* themselves did not know afterwards what they spoke, for they were attached to the supernal worlds while the *Shekhinah* spoke from within their throats." Compare to *Ma'or va-Shemesh* (Jerusalem: Even Israel, 1992), I, p. 127; Rivka Schatz Uffenheimer, *Hasidism as Mysticism: Quietistic Elements in Eighteenth-Century Hasidic Thought*, trans. Jonathan Chipman (Princeton: Princeton University Press; Jerusalem: The Magnes Press, 1993), pp. 200–01 and adduced in the English translation of Louis Jacobs, *Jewish Mystical Testimonies* (New York: Schocken Books, 1987), pp. 217–18.

The use of the past tense in this passage indicates the difference between the righteous acting today and the prophets who acted in the past. On this issue, see Moshe Idel, "The Interpretations of the Secret of Incest in Early Kabbalah" (in Hebrew), *Kabbalah* 12 (2004): 106 n. 92.

75. *Sefer Ma'arekhet ha-'Elohut*, fol. 98b. The term "cleaving of the mind"—*Devequt ha-Da'at*—is a clear example of nousanodia, despite the fact that at the beginning of the passage the soul is mentioned explicitly. The quote within this passage is Deuteronomy 4:4.

76. See Rabbi Ezra's passage translated in Moshe Idel, "Some Remarks on Ritual and Mysticism in Geronese Kabbalah," *Jewish Thought and Philosophy* III (1993): p. 124.

77. MS. Jerusalem 1959 80, fol. 200a. It seems that the term *Middah* implies a certain way of action, or a technique, to attain the spiritual experience. The quote in this passage is Genesis 5:22. For commentary on the phrase "as if," see n. 104.

78. *Zohar Hadash*, fol. 69ab. In Manichaeism, the soul is given a garment of light after death. See Manfred Heuser, "The Manichaean Myth according to Coptic Sources," in *Studies in Manichaean Literature and Art*, eds. Manferd Heuser and Hans-Joachim Klimkeit (Leiden: Brill, 1998), pp. 42–43. On luminous garments in early Kabbalah, see Gershom Scholem, "*Levush ha-Neshamot ve-Haluqa' de-Rabbanan*" (in Hebrew), *Tarbiz* 24 (1955): pp. 290–306; Elliot Wolfson, "The Secret of the Garment in Nahmanides," *Da'at* (English version) 24 (1990): pp. 29 and 47. For more on Manichaeism and the Zohar, see chapter 3, and Idel, "Some Remarks on Ritual," pp. 119–21.

The matter of "brilliance" is undoubtedly connected here to the concept of the *haluqa' de-Rabbanan*, as emphasized in Lurianic Kabbalah; this matter requires detailed study. See also Hugo Odeberg's introduction to *The Book of Enoch* (Cambridge: Cambridge University Press, 1928), pp. 122–23. For the use of the expression "Metatron" in order to indicate the most exalted part of the human soul, see a citation entitled "Midrash" in *Yalqut Reuveni* (Jerusalem, 1962), fol. 23a: "'And God created man in His image'—in the image and the image of Metatron. If man merits, he merits the image...the first God is the living God, [which is] an allusion to Metatron." See also chapter 3, n. 15.

79. Natan ben Sa`adyah Har'ar, *Le porte della Giustizia*, p. 385. The quote is Ezekiel 1:26. It should be noted that this verse is the proof text for the Midrashic dictum about the prophets that compares the form to the entity that forms them, adduced by Rabbi Nathan in the passage quoted from a book of Rabbi Isaac of Acre, in Rabbi Moses of Kiev. On the concept of "the point," which in Rabbi Abulafia's writings refers either to the agent intellect or to the human soul, see Moshe Idel, *Language, Torah and Hermeneutics in Abraham Abulafia*, trans. M. Kallus (Albany: State University of New York Press, 1989), pp. 40–41.

80. Natan ben Sa`adyah Har'ar, *Le porte della Giustizia*, p. 385.

81. *'Otzar Hayyim*, Ms. Moscow-Ginsburg 775, fol. 233b. I translated the rather exceptional formulation found in this version, which uses "Nought" in lieu of *'Ein Sof*, as is also the case in the version of this passage extant in Ms. Oxford-Bodleiana 1911, fol. 154b. "Nought" is *va-tidbbaq nefesh zo be-'ayin*; "palace" is *Heikhalah*. The latter is a recurrent image in Rabbi Isaac's writings on the body. See also the quote from an unnamed Kabbalist, adduced in Rabbi Nathan Ben Sa`adya's *Sha`arei Tzedeq*, in *Le porte della Giustizia*, p. 373, and in the anonymous *Peraqim be-Hatzlahah*, attributed to Maimonides, ed. D. Baneth (Jerusalem: Mekize Nirdamim, 1939), p. 17.

82. See Rabbi Levi Isaac of Berditchev, *Qedushat ha-Levi*, (Jerusalem: Makhon Qedushat Levi, 1993), p. 5.

83. Natan ben Sa`adyah Har`ar, *Le porte della Giustizia*, p. 467. I assume that this refers to the angelic powers.

84. Ibid., p. 475.

85. Meir Benayahu, ed., *Sefer Toldot ha-Ari* (Jerusalem: Makhon ben-Tzvi, 1960), p. 155. This hagiographic description left an indelible impression on the way in which the Besht has been portrayed. For more on this issue, see chapter 4. For an important passage by Rabbi Hayyim Vital dealing with the ascent of Moses in body and soul, which becomes an example for the Messiah, see Gershom Scholem, *Sabbatai Sevi: The Mystical Messiah*, trans. R. J. Z. Werblowsky (Princeton: Princeton University Press, 1973), p. 53.

86. Benayahu, *Sefer Toldot ha-Ari*, pp. 154–55.

87. *Sha`arei Qedushah*, Ms. British Library 749, fol. 16a, printed also in Rabbi Hayyim Vital, *Ketavim Hadashim*, ed. Nathanel Safrin (Jerusalem: Ahavat Shalom, 1988), p. 6. "As above" refers to a prescription copied earlier on the same page. For comments on the phrase "as if," see n. 104 below.

88. See Lawrence Fine, "Recitation of Mishnah as a Vehicle for Mystical Inspiration: A Contemplative Technique Taught by Hayyim Vital," *REJ* 141 (1982): pp. 190 and 198; and idem, *Physician of the Soul, Healer of the Cosmos: Isaac Luria and His Kabbalistic Fellowship* (Palo Alto, Cal.: Stanford University Press, 2003), pp. 290–91.

89. *Sefer ha-Heziyonot*, p. 112; Morris M. Faierstein, ed., *Jewish Mystical Autobiographies* (New York: Paulist Press, 1999), p. 136.

90. *Sefer ha-Heziyonot*, pp. 42 and 47–49.

91. See Dov Baer of Medzeritch, *Maggid Devarav le-Ya`aqov*, pp. 38–39. The quote is Ezekiel 1:26. It is important to emphasize that a distinguished disciple of the Great Maggid understood this verse as symbolizing the deep

affinity between the human and the divine. According to Rabbi Abraham Jehoshua Heschel of Apt, the man on the chariot is identical to the plene spelling of the Tetragrammaton and, at the same time, stems from the lower man, who generates or makes God by his performance of the commandments. This interpretation ostensibly reduces, or even obliterates, the distance between God and man.

Shortly before this excerpt, the Maggid refers to the descending contractions that permitted a union of God to man. Here, man returns to his origin, ascending the *scala contemplationis*, which implies gradual obliterations of the contractions, culminating in annihilation of the human existence.

The term translated as "speech" is *Dibbur*; I prefer the version found in a variant of this passage found in another collection of the teachings of the Great Maggid, *'Or ha-Torah* (Jerusalem, 1968), p. 73: *dibbur Malkhut*, or "speech" and "*Malkhut*," the initials of which—*D* and *M*—form parts of the word *'ADaM*. Thence, it seems that "speech" may represent here the sefirah of Tiferet; compare, however, Schatz-Uffenheimer's remark in her edition of Dov Baer of Medzeritch, *Maggid Devarav le-Ya`aqov* (Jerusalem: The Magnes Press, 1976). My interpretation turns *'ADaM* into a symbol for three aspects in the Godhead: the *'A*—master of the universe, that is, the transcendent aspect; and two immanent aspects—Malkhut and Tiferet. *DaM*, which is translated here as "Alpha," in Hebrew is blood. The Maggid uses a pun: the Hebrew term *'Aluf* is both master and champion but is also close to *'Alef*, the principle of the world. Compare also to Rabbi Levi Isaac of Berditchev's discussion in *Qedushat Levi*, fol. 64bc, where the reference to *'Alef* is explicit. The source is apparently *BT, Hagigah*, fol. 16a.

For parallels to this text in Hasidic literature, see Schatz-Uffenheimer, *Hasidism as Mysticism*, p. 213, n. 29. See also Gershom Scholem, *The Messianic Idea in Judaism* (New York: Schocken Books, 1972), pp. 226–27; Isaiah Tishby, *The Wisdom of the Zohar: An Anthology of Texts*, trans. D. Goldstein (London: Littman Library, 1991), vol. 2, pp. 1010–11, n. 354.

92. Num. 10:2.

93. See Tishby, *Wisdom of the Zohar*, vol. I, pp. 229–370; Idel, *Kabbalah: New Perspectives*, pp. 136–53.

94. Ioan P. Couliano, *Experiences de l'extase*, (Paris: Payot, 1984),pp. 119–144.

95. For more on this issue, see the concluding remarks in Moshe Idel, *Kabbalah and Eros* (forthcoming). For a description of the theosophical-theurgical Kabbalists by Rabbi Abulafia, who declares that they ascend from one light to another, see the passage translated and analyzed in Idel, *The Mystical Experience*, pp. 83–84.

96. Reprinted in Azulai, *Massekhet 'Avot* (Jerusalem, 1986), fol. 3a. The Hebrew term translated here as "entity" is *sibbah*. Cordovero also mentions the ascent from one `*Illah* to another. On "the source," see also Idel, *Kabbalah: New Perspectives*, pp. 42–46; and idem, "Universalization and Integration," pp. 28–33. On the pericope Terumah, see *Zohar* II, fol. 169a. The pertinent text is quoted by Rabbi Cordovero, but I do not deal with it here because, in my opinion, it is not the actual source of this view. See, however,

Zohar, I, fol. 43a; and Idel, *Kabbalah: New Perspectives*, p. 53. "The great pipe" in Hebrew is *bi-meqom ha-tzinor ha-gadol*. For more on this text in general, see Idel, *Hasidism*, pp. 100–01.

97. Gershom Scholem, *Researches in Sabbateanism* (in Hebrew), ed. Yehuda Liebes (Tel Aviv: Am Oved, 1991), pp. 214–15; and Idel, *Messianic Mystics*, pp. 193–94. The ninth sefirah, Yesod, is widely described as Tzaddiq, as we shall see in chapter 2.

For a Freudian interpretation of this passage, which emphasizes the importance of the mention of "his mother," see Avner Falk, "The Messiah and the Qelippoth: On the Mental Illness of Sabbatai Sevi," *Journal of Psychology and Judaism* 7:1 (1982): pp. 25–26. For another psychoanalytical interpretation of Sabbateanism, see Siegmund Hurwitz, "Sabbatai Zwi, Zur Psychologie der haeretischen Kabbala," *Studien zur analytischen Psychologie C. G. Jungs, Festschrift zum 80. Geburtstag von C. G. Jung* (Zurich: Rascher Verlag, 1956), vol. II, pp. 239–63.

98. Scholem, *Sabbatai Sevi*, pp. 119–23, 146–47 and 149; and Yehuda Liebes, *Studies in Jewish Myth and Jewish Messianism* (Albany: State University of New York Press, 1993), pp. 107–13.

99. This suggestion invites a more detailed investigation, which may find that the Sabbatean secret of the divinity changed as part of a development alongside the vector of time and of the ontic hierarchy of the sefirot. This means that the closer the messianic drama comes to the final stage, the higher the divine power that is appointed upon Sabbatai and constitutes the "secret of divinity."

100. Scholem, *Researches in Sabbateanism*, p. 222.

101. See Charles H. Talbet, "The Myth of a Descending-Ascending Redeemer in Mediterranean Antiquity," *New Testament Studies* 22 (1976): pp. 418–39.

102. See the citation adduced in the name of his grandfather by Rabbi Moshe Hayyim Efrayyim of Sudylkov, *Degel Mahaneh 'Efrayyim* (Jerusalem, 1995), p. 214.

103. Menahem Nahum of Chernobyl, *Me'or 'Einayyim* (Jerusalem, 1975) p. 123. See also Elliot R. Wolfson, *Circle in the Square* (Albany: State University of New York Press, 1995), p. 25. For more on the views of this master regarding the righteous and his task, see chapter 4.

The "Assembly of Israel" is translated from *Knesset Yisrael*. This is a cognomen for the last sefirah, which is commonly understood as the bride of God, and the union between them is conceived of as the main task of the theosophical–theurgical Kabbalah. The first quote in this passage is Isaiah 62:5. "Delight of all delights" is a recurring dictum in Hasidism since its very beginning, which was influenced by the anti-Maimonidean stance of the early fifteenth-century Catalan thinker, Rabbi Hasdai Crescas. Rabbi Menahem Nahum and his son Mordekhai were very fond of this formula. Interestingly enough, to the best of my knowledge, only Rabbi Menahem Nahum describes God by the term "the delight of all delights." See Menahem Nahum, *Me'or 'Einayyim*, p. 27. The Besht has been attributed a passage in which this dictum appears by Rabbi Aharon ha-Kohen of Apta, an early collector of the Besht's dicta; see his book,

Ner Mitzvah (Pietrkov, 1881), fol. 24b, written at the end of the eighteenth century.

On the history of the interpretations of the dictum, "let the words of the Torah be new," see Idel, *Absorbing Perfections*, pp. 370–89. "The creation of the world" is translated from *Ma'aseh bereshit.* "Yesterday that passed" is Psalm 90:4. "Israel is called a virgin" is translated from *Betullat Yisrael.*

104. On the language "as if," see R. J. Z. Werblowsky, *Joseph Karo: Lawyer and Mystic* (Oxford: Oxford University Press, 1962), pp. 69–70; Wolfson, "Weeping, Death," p. 232; Haviva Pedaya, "'*Ahuzim be-Dibbur*," *Tarbiz* 65 (1996): pp. 576–77, n. 21; Michael Fishbane, *The Exegetical Imagination: On Jewish Thought and Theology* (Cambridge: Harvard University Press, 1998), pp. 126– 31, 137–42, 144–46 and 148–50; and idem, *The Kiss of God: Spiritual and Mystical Death in Judaism* (Seattle: University of Washington Press, 1994), p. 45.

105. Y. E. E. Porush, ed., *Sullam ha-'Aliyah* (Jerusalem: Sha'arei Ziv, 1989), p. 73. On the expression "as if," which occurs three times in this passage, see section 4. Compare "the splendor and the radiance" to the passage extant above from the *Theology of Aristotle*. The sentence, "And it is...," reflects the impact of Rabbi Abulafia's *Hayyei ha-'Olam ha-Ba'*. "From one rank to another" is translated from *Mi-madregah le-madregah*. On this phrase, see section 5 and chapter 4, n. 7. The "supernal and hidden world of emanation" is the realm of the ten sefirot. The terms "human dominion" and "divine dominion" stem from Rabbi Nathan ben Sa'adya's *Sha'arei Tzedeq*. See Moshe Idel's introduction to Rabbi Nathan ben Sa'adya Harar, *Le porte della Giustizia*, pp. 276–87.

106. *Sha'arei Qedushah*, pp. 102–03. For an analysis of this passage, see Werblowsky, *Joseph Karo*, pp. 69–70; and Wolfson, *Through a Speculum*, pp. 320–23. I read "as if the soul exited it" as referring to the world, though it is also possible that the soul exited from the body of man. "From one root to another" is but another version of the ascent from one degree to another, as discussed above.

107. *Sha'arei Qedushah*, pp. 114–15.

108. Werblowsky, *Joseph Karo*, p. 70.

109. See, for example, Henry Corbin, *Alone with the Alone* (Princeton: Princeton University Press, 1998); and William Chittick, *Imaginal Worlds* (Albany: State University of New York Press, 1994).

110. Idel, *Studies in Ecstatic Kabbalah*, pp. 73–89.

111. Moshe Idel, "Kavvanah and Colors: A Neglected Kabbalistic *Responsum*," in *Tribute to Sara Studies in Jewish Philosophy and Kabbalah Presented to Professor Sara O. Heller Wilensky* (in Hebrew), eds. M. Idel, D. Dimant, and S. Rosenberg (Jerusalem: The Magnes Press, 1994), p. 5. On this issue, see also Moshe Idel, "Kabbalistic Prayer and Colors," in *Approaches to Judaism in Medieval Times*, ed. D. R. Blumenthal (Atlanta: Scholars Press, 1988), vol. III, pp. 17– 27. The quote at the end of the passage is Psalms 16:8.

112. Ms. British Library, Margoliouth 749, fol. 16a, printed in Rabbi Hayyim Vital, *Ketavim Hadashim*, p. 6.

113. See *The Book of Mystical Chapters: Meditations on the Soul's Ascent from the Desert Fathers and Other Early Christian Contemplatives*, trans. and intro. John Anthony McGuckin (Boston: Shambhala, 2002).

114. Nahmanides, on Leviticus 18:4.

115. Ms. Jerusalem, NUL 80 147, fols. 96b–97a; this passage was copied in the mid-sixteenth century in Safed by Rabbi ʻOvadiah Hamon, Ms. Oxford-Bodleiana 1597, fols. 58b–59a. The Hebrew original is printed in Idel, "Inquiries," pp. 212–13; and more recently, in Claude Sultan, *Levouch ha-Malkhout, Le vetement royal* (Ph.D. diss., University of Strasbourg, 1990), pp. 181–82.

   The "power of spirituality" is *Koah ruhaniyyut*. "An integral part" of Elijah is his angelic nature. It is in Elijah's name that letters of the Tetragrammaton are found. This is a theory found in several Kabbalistic sources. The divine names referred to in this passage play a central role in the theories of this book. The first quote is Ecclesiastes 10:20; the second, Deuteronomy 4:6. "My soul is bound to him" also refers to Elijah or to his name. "By his descending to earth together with him" refers to Elijah, who descends with the Messiah according to many traditions. Though the mythical return of the prophet with the Messiah is part and parcel of Jewish apocalyptics, here a more theosophical understanding of the event is found.

116. See Idel, "Inquiries," pp. 232–43; and idem, "Magic and Kabbalah in the Book of the Responding Entity," *The Solomon Goldman Lectures*, ed. M. Gruber (Chicago: Spertus College, 1993), vol. VI, pp. 125–38.

117. See Idel, *Enchanted Chains*.

118. Couliano, *Psychanodia*; and idem, *Experiences de l'extase*, pp. 153–72.

119. See Israel Levin, ed., *Igeret Hay ben Meqitz le-Abraham ibn Ezra* (Tel Aviv: University of Tel Aviv, 1983); and Aaron Hughes, "The Three Worlds of ibn Ezra's *Hay ben Meqitz*," *Journal of Jewish Thought and Philosophy* 11:1 (2002): pp. 1–25. A translation of Avicenna's book in Hebrew, together with a commentary by ibn Zayla, is available under the title *Hay ben Meqitz: The Living, the Son of the Awaker*, printed by David Kaufmann, *Qovetz alYad* (Berlin: Mekize Nirdamim, 1886), vol. II, pp. 1–29.

120. See *A Valley of Vision: The Heavenly Journey of Abraham ben Hananiah Yagel*, trans. David B. Ruderman (Philadelphia: University of Pennsylvania Press, 1990). On Yagel's sources, see Ruderman's introduction, pp. 28–50.

121. For Arabic and Jewish sources dealing with this issue, see chapters 3 and 5.

CHAPTER 2:

On Cosmic Pillars in Jewish Sources

1. The Pillar in the Work of Mircea Eliade and Ioan P. Culianu

In the following chapters, I will address a topic that has been neglected in the study of Judaism in general and of Kabbalah in particular. Pillars are mentioned in a variety of contexts in the Bible. Most conspicuous are the two pillars of fire and smoke that led the people of Israel out of Egypt, the two pillars of the temple in Jerusalem named Yakhin and Bo'az, and others found in rabbinic and Kabbalistic literature to be analyzed below. The vast interpretive literature on the Bible and rabbinic discussions supply numerous treatments on this theme, but there is no comprehensive monograph on the topic. In Kabbalistic writings, the term "pillar" occurs thousands of times in descriptions of the architecture of the divine world, but again, no academic analysis of this issue is available. Though the study of Judaism, and even more so of Kabbalah, is relatively new, this absence is too conspicuous to be attributed simply to the desiderata that await scholarly engagement. My assumption is that the concreteness of these figures is conceived—perhaps unconsciously—as unsuitable to the basic picture of Jewish thought that is imagined by scholars as being more "spiritual" or "intellectual." This bias can be discerned in other cases as well, such as the marginalization of the study of Jewish magic. Here I will use a perspectivistic approach, as discussed in the introduction, to address a few aspects of the pillar primarily in Jewish mysticism, which has been inspired by my acquaintance with analyses of this topic in Romanian folklore.

In his monograph on Shamanism, Mircea Eliade describes at length the importance of the theme of the pillar in the cosmology and ecstatic experiences of archaic religions, especially that of Siberian and Northern American tribes.[1] In 1970 Eliade wrote a play entitled *Coloana nes-fîrşita*, "The Endless Column," that deals with Constantin Brancusi's famous sculpture *Coloana infinita*. In his diary, Eliade elaborates upon the similarity between Brancusi's sculpture and megalithic concepts.[2]

Eliade distinguishes between the cosmological aspect of the pillar as *axis mundi*, on the one hand, and its function as a means to ascend to supernal worlds, on the other, in archaic societies' world views. While the cosmic structure of the world implies that the pillar is accessible to the entire archaic society, it is only a few elite, or the shamans, who resort to it *de facto* for their otherworldly journeys.[3] The practices of the elite led to a transformation of the "cosmo-theological concept into a concrete mystical experience."[4] Later, Eliade describes such experiences as "personal and ecstatic" as a result of the interiorization of tribal ideologies or mythologies.[5] More recently, the theme of the cosmic pillar or column has attracted the attention of two other Romanian scholars: Sergiu Al-George and Romulus Vulcanescu.[6] In the next chapter, I shall concern myself with the theme of the journey on the posthumous eschatological pillar, which is reminiscent of Eliade's descriptions of features of archaic religions, though never—insofar as I am acquainted with his writings—of his depictions of Judaism.

The post-mortem ascent by a pillar from one world to another is absent in Ioan P. Culianu's discussions of Jewish sources dealing with the ascent of the soul. Interested more in planes, heavens or bridges as described by Jewish literature of late antiquity, Culianu almost completely ignores the importance of the pillar, which is so cardinal in Eliade's analyses. The divergence between the two scholars may reflect an essential difference in their understanding of religion: more rural in the case of Eliade, and more urban in the case of Culianu. Why Eliade ignored the pillar in Jewish sources is a much more complex story, a succinct survey of which will be offered below.

Though I am more concerned with the ascensional understanding of the pillar in Jewish mysticism, as elaborated in the next two chapters, I will first survey other interpretations of the pillar as a cosmic entity in Jewish sources. Only this version of the pillar can explain its purpose as the means for ascent from one world to another.

2. THE COSMIC PILLAR IN RABBINIC TEXTS

Many of the following discussions refer to Proverbs 10:25 as a proof text for the cosmic understanding of the pillar. In this verse, the righteous are described as lasting as long as the world—or forever—in contradistinction to the wicked, who perish after a storm. This exemplifies the Bible's emphasis on abundance and vitality in characterizing the righteous, particularly notable in Psalm 1. The Hebrew form *Yesod* `Olam* found in Proverbs 10 describing the righteous can be read in two ways: as the foundation of the world or as the foundation forever. The former understanding the word `Olam* is consonant with rabbinic Hebrew; the latter, with biblical Hebrew.[7] It is, therefore, only according to a rabbinic understanding of the biblical phrase that the righteous may be interpreted as identical to the foundation that supports the world, and only in conjunction with the interpretation of `Olam* as world does *Yesod* indicate an architectural construct underlying the phrase, giving the righteous a cosmic dimension.

The image of a cosmic pillar is found in early rabbinic Judaism as the column—`amud*—upon which the earth stands, which is referred to as the righteous, *Tzaddiq.* A tradition in the name of Rabbi Eleazar ben Shamo`a is found to this effect in two late antiquity sources.[8] While the biblical verse in Proverbs deals with the righteous lasting in time, and the word "foundation" describes his durability, in the two rabbinic sources, the pillar is the main topic of discussion. This is gleaned from the context, in which seven pillars are invoked in discussions on the way the earth stands. As a side note, the theory of the seven firmaments is mentioned in these discussions, though there is no explicit connection between the two topics. As we shall see below, they are united in the *Slavonic Book of Enoch* and in several medieval accounts. Thus, the term *Yesod* in the biblical verse is understood as "pillar," and the righteous is identified with both pillar and foundation. The term *Tzaddiq* does not designate a human righteousness, but a cosmic pillar. The meaning of this passage is that the existence of a relatively stable column plays a major role in the architecture of the world. In other words, the Hagigah, a short but highly influential passage, is a part of mythical cosmology rather than a mode of making sense of religious behavior. To be clear, the basic context of the discussion is cosmology, and its influence on the way in which the righteous should be understood is only an aside. It seems therefore that the relationship between the righteous and the world reflects the role relegated to Atlas in myth.[9]

In other rabbinic sources, however, we find a view according to which the good deeds of exceptional human beings sustain the world, which has been created for the sake of the righteous.[10] This ethical understanding differs from the temporal–biblical and other rabbinic–architectural interpretations, as it allows a dynamic affinity between the righteous and the existence of the world. An interesting parallel to these stances is found in a late midrashic compilation entitled *'Aggadat Bereshit*, in which the righteous is described as causing the world to stand upon its foundation—*ma'amid 'et ha-'olam 'al yesodo*—no doubt a reworking of the verse from Proverbs.[11] What is particularly interesting in this example is the use of the term *ma'amid*—the *hiphil* active form of the verb *'MD*, which is the root of *'amud*, or pillar—together with the expression *Yesod 'Olam*. This formulation ascribes a more active role to the pillar: the world does not just rest upon but rather is sustained by it. In this context, there is a clear parallel in the Midrash on Psalms 1:15 between the righteous and pillars, and though the cosmic dimension of this parallelism is probably missing, the proper names of tzaddiqim are mentioned.[12] Thus, the nexus between the righteous and the pillar is a matter not only of a generic parallelism but also of specific persons. It should be mentioned that the manner in which the righteous is presented in these cases is reminiscent of the way in which the Torah and its commandments are envisioned as a cosmic entity by rabbinic authors.[13] It seems that this similarity reflects a hidden ancient debate between one view, in which the Torah is the center, and another, in which the performance of the commandments by the righteous and the special status acquired by them are concerned.

At least in some cases, the cosmic function of the righteous should be read not in a metaphorical but rather in a more dynamic manner, due to views found elsewhere in the Talmud. A passage that had widespread repercussions states that: "Rava said: If the righteous wished, they could create a world, for it is written: 'Your iniquities have separated you from your God.' For Rava created a man [*gavra'*] and sent him to Rabbi Zeira. The Rabbi spoke to him but he did not answer. Then he said: 'You are [coming] from the pietists: Return to your dust.'"[14] Such texts assume that the tzaddiq is not only a societal actor but also a holy man whose deeds have cosmic dimensions. Indeed, according to some statements found in rabbinic literature, it is plausible that the tzaddiqim reflect some form of the cosmic function of the thirty-six deans according to late-antiquity Hellenistic astrology.[15] As Gershom Scholem points out, the concept of the supernal righteous as an instrument of creation also is found in a source of Jewish extraction, the apocryphal *Slavonic Book of Enoch*, the date of which is still unclear.[16] Scholem brings this text into his analysis of a passage in *Sefer ha-Bahir*. In chapter eleven of the former work, God—the speaker in the following passage—reveals to Enoch an account of the secrets of the acts of creation:

> Before all visible things were, the light opened and I, in the middle of the light, was traveling like one of the invisible things, as the sun goes from East to West, and from West to East. The sun found repose, but I did not find repose because everything was formless. Having thought to create the foundation for visible creation, I ordered that from the depths that were mounting up, one of the invisible things should become visible. Adonil went out, being extraordinarily big. I looked at it, and behold, it had in his belly the Great Aion. I told him: "Adoil, give birth and what you deliver will be visible!" It delivered and from it the Great Aion was born, and it sustains all the creation that I wanted to create. "And I saw that it is good" and I made my throne and sat on it. To the light I said: "Ascend higher, and fix thyself and become the foundation of all the things on high!"[17]

Later in chapter seventeen, the connection between the Great Aion and the righteous is discussed in the context of the end of days: "And all the righteous that will escape the Great Judgment of the Lord will join the Great Aion, and at the same time the Aion will join the righteous, and they will be eternal… They will have for always a great light and an indestructible wall, and they will have a great Paradise, the shelter of an eternal habitation. Happy are the righteous who will escape the Great Judgment. For their faces will shine like the Sun."[18]

Let us start with the observation that three of the main concepts found in the verse from Proverbs—righteous, foundation and world—play major roles in these two passages. The second deals with this verse not in an exegetical manner, but by freely appropriating these concepts. The first passage reflects the manner in which God explains to Enoch the details of the act of creation in the first chapter of Genesis, particularly verse three, dealing with light.

Let me attempt to elucidate the manner in which light is understood in the above passages. It is first split into two, God being in the center. Then he commanded the light to ascend on high. In the eschaton, the light, as the Great Aion, becomes available to the righteous who, on the one hand, are described as united with this Aion and, on the other hand, have their faces illuminated by it. This account is reminiscent of the myth found in *BT, Hagigah*, fol. 12a, about the light of creation that has been stored and is reserved for the righteous at the end of days. The rabbinic storing of light parallels the ascent of the light in the Slavonic Enoch.[19] Similar to rabbinic personal eschatology, in the Slavonic Enoch the righteous obtain some form of luminosity.[20] What seems to be missing in rabbinic literature is the view that the righteous become the Great Aion, which "passes for the righteous." If we assume that this Aion is the foundation, as portrayed in chapter eleven of the Slavonic Enoch, the righteous become part of the foundation in some way, and they ascend to the status of being within the supernal realm. In other words, the righteous become the foundation described in the account of the creation of the world. It is as if the ancient Jewish author of the Slavonic Enoch read the words *tzaddiq* and *yesod*, from the verse of Proverbs, as "the righteous become the foundation." In this context, the third word in the verse, `olam, understood as time, may be reflected by the term Aion. Or, to formulate it in a different manner, light, which is the first creation in Genesis, is understood not just as the first of many discrete acts of creation, but also as the beginning of a gradual process that is grounded in the basic importance of light as the foundation of what evolves later.

If my conjecture is correct, then the discussion in chapter seventeen of the Slavonic Enoch may be considered as a sort of early Midrash on the verse from Proverbs, attributing a cosmic dimension to it, just as the passage from chapter eleven constitutes some form of Midrash on Genesis 1:3. As Scholem points out, additional details of the account of creation, such as the resort to stones as the foundation for subsequent creations, are connected to another discussion in Hagigah, fol. 12a.[21] Thus, it seems that there are parallels between the Slavonic Enoch and three different treatments of topics related to cosmology found in two excerpts of BT, Hagigah. However, while in Talmudic discussions the three excerpts are not considered to be a unified narrative, this is the case in the apocryphal book. Interestingly enough, in chapter eleven God tells Enoch that the account described is a secret unknown even to the angels, and in rabbinic literature, too, the creation of light is treated as though a secret topic.[22]

Let me highlight what seems to be an important dimension of these discussions. I have presented interpretations of the terms *Yesod* and `*Olam* as semantic shifts that allow the insertion of new dimensions into biblical verse. In my opinion, these semantic shifts do not introduce new concepts into but rather facilitate the anchoring of these concepts in the verse that serves as proof text. Only because these already existed does the semantic shift become instrumental in conveying them. The implication of this statement is that the archaic vision of the pillar as *axis mundi* did not emerge in Judaism as the result of a systemic development based upon linguistic changes. It is more reasonable to assume that it reflects the stance introduced in this discussion related to the term `amud found in Hagigah. The basic carrier of the cosmic dimension is, in this case, a term that does not occur in the biblical verse but organizes the cosmic reinterpretation of that verse.

A certain modest beginning of a cosmic vision of the pillar unrelated to the righteous is found in *Genesis Rabba'*, where the pillar of cloud is understood explicitly as the angel of God.[23] This type of apotheosis of the righteous and the assumption that he exists on a supernal plane of existence is nevertheless reminiscent of a tradition known in the Middle Ages; Philo of Alexandria describes the pillar of fire as an angel.[24]

According to medieval *ha-Midrash ha-Gadol* on Genesis 5:24, a verse that deals with Enoch, three persons are described as ascending on high—Enoch, Moses and Elijah—and in this context it is said that "all the righteous ascend and serve on high."[25] Interestingly enough, the verse adduced as a proof text, Zekharia 3:7, is: "I shall give you access among these who stand by [*ha-`omedim*]"—namely the angels, according to rabbinic tradition.[26] Thus the affinity between angelic powers and the concept of standing—from which the noun `amud stems— is well known in rabbinic sources and could allow for the development of angels as pillars.

3. THE PILLAR IN THE BOOK OF BAHIR

Synthesis between the architectural–static and the ritualistic–dynamic understandings of the terms pillar and righteous is found in an influential passage of the *Book of Bahir*, an important Kabbalistic work edited in the late twelfth or very early thirteenth century, presumably in Provence. As pointed out by other scholars, this treatise is a collection of various traditions that draw from Oriental—namely, Near Eastern— sources that reached Europe and were edited, integrating some speculative traditions found in Provence.[27] The passage conveys that:

There is a pillar from earth to heaven, and its name is *Tzaddiq*, according to the name of righteous men. And when there are righteous men in the world, then the pillar is strengthened, but if not—it becomes weak. And it supports the entire world, as it is written: "the righteous are the foundation of the world." But if it is weakened, it cannot support the world. This is the reason why even if there is only one righteous [in the world], he maintains the world.[28]

First and foremost, unlike the rabbinic vision of the pillar that sustains the world, here the pillar starts from the world and reaches heaven, presumably sustaining the latter, in a manner reminiscent of Atlas. Thus, it seems that this may be the first formulation of an *axis mundi*, which deals not only with cosmology, but also with a structure that brings together different planes of reality. It is only later in the Bahir passage that the Talmudic theme of sustaining the world occurs. The focus of this passage is the `amud: unlike the short occurrence in the Talmudic text, it stands at the center of a more elaborate discussion. Furthermore, there is clear justification for the use of the epitheton *Tzaddiq* to indicate the cosmic pillar. The static, architectural, cosmic device of the Hagigah passage now becomes dependent upon the deeds of the righteous human, as is the case in the *Yuma'* fol. 38b passage, to be discussed below. In other words, the pillar of the world depends upon what happens within the world: if there are righteous humans, it is strengthened. Within the context of the Bahir, this affinity is not dependent upon a certain theology or theosophy, because it only reaches heaven. Though different from the rabbinic sources, the above passage does not transcend the intellectual horizon of what is found in rabbinic sources or in the Slavonic Enoch. Rather, it binds loose ends and rounds out different tendencies found in divergent approaches, which is characteristic of rabbinic conciseness in discussions on non-Halakhic topics.

What seems to be new in this passage is the assumption of a dual status of the righteous: there are righteous men in the world, but there is also a cosmic righteous; the former depend on the latter, and it is called by its name. The question is: what is the meaning of this affinity? Do the two entities share a generic term, or does the cosmic pillar adopt the name of the righteous through generations? The former possibility seems to be much more plausible and is consonant with the passage from chapter seventeen of the Slavonic Enoch adduced above, according to which the Great Aion, which is identical to the foundation, passes for the righteous. Though this is a rather vague statement, there can be no doubt that an identity exists between the righteous and the supernal entity. And if this reading it correct, then we may suppose a common source for the Bahir statement and the apocryphal book.

According to Scholem, the above Bahir passage may have two possible meanings: cosmic and sexual.[29] There is little doubt concerning the validity of the cosmic dimension of the pillar. The sexual, however, is more problematic, judging on the basis of this specific passage alone. The formulation that the pillar extends from earth to heaven problematizes the phallic aspect but reinforces the cosmic one. The process of the strengthening and weakening of the pillar, which is adduced by Scholem in order to make this claim, is a typical rabbinic approach, connecting religious deeds below to the divine powers on high, an approach I call theurgical.[30] The cosmic, non-sexual description of the pillar is carried through to another paragraph found in the same book. When dealing with the theosophical system, consisting of ten powers, an anonymous Kabbalist describes the eighth of these powers as follows:

> The Holy One, blessed be He, has the righteous in His world, and he is fond of him because he maintains the entire world. He [the righteous] is its foundation and he provides for it, and lets it grow and cultivates it and guards it. He is loved and treasured above, loved and treasured below; feared and sublime above, feared and sublime below. He is comely and accepted above, comely and accepted below. And he is the foundation of all souls.[31]

Here, the righteous is less plausibly the mortal and thus transient human righteous, as Scholem assumes,[32] or even the cosmic righteous, as in the passage from the same book discussed earlier, but rather an entity that is part of the divine sphere—it is a name for a divine-like power. I take the phrase "His world" to indicate not the world created by God in general, but the specific intra-divine world, the realm of the ten divine powers. The formulation used here is reminiscent of another in the same book: "The Holy One, blessed be He, has a tree."[33] Here the tree constitutes a theosophical structure. In both cases, there is differentiation between the mundane righteous and the tree, and those found on another plane of existence. This supernal existence is the reason why the righteous is glorified. The world is both sustained and suspended by the pillar. In Talmudic discussions, the emphasis is on the mundane activity that sustains and the supporting activity that is similar to the relationship between Atlas and the world. Here, however, the higher power holds what is beneath it, in a manner characteristic of earlier Heikhalot literature.

My assumption is that the passage deals with two different sorts of activity: the first is the material impact of the eighth power in this world, and the second deals with the provision of souls. In both cases, the supernal righteous provide the lower world with whatever necessary, which indicates not only some form of static cosmology, but also an on-going process of providing for the lower world by a higher power. A vertical and downward vector is involved that does not resort to the image of the pillar, unlike the upward vector found in rabbinic discussions of the righteous as a cosmic pillar.

The final sentence in this passage deals with the foundation of souls and has an important parallel to the theosophical tree: "from there the souls are floating [emerging]."[34] Here again, the tree and the intra-divine pillar function in the same manner. However, both the image of the foundation of the souls and that of the source of their emergence are part of the descending vector, related to cosmogony. To the best of my knowledge, in these passages of the Bahir neither the tree nor the pillar serves as a vehicle by which one returns to the source, or what shall be described in the next chapter as the eschatological pillar; hence Scholem's parallel between the Bahir and the Manichaean "column of splendor," interesting as it is for later forms of Kabbalah, does not assist us with a better understanding of the Bahir.[35]

There can be no doubt that mention of the souls in the Bahir has sexual connotations, since the paragraph that immediately precedes it deals with the descent of semen. The seventh divine power is described as the spinal column, while the eighth is portrayed as the *membrum virile*.[36] Last but not least, the identity between the concept of the pillar and of the cosmic tree, which in later Kabbalistic texts is related to the souls as well, is explicitly found elsewhere in the Bahir.[37]

To summarize the distinctions proposed above, in the Bahir there are two different concepts of the pillar: one cosmological, dealing with a column that stretches from earth to heaven, and the other theosophical, describing an active entity that is part of the divine world. The different types of pillars are not juxtaposed, and no attempt is made to offer a unified vision providing a continuum from one pillar to the other. This should not be surprising, since the Bahir also does not provide a coherent picture of the higher or lower world.

4. THE PILLAR IN EARLY KABBALAH

From two early Kabbalistic documents, we find similar attempts to harmonize the two different traditions found in BT, Hagigah about one or all of the seven pillars upon which the world stands. Rabbi Isaac Sagi Nahor, the dominant Provencal Kabbalist, identifies the seven great pillars mentioned in *Sefer Yetzirah* 2:5 with the seven sefirot, one of which is "*Yesod 'Olam*, a power which belongs to the six extremities, which is set in judgment."[38] In my opinion, the affinity between one of the pillars and the phrase from Proverbs 10:25 demonstrates the fact that the Talmudic view underlies the discussion. More explicit is the stance of a contemporary of Rabbi Isaac, the Barcelonese Rabbi Yehudah ben Yaqar, originally from Provence, who proposes a harmonistic approach and introduces the topic of Sabbath as Yesod and the six days of the week.[39] Thus, early in the history of Kabbalistic theosophy, three different Kabbalists believed that the one single pillar pointed to the ninth sefirah, understood also as the righteous. Let me highlight the fact that in the Provencal and Geronese texts adduced above, the term "pillar" does not occur in the sense used in the Bahir. I assume that in this particular case, as in many others, the Kabbalah of the Bahir and that of Rabbi Isaac Sagi Nahor represent different and basically independent types of theosophy. In the work of two followers of Rabbi Isaac's theosophical Kabbalah, there are discussions in which theosophical understandings of the tzaddiq are present, though without the sexual connotations of the pillar concept portrayed in the Bahir. So, for example, Rabbi Ezra of Gerona describes the flow of water from paradise as a symbol of the sefirotic realm as follows:

All these are supplied by that spring which proceeds from Wisdom's paradise, within which souls flower in joy. It flows forth without ceasing either day or night; on its account the world is sustained. As our sages said in the tractate *Yuma'*: "On account of the righteous one is the world created and sustained," as it says: "The righteous one is the world's foundation." Our sages also said concerning this:

"The circumference of the tree of life is a journey of five hundred years, and all of the waters are divided forth from it."[40]

Rabbi Ezra looks for proof texts in *Yuma'* and in *Genesis Rabba*, but he does not refer to more theosophical sources, such as the book of Bahir. And despite the garden imagery and the topic of water, he does not refer to the theme of the pillar. In his *Commentary on the Account of Creation*, however, he describes three pillars: the first two are viewed as the pillars of heaven, which correspond to the sefirot of Netzah and Hod, and a third, the righteous one that is the pillar that sustains the world, which corresponds to the sefirah of Yesod.[41] Probably due to the impact of Rabbi Ezra, the short reference by Rabbi Jacob ben Sheshet to three pillars that are parallel to the daily recitation of the eighteen benedictions—known as `amidah (the last being parallel to the ninth sefirah, the righteous as the foundation of the world)—also has nothing to do with the Bahir.[42] Interestingly enough, in their commentaries on the Talmudic `Aggadot, Rabbi Ezra and his companion in Gerona, Rabbi Azriel, skip the Hagigah statement. Therefore, in the first generation of theosophical Kabbalists, those of Provencal and Gerona do not adopt the view of the pillar as elaborated by the Bahir, even where they interpret rabbinic statements on the topic. This is also the case in contemporary Jewish esotericism composed in Germany, where a different type of treatment of the pillar is discerned, as we shall see in the next section. To the best of my knowledge, and according to Scholem's list of those who were acquainted with this paragraph of the Bahir, no thirteenth-century Kabbalist cited it verbatim.[43]

The image of the pillar occurs in a short Kabbalistic prayer belonging to a group of writings related to an enigmatic book entitled *Sefer ha-`Iyyun*, the Book of Contemplation, the date and place of composition of which are still uncertain.[44] When dealing with the sefirah of Tiferet, the anonymous author uses the terms `Amud ha-Ne'eman, the faithful pillar, and `Amud ha-Tavekh, the central pillar. The second designation is expressly related to the tree of life and to paradise.[45] It is reasonable to assume that this sefirotic identification had an impact on the later layer of the Zohar, where the median pillar is identified with the sefirah of Tiferet.[46]

To address a question posed above concerning the possibility that, according to the passage from the Bahir, the pillar has a proper name related to the living righteous, I assume that a personal name is transferred to the pillar, and in my opinion, such a view is corroborated by an anonymous tradition preserved by a presumably Geronese Kabbalist. In a text reprinted by Scholem, it is said that:

[a] I heard that about him it is hinted at [in the verse] "and the righteous is the foundation of the world." For [the sake of] one [single] righteous the world is maintained and it is Enoch the son of Yared. [b] And there are those that intend to him in their prayer. And they gave a rationale for their words, saying that because they are impure and abject, how they may think to pray to Causa Causarum. And since there is a minister that is appointed over the issues of [this] world, we should pray to him.[47]

The conciseness of this tradition prevents an unequivocal understanding of this dense passage. It is hard to determine if Enoch is conceived in sentence (a) as a human righteous, in accordance with the source that undeniably underlies this sentence, *Yuma'*, fol. 38b, or if the vision of Enoch as a minister, *sar*, or as an angel found in (b) also reflects the meaning of (a). If the second understanding is adopted, then the minister is presumably the prince of the world and thus the righteous upon which it stands. More material on this topic will be presented in the next section.

There is a theological issue that is more evident in the above testimony than in other cases: this passage reflects an interesting case of what Culianu describes as ditheism, Hurtado calls binitarianism, Segal refers to as two powers in heaven, and Stroumsa, as hierarchical duality.[48] As Culianu has pointed out, the term "dualism" does not fit the assumption that there is no polarity of a good and a bad deity involved in some ancient Jewish sources, but it is more a matter of attempting to transfer some anthropomorphic expressions from the supreme deity to a lower divine entity, or an angel, which assumes the status of creator or revelator or becomes the object of profound religious reverence. In any case, I propose combining Culianu's and Stroumsa's proposals in order to better illuminate the phenomenon described below: hierarchical ditheism. This assumes the existence of a high divinity and an archangel, which is conceived in basically positive terms and fulfills some roles attributed in the Hebrew Bible to God. In late antiquity, there are several testimonies to the concept of a great angel in sectarian Judaism, that may allow this hierarchical ditheism.[49]

5. The Pillar and Enoch-Metatron in Ashkenazi Esotericism

The cosmic stance of the pillar—it holds the world—parallels some discussions of Metatron. In some sources, while Enoch is ascending, the size of the archangel is enhanced until it reaches the dimensions of the entire world.[50] To be sure, there is no explicit affinity between the two topics in late antiquity texts, but in some sources contemporary to the anonymous Kabbalist cited above, the nexus between the two is quite explicit.

According to a tradition found in a thirteenth-century Ashkenazi passage, the term "pillar" in the Hagigah text, which is understood as the righteous, is identified as an angel that shakes the world once every seventy years.[51] The identity of the angel is not explicit. But in another Ashkenazi treatise belonging to a circle other than that of Rabbi Eleazar, a nexus between the pillar as the righteous and Metatron seems to be quite possible. In the *Commentary on the Haftarah*, authored in my opinion by Rabbi Nehemiah ben Shlomo ha-Navi', the Ashkenazi figure writes on one of the names of Metatron as follows: "*Ve-Tzaddiq*—because a pillar seizes the world and its name is *Tzaddiq*, and it is seizing the world by the right hand, as it is said: 'And the righteous is the foundation of the world.'"[52] A few lines before this passage, the identity of the entity that seizes the world is revealed in a somewhat more explicit manner: "*ve-'Akhy'el* in gematria [amounts to] *'Ofan*, and in gematria *Yuppiy'el* and this is the name of the angel of the countenance, and this is the meaning of the statement that there is an *'Ofan* on high and the arm of Metatron is linked to the *'Ofan*, and it seizes the world. And the storm is going from the *'Ofan* to the arm of the Holy one, blessed be He, as it is said: 'and under the arms, the world [is found].'"[53]

The significance attributed by the anonymous author to the string of numerical equivalences of these words is not totally clear. They may indicate the identity among the three terms, which I find difficult in the hierarchy explicit in the passage, or they may refer to the relationship among them, which I find more plausible. According to the latter reading, the name of the angel of presence is equivalent to the term *'Ofan* because it is dependent on, or linked to, that angelic figure. Likewise, I would read the first name, *ve-'Akhy'el*, as referring to God, in a manner reminiscent of what is written in precisely this context, "*ve-'Ay'el* amounts in gematria *ha-Gadol*, because God is great."[54] According to another statement, *ve-'Akhy'el* is the mystical name of the right hand of God.[55] The remaining question to be resolved is what the specific meaning of the arm is. According to this passage, the world is held by the arm, and the arm, which is also a pillar, is linked to the 'Ofan. I am not sure that I can provide a visual representation of the relationship among the four factors mentioned above: God, 'Ofan, Metatron and the world. Given the prominence of the verb *TPS*, to seize, in connection to an arm, I am inclined to relate this passage to a misunderstood Heikhalot passage describing another angel, *'Anafiel*, as holding the world in his hand in a manner reminiscent of Apollo in some mosaics from the Hellenistic period.[56] However, for our purposes, it will suffice to point out that Metatron, or his right hand, is identified as the cosmic pillar. Later on in this treatise, it is written that "the pillar of the world is called *Tzaddiq*, the foundation of the world, [and] it is linked to the cherub, and *'Adaneyah* is the pillar, as it is written 'whereupon are its foundations [*'Adaneyah*] fastened.'"[57]

The plural form of *'Eden*, or foundation stone—*'Adaneiah*—has been understood as a proper name for the pillar. Like in the earlier sentence, this entity is linked to a supernal entity, a cherub, quite reminiscent of the 'Ofan. We witness here a specific hierarchy constituted by three beings: God, an angelic figure ('Ofan or, alternatively, a cherub) and the lower cosmic entity designated as Metatron, which is also the pillar and the righteous. Unlike the rabbinic text, which does not create any specific link between the pillar and God, in this case, a certain continuum and similarity between them has been articulated. They are connected by an angelic median figure, and both are described anthropomorphically. This cosmic pillar-righteous is obviously connected to the world, and I assume that in a way, Metatron is understood as the angel appointed to and also sustaining the world. However, in this medieval text, the strong linkage of the angel to God has been emphasized by describing it as depending upon the arm of God. In a way, Metatron is a reverberation on a lower plane of a part of the divine structure. Elsewhere in the same treatise, there is a parallelism between the divine form and the angelic world.[58] In the immediate vicinity of the discussions about the pillar and the angels, the anonymous author makes another comment on the affinity between the two: since the angels are portrayed in some places in rabbinic literature as standing, having no knees and thus being inflexible, the Ashkenazi writer describes them as being like "pillar[s] of iron."[59]

Some interesting parallels to these passages are found in an anonymous manuscript related to Heikhalot literature that eliminates the
cherub as an intermediary between God's arm and that of Metatron. In
this fragment Yuppiel is identified with Metatron.[60]

In another Ashkenazi treatise called *The Seventy Names of Metatron*,
authored by the same Rabbi Nehemiah, a view of Metatron understood
as the righteous is accompanied by the view that this angel and God
seize the world in their hands.[61] Especially interesting is the formulation
according to which one of these names amounts to the numerical value
of the following Hebrew phrase: "'The righteous, that is the foundation
of the world, comes to me.' Because it supports the pillar whose name
is righteous, and the entire world it supports with it."[62] Closer to the
Commentary on the Haftarah is a version found in a manuscript of the
Commentary on the Seventy Names of Metatron, where Yuppiel is described as amounting in gematria to "'*Ofan*...since the entire world
stands upon a pillar named righteous...and Yuppiel is linked to the fin-
ger of the Holy One, blessed be He."[63] My assumption is that this is a
powerful parallel to the Ashkenazi texts adduced above, and we may assume that in one of the groups of Ashkenazi esoteric authors, a hierarchy based on three supernal entities connected among themselves and
related to the concept of cosmic pillar was articulated. A subordination
of the angel of the countenance to the cherub also is found in a late
thirteenth-century Ashkenazi text, which demonstrates acquaintance
with theosophical Kabbalah.[64]

6. The Zohar and the Luminous Pillar

Among works that demonstrate fascination with the theme of the cosmic pillar, the Zohar is indubitably the most prominent. Various terms
related to the pillar are found in this vast body of Kabbalistic literature,
and I will not even attempt to exhaust them here. There are hundreds
of discussions gravitating around this concept, but I shall address here
only its cosmic understanding, leaving the eschatological for the next
chapter.

Following the lead of two early thirteenth-century Kabbalists, Rabbi
Isaac Sagi Nahor and Rabbi Yehudah ben Yaqar,[65] the former of whom
has been discussed above, both the Zohar and de Leon's Hebrew writings suggest a solution to the discrepancy between two rabbinic stances.
One view believes the world is sustained by seven pillars; the other,

which will concern us in this chapter, that the world stands on a single pillar. According to the theosophical code, the single pillar is believed to point to the sefirah of Yesod, while the six others are related to the six lower sefirot that are thought to be grounded in the sefirah of Yesod.[66] The sefirotic understanding reflects an intra-divine appropriation of cosmological theories stemming from the different Talmudic discussions in Hagigah, upon which some forms of coherence have been imposed by means of the theosophical code. It is plausible to envision the relationship between the single pillar and the other six as one between the center and six extremities that are part of the circumference of a circle.

According to its medieval significance, by the second half of the thirteenth century the term `amud refered to the center of a circle.[67] Like the pillar sustaining the world, the pillar as the center sustains the circle. Designs reflecting the geometrical relationship among the seven lower sefirot are known from late thirteenth-century Castile in the very circle of the Zohar.[68] In the so-called *Midrash ha-Ne`elam* on the Song of Songs, there is a passage dealing with the seat of glory that rests on four pillars, each of which is held up by twelve supporting pillars. For our purposes, it should be noted that one of them is called the "median pillar," `amuda' de-'emtza`ita'.[69] Interestingly enough, letters of the Hebrew alphabet are inscribed on each of these pillars.

In other Zoharic discussions, the concept of the pillar is interpreted symbolically as pointing to the ninth divine manifestation or power, identified with the divine phallus and with the concept of righteousness. This is especially evident in many discussions in the Zohar, the most explicit of which is found in *Zohar*, I, fol. 45a, where Joseph, the prototype of righteousness, is described as the pillar of the world, `amuda' de-`alma'. This propensity for emphasizing the phallic nature of the ninth sefirah is also evident in Rabbi Moses de Leon's writings.[70]

In the last layer of Zoharic literature, in a composition called *Tiqqunei Zohar*, the median pillar is described as a structure emerging from the union of the seven lower sefirot: "The son is the union of father and mother, he is a pillar that supports everything like heaven and earth, as it is said that the world stands on a pillar, as it is said 'the righteous is the foundation of the world,' so [too] are father and mother standing on the median pillar, which is the union of mother and daughter, as in *HWH*."[71] This transposition of the organic vision of the pillar as a son to the cosmic sustaining function translates the rabbinic type of discourse into a theosophical one, pointing to the relationship between various levels of sefirot in the supernal world. As we shall see below, this process of transposing discussions dealing with lower levels of reality to higher ones is part of the semantic strategy characteristic of the last layer of the Zohar.

In another composition belonging to this layer called *Ra'aya' Meheimna'*, there is a clear affinity between the median pillar and the angel Metatron. The pillar is described as the sefirah of Tiferet, the center of the lower seven sefirot (as seen above in some earlier Kabbalistic writings), but connected to the sefirah of Yesod. This nexus between the median pillar and the six other sefirot is linked to a view found in some Kabbalistic writings that describe Metatron as sometimes being spelled with six consonants, and in other instances, with seven—Mytatron.[72] This twofold affinity suggests an analogy between the angel Metatron and the median pillar; its name is in the name of its master,[73] and this master is Tiferet, the king and Adam. Likewise, Metatron is described in this context as being created in the image of its master. This is the reason why Metatron exists as the median pillar in the non-sefirotic realm, where it needs protection against the evil powers described as shells. In this context, the angel is associated with the divine throne,[74] while later in the discussion, Metatron is described as the "horse of *Tiferet*" and its garment.[75] Either way, an affinity is created between the median pillar and Metatron: they are not only similar but also intertwined. Though I have not found a clear-cut statement referring to Metatron as the cosmic pillar, as in Hasidei Ashkenaz, I believe that the later layer of the Zohar comes very close to suggesting this.

Another interesting connection found in the Zohar is among light, the foundation and the righteous, which occurs in the first layer, the *Midrash ha-Ne'elam*, where an anonymous Kabbalist explains an exegetical action that creates this series of identifications: he mentions the verse from Psalms 93:11, in which the righteous is related expressly to light. Moreover, the term *Yesod*—foundation—is interpreted as "element," and light is described as such.[76] In the main layer of the Zohar, this affinity is elaborated as follows: "'And God says that the light is good.'—This is the median pillar [*'amuda' de-'emtza'ita'*], because it is good, it illumines on high and below, and to all other sides according to the secret of *YHWH*, the name that holds all the sides."[77] What is pertinent to our purpose is what seems to me explicit: the identification of the term light in the biblical verse with the median pillar. I assume that this passage should be read as pointing symbolically to the sefirah of Yesod. The nexus between the median pillar and light is also quite evident from a discussion found some lines later in the same Zoharic treatise, where it is identified with the sefirah of Yesod.[78] I believe that this understanding of the verse from Genesis is related to the Midrashic interpretation of the deeds of the righteous.[79] Pillars of light are mentioned in many other instances in this literature,[80] and discussions assigning the pillars the role of maintaining the world, apparently as symbols for the seven lower sefirot, are reflected in turn by the study of the Torah by Israel.[81]

A similar interpretation of the pillar as light is found in the writings of Rabbi Todros ben Joseph ha-Levi Abulafia, a contemporary of the circle of Kabbalists from which the book of the Zohar emerged and one of the first authors who ever quoted it.[82] In his *'Otzar ha-Kavod*, a commentary on the Talmudic *'Aggadot*, he interprets the dictum from Hagigah about the pillar as follows: "I had already spoken about it in several places. Know that it is the light, about which it has been said, 'It is good' and it stands ['*omed*] between heaven and earth...and from there the souls are emerging as it is said, 'The righteous lives by his faith.' And about him it has been said, 'If not for my covenant day and night, I would not promulgate the orders of heaven and earth.' This means that it is the foundation of the world."[83] This is no doubt a theosophical presentation of the pillar that combines elements found in the Bahir. However, unlike that earlier book and closer to the Zohar, the pillar is related by Rabbi Todros Abulafia to light and to goodness, as if in evident understanding of Genesis 1:3. Interestingly enough, he understands the view of Hagigah as referring not to the pillar that holds the world, but as standing between heaven and earth, apparently as an entity descending from heaven. The world or earth is, so it seems, suspended from the descending pillar, as is the case in the second passage adduced above from *Sefer ha-Bahir*. However, both earth and heaven here are symbols for Tiferet and Malkhut, and the righteous stands for Yesod, which is the median power between the two sefirot. The cosmic stance of the Bahir has been interpreted theosophically—again following the views of the Bahir in other discussions—changing the cosmic dimension into an intra-divine function.

7. The Human Righteous as a Pillar in the Zohar

In several instances not necessarily related to Jewish mysticism, important figures like the patriarchs have been described as the pillars of the world, `amudei `olam.[84] This expression reverberates later in many schools of Jewish literature, including in Rabbi Moses de Leon's writings and in the Zohar.[85] In some parts of the Zohar, however, especially in that called the *Idra'*, the pillar theme recurs. The main protagonist of the Zohar, Rabbi Shimeon bar Yohai, the second century legalistic and mystical–magical figure to whom the book has been ascribed, is described as "the pillar of the world," *qayyema' de-`alma'*. This stance emerges in the *Midrash ha-Ne`elam*, the earliest layer of the Zohar,[86] and he describes himself as "standing on a pillar."[87] My colleague, Yehuda Liebes, has dedicated an important and original study to this theme, in which he suggests, *inter alia*, an affinity between this Shimeon and the pillar on the one hand and the much earlier and famous phenomenon of Simeon the Stylist, a saintly figure sitting upon a column, on the other.[88] In any case, according to other statements, Shimeon expressly describes himself as identical to the pillar that sustains the world in contexts that have phallic valences.[89] In another discussion in the Zohar, the appearance of a pillar of cloud is mentioned as a follow up to Rabbi Shimeon's exposition on the Torah: "We have seen a pillar of cloud fixed from above to low, and splendor is shining within the pillar."[90]

Whether in the form of descending or sustaining pillars, it is the world that benefits from the role played by the pillar according to the above sources. Souls are indeed mentioned sometimes, but only as emanating from the descending pillar, the sefirah of Yesod, and never as ascending either of the two. I also assume that succinct references to the soul are part of cosmological treatments and are not concerned with descriptions of mystical experiences in any way. Such descriptions are part of the much more elaborate concern with a cosmic picture of the world that emerged in the Middle Ages in both South and North European Jewish cultures.

It may be said that the Zohar adduced different Kabbalistic understandings of already existing cosmological and theosophical pillars. Thus, it constitutes a compendium of some earlier Kabbalistic views that are not always concordant with one another. By and large, the schemes within which the pillar occurs in the above discussions reflect cosmological and theogonic pictures. They are concerned with two major topics: how the pillar sustains or if it suspends. They are elements of larger maps of higher worlds, which can be described as the cosmological and the theosophical *imaginaire*. These maps may or may not be used by Kabbalists in their search for spiritual experiences, and we shall explore this issue in the following two chapters.

NOTES

1. Mircea Eliade, *Shamanism: Archaic Techniques of Ecstasy* (Princeton: Princeton University Press, 1974), pp. 259–66. See also idem, *Images and Symbols: Studies in Religious Symbolism* (Princeton: Bollingen Series, Princeton University Press, 1991), pp. 41–51; idem, *Rites and Symbols of Initiation: The Mysteries of Birth and Rebirth* (New York: Harper Torchbooks, 1958), pp. 69–70; and idem, *Patterns in Comparative Religion*, trans. Rosemary Sheed (New York: Meridian Books, 1972), pp. 106, 299, 300 and 380.

2. Mircea Eliade, *No Souvenirs: Journal, 1957–1969* (San Francisco: Harper and Row, 1977), pp. 167 and 292–93.

3. Eliade, *Shamanism*, p. 265.

4. Ibid. Emphasis in the original. See also pp. 411 and 494.

5. Ibid., p. 266.

6. See Sergiu Al-George, *Arhaic și Universal: India in constiinta romineasca* (Bucharest: Editura Herld, n.d.), pp. 17–108; and Romulus Vulcanescu, *Coloana Cerului* (Bucharest: Editura Academiei, 1972). See also the more recent discussion of the pillar theme in Andrei Oisteanu, *Cosmos vs. Chaos: Myth and Magic in Romanian Traditional Culture* (Bucharest: The Romanian Cultural Foundation Publishing House, 1999), pp. 114–58. For Culianu's short treatment of the topic of the column of light, see Ioan P. Culianu, *Iocari serio, Știinta si arta in gindirea Renașterii* (Iasi: Polirom, 2003), pp. 172–73.

7. See Rabbi Abraham ibn Ezra's commentary on Psalm 112:6, where he interprets the phrase from Proverbs in a temporal manner.

8. See, *BT, Hagigah*, fol. 12b; and Shlomo Buber, ed., *Midrash Tehilim* (Vilnius: Reem, 1891), on Psalms 136:5, p. 520.

9. As is well known, the mythical picture of Atlas as bearer of the world had a deep impact on the concept of the pillar or column of glory in Manichaeism. See A. V. Williams Jackson, *Researches in Manichaeism* (New York: Columbia University Press, 1932), pp. 299–303. See also Paul, who calls the Church "the pillar and ground of the truth," I Tim., iii, 15; compare to Mark, xvi, 16; Rom., x, 17; Acts, xv, 28. For a bibliography of studies on the apostles as pillars, see Larry W. Hortado, *Lord Jesus Christ, Devotion to Jesus in Early Christianity* (Grand Rapids, Mich. and Cambridge, Engl.: Eerdmans, 2003), p. 158, n. 6.

10. See, for example, *BT, Yuma'*, fol. 38b, *Yalqut Shime'oni*, on Genesis, par. 5; on Samuel I, par. 86; on Proverbs, par. 947; and Rabbi Bahya ben Asher's commentary on Deuteronomy 29:9. For more on this issue, see Ephraim E. Urbach, *The Sages: Their Concepts and Beliefs*, trans. I. Abrahams (Jerusalem: The Magnes Press, 1979), pp. 487–88; R. Mach, *Der Zaddik in Talmud und Midrasch* (Leiden: Brill, 1957), pp. 109–10 and 134–35; and Yehuda Liebes, "The Messiah of the Zohar," in *The Messianic Idea in Israel* (in Hebrew) (Jerusalem: Israel Academy for Sciences and Humanities, 1982), pp. 120–21 and nn. therein. On an earlier connection in Qumran literature between 'amud and *Yesod*, see Crispin H. T. Fletcher-Louis, *All the Glory of Adam: Liturgical Anthropology in the Dead Sea Scrolls*, Studies on the Texts of the Desert of Judah, No. 42 (Leiden: Brill, 2001), p. 383.

11. See Salomon Buber, ed., *Agadath Bereshith* (Cracow: Josef Fischer, 1903), chapter 50, p. 100; and Mach, *Der Zaddik*, p. 134, n. 1.

12. *Midrash tehilim*, ed. S. Buber (Vilnius: Reem, 1891), fol. 8a.

13. See Urbach, *Sages*, pp. 286–87; and Mircea Eliade, *A History of Religious Ideas*, trans. W. R. Task (Chicago: Chicago University Press, 1978), vol. II, p. 274.

14. *BT, Sanhedrin*, fol. 65b; Mach, *Der Zaddik*, p. 111; and Moshe Idel, *Golem: Jewish Magical and Mystical Traditions on the Artificial Anthropoid* (Albany: State University of New York Press, 1990), pp. 27–30. The first quote in this passage is Jesaiah 59:2.

15. See the sources adduced by Mach, *Der Zaddik*, pp. 136–38; Moshe Beer, "Regarding the Source of the Number of the 36 Tzaddiqim" (in Hebrew), *Bar-Ilan, Annual of Bar-Ilan University* I (1963), pp. 172–76; and Meir Bar-Ilan, *Genesis's Numerology* (in Hebrew) (Rehovot, 2003), p. 117.

16. See Gershom Scholem, *On the Mystical Shape of the Godhead* (New York: Schocken Books, 1991), pp. 99–100.

17. A. Vaillant, ed., *Le livre des secrets d'Hénoch: Texte slave et traduction française* (Paris: Institut d'Etudes Slaves, 1952), chapter 11, pp. 29–31; Alexander Altmann, "A Note on the Rabbinic Doctrine of Creation," and *Journal of Jewish Studies* 6/7 (1955/1956): pp. 198 and 221. For the creation from formless into form, see ibid., pp. 195–96, where Slavonic Enoch 24:2 is referred to as indicating *creatio ex nihilo*, though I assume that our text refers to creation from a preexistent invisible entity, like in the Greek theories mentioned by Altmann. According to some versions, the Great Aion is translated as the "great light." On the Great Aion, see Shlomo Pines, "Eschatology and the Concept of Time in the Slavonic Book of Enoch," in *Types of Redemption*, eds. R. J. Z. Werblowsky and C. Jouco Bleeker (Brill: Leiden, 1970), p. 76, n. 17 and p. 79, n. 33. The second quote perhaps refers to Genesis 1:3.

18. Vaillant, *Le livre des secrets d'Hénoch*, chapter 17, p. 63; compare with Pines, "Eschatology," p. 78; and Gershom Scholem, *Origins of the Kabbalah*, ed. R. Z. J. Werblowsky, trans. A. Arkush (Philadelphia: Jewish Publishing Society and Princeton University Press, 1987), p. 74.

19. See also Scholem's short hint in *Origins of the Kabbalah*, p. 73.

20. See Moshe Idel, "Enoch is Metatron," *Immanuel* 24/25 (1990): p. 224; idem, "Adam and Enoch according to St. Ephrem the Syrian," *Kabbalah* 6 (2001): pp. 187–88; Phillip Alexander, "From Son of Adam to a Second God: Transformation of the Biblical Enoch," in *Biblical Figures Outside the Bible*, ed. M. E. Stone and T. A. Bergen (Harrisburg: Trinity Press International, 1998), p. 111; Andrei Orlov, "'Without Measure and Without Analogy': The Tradition of the Divine Body in *2 (Slavonic) Enoch*," *Journal of Jewish Studies* (forthcoming); and idem, "On the Polemical Nature of *2 (Slavonic) Enoch*: A Reply to C. Boettrich," *Journal for the Study of Judaism* 34 (2003): pp. 274–303.

21. See Scholem, *Origins of the Kabbalah*, pp. 73–74.

22. See the Midrashic texts discussed by Altmann, "A Note," pp. 196–97.

23. *Genesis Rabba'*, 35, eds. Theodor and Albeck (Jerusalem: Wahrmann Books, Jerusalem, 1965) vol. I, p. 333. See also the discussion of Ashkenazi esotericism below.

24. Philo of Alexandria, *De Vita Mosis*, I:29.

25. See M. Margolioth, ed., *Ha-Midrash ha-Gadol* (Jerusalem: Mossad ha-Rav Kook, 1975), on Genesis, p. 132.

26. See the various traditions printed in Jacob Gellis, ed., *Tossafot ha-Shalem* (Jerusalem: Mifal Tosafot Shalem, 1982), vol. I, pp. 177–78. On Enoch in Midrashic literature, see Daniel Sperber, *Massekhet Derekh 'Eretz Zuta*, 3rd ed. (Jerusalem: Zur Ot, 1994), pp. 84–85.

27. See Scholem, *Origins of the Kabbalah*, pp. 49–148; Haviva Pedaya, "The Provencal Stratum in the Redaction of Sefer ha-Bahir" (in Hebrew), *Jerusalem Studies in Jewish Thought* 9 (1990): pp. 139–64; and Ronit Meroz, "On the Time and Place of Some of *Sefer ha-Bahir*" (in Hebrew), *Daat* 49 (2002): pp. 137–80.

28. Daniel Abrams, ed., *The Book of Bahir* (Los Angeles: The Cherub Press, 1994), para. 71, pp. 160–61; Scholem, *On the Mystical Shape*, p. 95; idem, *Origins of the Kabbalah*, pp. 152–54; Elliot R. Wolfson, *Along the Path* (Albany: State University of New York Press, 1995), pp. 71–72; Gershom Scholem, *Das Buch Bahir* (Darmstadt: Wissenschaftliche Buchgesellschaft, 1970), p. 74. See also Arthur Green, "The Zaddiq as *Axis Mundi* in Later Judaism," *Journal of the American Academy of Religion* XLV:3 (1977): p. 333; and Michael Fishbane, *Biblical Myth and Rabbinic Mythmaking* (Oxford: Oxford University Press, 2003), pp. 258–60. The quote is Proverbs 10:25.

29. See Scholem, *Origins of the Kabbalah*, p. 153.

30. See Moshe Idel, *Kabbalah: New Perspectives* (New Haven: Yale University Press, 1988), p. 157.

31. Abrams, ed., *Book of Bahir*, pp. 188–89, n. 105; and Scholem, *On the Mystical Shape*, pp. 94–95. My translation and interpretation differ substantially from Scholem's in this book and is closer to both the translation and interpretation in Scholem, *Origins of the Kabbalah*, pp. 155–56. See also Liebes, "Messiah of the Zohar," p. 121–22, for this passage in Rabbi

Meir ibn Gabbai's influential `Avodat ha-Qodesh (Jerusalem: Levin-Epstein, 1973), I:26, and III:8.

32. Scholem, On the Mystical Shape, pp. 94–95.

33. Abrams, Book of Bahir, no. 64, pp. 155–57, and no. 14, p. 125.

34. Ibid., no. 14, p. 125. See also Scholem, Origins of the Kabbalah, p. 156–57.

35. Scholem, Origins of the Kabbalah, p. 153.

36. See Scholem, On the Mystical Shape, pp. 93–97; and idem, Origins of the Kabbalah, p. 154; compare especially to Abrams, Book of Bahir, no. 123, pp. 206–07.

37. See Scholem, Origins of the Kabbalah, pp. 71–80 and 153; Yehuda Liebes, Studies in the Zohar (Albany: State University of New York, 1993), p. 14; and the passage adduced in chapter 3 from Seder Gan `Eden.

38. See Mark Sendor, The Emergence of Provencal Kabbalah: R. Isaak the Blind's Commentary on Sefer Yezirah (Ph.D. diss., Harvard University, 1994), part II, pp. 114–15. See also part I, p. 356, n. 240 and p. 358, n. 246.

39. See chapter 3.

40. Rabbi Ezra ben Solomon of Gerona, Commentary on Song of Songs and Other Kabbalistic Commentaries, trans. Seth Brody (Kalamazoo, Mich.: Medieval Institute Publications, 1999), pp. 86–87; and Georges Vajda, Le commentaire d'Ezra de Gerone sur le cantique des cantiques (Paris: Aubier, 1969), p. 89. The first quote is from Yuma', fol. 38b; the second, Genesis Rabba' 15:7.

41. See Ezra ben Solomon, Commentary, pp. 230–31.

42. See Y. A. Vajda, ed., Meshiv Devarim Nekhohim (Jerusalem: Israeli Academy of Science, 1968), p. 185.

43. See Scholem, Das Buch Bahir, pp. 112–13.

44. See Mark Verman, The Book of Contemplation: Medieval Jewish Mystical Sources (Albany: State University of New York Press, 1992).

45. Printed in Adolph Jellinek, Auswahl Kabbalistischer Mystik (Leipzig: A. M. Colditz, 1853), vol. 1, p. ix.

46. I do not accept the view of David Neumark, who describes what he calls the doctrine of the median pillar, `Amuda' de-'Emtza`ita', as containing the sefirot Keter, Hokhmah, Binah, Tiferet, Yesod and Malkhut as a central view in Kabbalah. See his Toledot ha-Philosophia be-Yahadut, reprint (Jerusalem: Maqor, 1971), I, p. 237. See also chapter 3 in the current study. In discussions of Zoharic phrases related to the pillar, I prefer the term "median" rather than "central," found in Matt's translation of the Zohar, since I am concerned with the theosophical understanding of the pillar not only as the center of the structure of the seven lower sefirot, but also as a mediating power, which facilitates the transition from one degree to another.

47. Reishit ha-Qabbalah (Tel Aviv/Jerusalem: Schocken, 1948), pp. 252–53; and Moshe Idel, "Kabbalistic Prayer in Provence" (in Hebrew), Tarbiz 62 (1993): pp. 272–73. The quote is Proverbs 10:25. "For one righteous the world is maintained" is BT, Yuma', fol. 38b. For a much more detailed analysis of this text, see the appendix in Moshe Idel, BEN: Sonship and Jewish Mysticism (forthcoming).

48. Ioan P. Couliano, *Experiences de l'extase: Extase, Ascension et recit visionaire de l'Hellenisme au Moyen Age* (Paris: Payot, 1984), pp. 70–71; Larry Hurtado, *One God One Lord: Early Christian Devotion and Ancient Jewish Monotheism* (Philadelphia: Fortress Press, 1988); Allan F. Segal, *Two Powers in Heaven* (Leiden: Brill, 1978); and Gedaliahu A. G. Stroumsa, *Another Seed: Studies in Gnostic Mythology* (Leiden: Brill, 1984), p. 172.

49. See John J. Collins, "Messianism in the Maccabean Period," in *Judaisms and Their Messiahs at the Turn of the Christian Era*, eds. J. Neusner, W. Green, and E. S. Frerichs (Cambridge: Cambridge University Press, 1987), pp. 98–103; H. A. Wolfson, "The Pre-Existent Angel of the Magharians and al-Nahawandi," *JQR* [NS] 51 (1960–61): pp. 89–106; Jarl E. Fossum, *The Name of God and the Angel of the Lord: Samaritan and Jewish Concepts of Intermediation and the Origin of Gnosticism* (Tuebingen: J. C. B. Mohr, 1985), pp. 18, 329–32 and 337; idem, "The Magharians: A Pre-Christian Jewish Sect and Its Significance for the Study of Gnosticism and Christianity," *Henoch* IX (1989): pp. 303–43; Segal, *Two Powers*; Shlomo Pines, "God, the Divine Glory, and the Angels according to a Second-Century Theology," in *The Beginnings of Jewish Mysticism in Medieval Europe* (in Hebrew), ed. J. Dan (Jerusalem: Institute for Jewish Studies, 1987), pp. 1–14; Ioan P. Couliano, *The Tree of Gnosis*, trans. Hillary Wiener and Ioan P. Couliano (San Francisco: Harper, 1992), p. 5; Scholem, *Origins of the Kabbalah*, pp. 211–12; Moshe Idel, *Messianic Mystics* (New Haven: Yale University Press, 1998), pp. 342–43, n. 52; Margaret Barker, "Temple Imagery in Philo: An Indication of the Origin of the Logos?" in *Templum Amicitiae: Essays on the Second Temple Presented to Ernst Bammel*, ed. William Horbury (Sheffield: JSOT Press, 1991), pp. 70–78; and more recently, Yoram Erder, "The Prince 'Mastemah' in a Karaite Work" (in Hebrew), *Meggilot* I (2002): pp. 243–46.

50. See Nicholas Sed, *La mystique cosmologique juive* (Paris: Mouton, 1981), pp. 286–87.

51. See Rabbi Abraham ben Azriel, `Arugat ha-Bosem*, ed. E. E. Urbach (Jerusalem: Mekize Nirdamim, 1947), vol. II, p. 195. For a citation of the Talmudic passage without any significant interpretation, see Rabbi Eleazar of Worms's *Sodei Razayya*, ed. Shalom Weiss (Jerusalem: Sha`arey Ziv, 1991), p. 37.

52. Ms. Berlin, Or. 942, fol. 153b.

53. Ibid. Each of the three Hebrew terms: *'Ofan, Yuppi'el* and *ve-`Aki'el*, amounts in gematriah 137. "The angel of the countenance" is translated from *Sar ha-Panim*. On "The arm of the Holy One," compare to *BT, Hagigah*, fol. 12b. The closing quote is Deuteronomy 33:27.

54. Ibidem. The numerical value of the two Hebrew words is identical: 48.

55. Ms. Berlin, Or. 942, fol. 153. See also Moshe Idel, "The World of Angels in Human Shape" (in Hebrew), *Jerusalem Studies in Jewish Thought* 4 (1986): p. 8.

56. I delivered a lecture on this topic at the conference of the Dinur Center at the Hebrew University in 2000, and I hope to elaborate upon this issue elsewhere.

57. Ms. Berlin, Or. 942, fol. 155b. A question on which I cannot elaborate here is the possible contribution of this passage, and some other occurrences in the same text, to the concept of cherub in Ashkenazi esoteric literature. See Joseph Dan, *The "Unique Cherub" Circle: A School of Jewish Mystics and Esoterics in Medieval Germany* (Tuebingen: J. C. B. Mohr, 1999); Wolfson, *Along the Path*, especially pp. 61–62. The quote is Job 38:5.

58. See Idel, "World of Angels," pp. 1–15.

59. Ms. Berlin, Or. 942, fol. 153a.

60. See Ms. Jerusalem, NUL 4* 6246, fols. 5b–6a. This text has been printed in Shlomo Musajoff, *Merkavah Shelemah* (Jerusalem: Solomon, 1921). I hope to elaborate on these texts in a separate study.

61. See Rabbi Abraham Hamoi, ed., *Sefer ha-Hesheq* (Livorno, 1858), *Sefer Beit Din*, fol. 3b, no. 22; fol. 4a, no. 24; fol. 4b, no. 30; fol. 6b, no. 49; fol. 8a, no. 61; and fol. 9b, no. 76. On the various versions of this treatise, see Joseph Dan, *The Esoteric Theology of Ashkenazi Hasidism* (Jerusalem: Mossad Bialik, 1968), pp. 220–21; idem, "The Seventy Names of Metatron," *Proceedings of the Eighth World Congress of Jewish Studies*, Division C (Jerusalem: World Union of Jewish Studies, 1982), pp. 19–23; Yehuda Liebes, "The Angels of the Shofar and Yeshua Sar ha-Panim" (in Hebrew), in *Early Jewish Mysticism*, ed. J. Dan (Jerusalem: Institute for Jewish Studies, 1987), pp. 171–96; Daniel Abrams, "The Boundaries of Divine Ontology: The Inclusion and Exclusion of Metatron in the Godhead," *HTR* 87 (1994): p. 301, n. 33, pp. 302–05; Elliot R. Wolfson, "Metatron and Shi`ur Qomah in the Writings of Haside Ashkenaz," in *Mysticism, Magic and Kabbalah in Ashkenazi Judaism*, eds. K. and E. Groezinger and J. Dan (Berlin, New York: Walter de Gruyter, 1995), pp. 60–92.

62. Hamoi, *Sefer ha-Hesheq*, fol. 6b, no. 50.

63. Ms. Roma-Angelica 46, fol. 35a; and another version of this material in Ms. New York, JTS 2026, fol. 8a.

64. *Reishit ha-Qabbalah* (Tel Aviv and Jerusalem: Schocken, 1948), pp. 213–14 and 219; and Idel, "The World of Angels," pp. 10–11.

65. See chapter 3.

66. See Rabbi Moshe de Leon, *The Book of the Pomegranate*, coll. and ed. Elliot R. Wolfson (Atlanta, Ga.: The Scholars Press, 1988), p. 199, n. to l. 10, and p. 227. See especially *Zohar* III, fol. 69a, translated into Hebrew in Rabbi David ben Yehudah he-Hasid, *Mar'ot ha-Zove'ot*, ed. Daniel Matt (Chico, Cal.: Scholars Press, 1982), p. 12; and Rabbi Moshe de Leon, *Sheqel ha-Qodesh*, ed. Charles Mopsik (Los Angeles: Cherub Press, 1996), p. 90.

67. See the anonymous *Sefer ha-Yashar* (Jerusalem: Eshkol, 1967), chapter 5, p. 56.

68. See Elliot Ginsburg, *The Sabbath in the Classical Kabbalah* (Albany: State University of New York Press, 1989), pp. 87–92.

69. *Zohar Hadash*, fol. 68c.

70. See, for example, Scholem, *On the Mystical Shape*, pp. 95–101; idem, "Two Treatises," pp. 338–40; Liebes, *Studies in the Zohar*, pp. 12–19; and Wolfson, *Along the Path*, pp. 100 and 101.

71. *Tiqqunei Zohar*, *Tiqqun* 69, fol. 99a. The two letters *H* of the Tetragrammaton *YHWH* symbolize the sefirot of Binah and Malkhut, which correspond to mother and daughter respectively, who are united by the letter *W*, which is a symbol of the son.

72. According to some texts, the spelling of Metatron with six consonants reflects the diminished plight of the angel, who ascends in order to receive influx from above, and then the name of the angel is spelled with seven consonants. See, for example, Gershom Scholem, "On the Study of the Kabbalah of R. Isaac ben Jacob ha-Cohen" (in Hebrew), *Tarbiz* 2 (1931): pp. 215–16, nn. 96–97.

73. *BT, Sanhedrin* 38b. This view understood theosophically as dealing with divine powers is approximated in a contemporary discussion of Rabbi Shem Tov ibn Gaon in his commentary on Nahmanides's secrets, *Keter Shem Tov*, Ms. Paris BN 774, fol. 75a; see also fol. 84b, where the righteous, namely the ninth sefirah, is described as comprised in the tenth sefirah, from which it can be conferred that the name of the master is comprised within that of his disciple.

74. *Zohar* III, fol. 227a.

75. Ibid., fol. 228b.

76. See *Zohar Hadash*, fol. 7d.

77. *Zohar* I, fols. 16b and 17a; Matt, *The Zohar*, I, pp. 125 and 127. See also Scholem, *On the Mystical Shape*, pp. 107–08; Tishby, *Wisdom of the Zohar*, I, p. 316. The quote is Genesis 1:3. "Illumines" is translated from *'anhir*. According to other versions of this passage, especially that of Rabbi Menahem Recanati, there is another verb here: *'adliq*—it lightens. Scholem, in his handwritten notes to the *Zohar ad locum*, prefers this second version.

78. *Zohar* I, fol. 17a; and Tishby, *Wisdom of the Zohar*, II, p. 317.

79. See *Genesis Rabba* 3:23.

80. See, for example, *Zohar* III, fol. 170a.

81. See *Zohar* I, fol. 77a; and Tishby, *Wisdom of the Zohar*, II, pp. 569–70.

82. See Liebes, *Studies in the Zohar*, pp. 135–38.

83. Rabbi Todros ben Joseph ha-Levi Abulafia, *'Otzar ha-Kavod* (Warsaw, 1879), fol. 23a. Though he mentions other references, I have not found any additional discussions by Rabbi Todros Abulafia in his writings on the Hagigah text. The first quote is Genesis 1:3. The light "stands between heaven and earth" in other manuscripts as well; see, for example, Ms. Vatican 229, fol. 220b; and Abulafia's other book, *Sha'ar ha-Razim*, ed. Kushnir Oron (Jerusalem: Bialik Institute, 1989), pp. 128–130. In Hebrew, "emerging" is *Porhim*. The second quote is Habakkuk 2:4. The third quote is Jeremiah 33:25.

84. *Midrash on Psalms* 1:15, fol. 8a; and the important remark of Louis Ginzberg, *The Legends of the Jews* (Philadelphia: Jewish Publication Society, 1968), vol. V, p. 12, n. 28.

85. See de Leon's *Sheqel ha-Qodesh*, p. 90; and *Midrash ha-Ne'elam* on Lamentations, *Zohar Hadash*, fol. 93b.

86. See *Zohar Hadash*, fol. 18d; and Green, "Zaddiq," p. 335.

87. *Zohar* III, fol. 127b.

88. See Liebes, "Messiah of the Zohar," pp. 227–29.

89. See ibid., pp. 122–23; and Elliot R. Wolfson, *Through a Speculum that Shines: Vision and Imagination in Medieval Jewish Mysticism* (Princeton: Princeton University Press, 1994), pp. 371, n. 155; and pp. 377–78.

90. *Zohar* II, fol. 149a.

CHAPTER 3:

The Eschatological Pillar of the Souls in Zoharic Literature

1. The Pillar and the Two Paradises

Unlike the works of other Kabbalistic schools before the 1280s, it is only in the book of the Zohar that an important additional function of a pillar is evident. In some of parts of the Zohar the pillar recurrently serves as a conduit for the ascent of the souls of the deceased righteous from a lower paradise to a higher one. This eschatological function will be the subject of this chapter.

Some time before 1270, the theory of two paradises became part and parcel of the eschatology of Rabbi Moses ben Nahman—known by the pseudonym Nahmanides—particularly evident in the last section of his book, *Torat ha-'Adam*.[1] He appears to be the first Jewish author to adopt an explicit theory of a double paradise: the terrestrial and the supernal. Immediately afterwards, the philosopher Rabbi Hillel ben Shmuel of Verona quoted this theory from one of the many Christian sources that, since the Isidore of Seville in the seventh century, discussed the double paradise.[2] Hence, Rabbi Hillel's source for this theory was probably that of Nahmanides,[3] as was the case with other theological issues.[4] Nahmanides, who died in 1270, deeply influenced many Kabbalistic understandings of personal eschatology, one of the most important of which was that of a group active in Castile a generation after his death.[5] Pillars appear in some Christian sources, and according to such texts, the names of the righteous are inscribed upon them.[6] However, in one of the early medieval treatises related to Heikhalot literature, *Midrash Alpha Beitot*, God is described as moving from one place to another, each described as a separate entity and as related to paradise.[7]

The Zohar demonstrates acquaintance with and citations of different passages from Hagigah discussions on the pillar. This is most obvious in the first layer of the book, entitled *Midrash ha-Ne`elam*.[8]

However, in the later layers, one finds a theory of the pillar as a column that connects the two paradises and serves as the mode for the process of continuous ascent and descent of souls from one to the other in privileged moments in time. This theory is elaborated in two Kabbalistic sources written in Castile before 1300: numerous discussions are found in the Zohar, and short passages referencing this theory appear in a pseudepigraphic Midrash composed by members of the circle of the Zohar. These seem to represent a Kabbalistic view that breaks with that of earlier Kabbalistic material and is characterized by an insistence upon the eschatological role of the pillar. To be sure, the pillar—actually two pillars, one of fire and the other of smoke—fulfilled a role in the Israelites' journey in the desert, which was part of an eschatological enterprise beginning with the exodus from Egypt. Moreover, as the biblical verses claim, those pillars represent the guidance of God during the long journey, and they constitute, in a way, a direct divine intervention in the order of nature. According to some early Jewish and Christian sources, the pillars played an eschatological role in national redemption.[9] Such a stance is found in some apocalyptic writings composed in the early Middle Ages, in which the pillar of fire reappears as part of the eschatological scenario.[10] However, these sources deal with historical events imagined to take place in this world at the end of time. Below we are concerned with ascents of the souls of the departed righteous and thus with personal forms of eschatology.

Before addressing the main topic under scrutiny, it should be noted that in a relatively early Zoharic composition entitled the *Midrash ha-Ne'elam* on the book of Ruth, there is a rather detailed description of paradise. This is from the perspective of a certain Rabbi Perahiyya, who was granted a tour of heaven during his lifetime. He and his guide, a dead scholar who took him on this tour, did not accomplish a posthumous ascension but instead entered a cave, the gates of which protect paradise.[11] Despite the relatively long description of paradise, not a single eschatological pillar appears, though seven pillars and even the foundation as the righteous—themes discussed in chapter two—are mentioned elsewhere in the same composition without any connection to paradise.[12] The absence of the motif of ascent of the soul in this context is even more interesting given the etymology of Rabbi "Perahiyya," which can be interpreted as the rabbi "who floats in the air."[13] Elsewhere in the same treatise, the ascent of souls toward the firmament again has nothing to do with a pillar.[14]

2. THE ESCHATOLOGICAL INTER-PARADISIACAL PILLAR

In the later layer that constitutes the main bulk of the Zohar by an anonymous Kabbalist, which presumably was written after the *Midrash ha-Ne'elam* on the book of Ruth, we learn that:

> In the middle of that firmament there is an opening that corresponds to that opening of the supernal palace, since from that opening the souls float from the inferior to the superior, by means of that pillar that is fixed in the garden, up to that opening. In that firmament within the opening that is in the middle of the firmament of the garden, three colors of light that are comprised as one are entering, and they illumine the colors of that pillar. Then the pillar is sparking and becoming incandescent in the numerous colors that it incandesces. And the righteous [souls] are illumined from that supernal brilliance all the time. But each Sabbath and first day of the month the Shekhinah reveals Herself in that firmament more than during other times, and all the righteous are coming to bow to Her.[15]

According to another passage, the anonymous Kabbalist writes that the souls are purified, and this is the reason why they are capable of ascending "in that opening in the middle of the firmament, and there is a pillar that stands in the middle of the garden.... And the ascent is by means of that pillar within that opening of the firmament."[16] This pillar is called "the foundation of the mount of Zion" elsewhere in the Zohar.[17] All these sources indicate a connection between the pillar and the concept of the center. The affinity between the pillar and the foundation of the mountain of Zion is again proof for the nexus between the pillar and the cosmic center, since Jerusalem has been interpreted as the center of the world. Interestingly enough, the opening in the middle of the firmament is reminiscent of the "central opening" mentioned in Mircea Eliade's book on Shamanism.[18]

This pillar, however, is not a regular *axis mundi*—a column that unifies all the realms of the universe—but rather a column that links only the two paradises and allows the ascent of souls from one to the other. The phrase "mount of Zion" should be understood to symbolize a supernal power rather than a location in the mundane world. However, it is clear that for many Kabbalists, including Nahmanides and members of the Zohar circle, the lower paradise was conceived to be part of the mundane world, as some passages dealing with attempts to reach this place by living persons demonstrate.[19] Just as in some shamanic views, the pillar is described as the means of the ascent—and also descent—of souls. While for the shamans the ascent is performed by a living expert, in the Zohar this task is accomplished only by the souls of the deceased righteous. In the relevant passages, the concept of the middle of the garden is a recurrent issue. Since the garden mentioned here indubitably refers to paradise, the column or pillar at its center is unmistakably identical to the biblical tree of life, a theme that emerges in later commentaries on the Zohar. This motif is also reminiscent of shamanic cosmic trees.[20]

The paradisiacal role of the pillar is in line with the Zoharic absorption of the lower world into the supernal one. This means that even a concept like the mundane world has meaning as a divine power, which while on high is designated as such. Being paradigmatic, the supernal world includes the lower world, and the Platonic opposition between them is less stringent in Zoharic Kabbalah. In lieu of a worldview based on strict parallelism, the main trends of Kabbalistic approaches assume the active interaction between these two worlds—what I propose calling a correlative approach.[21] In another Zoharic composition, the Heikhalot of a portion of Genesis, the seventh supernal palace is described as follows: "The seventh palace is the most hidden and occult of all the palaces. In the center of that palace a pillar ['amuda'] stands that consists of many colors: green, white, red [and] black. And when the [high] souls [nishmatin] ascend, they enter that palace."[22] From a terminological point of view, it is neither paradise that is mentioned here nor the ascent from the lower to the higher paradise, but rather the entrance to the highest of the seven palaces. Nevertheless, it is clear from the context that in the lower paradise there are seven palaces just as there are on high. According to a later discussion, a pillar is found in the center of the first supernal palace, and it seems to penetrate vertically toward the highest, seventh palace.[23] As seen in the passage above, the lower paradise has an opening corresponding to an opening found in the supernal paradise. Thus, we may assume that the pillar is an axis that penetrates the entire world, beginning with the lower paradise and reaching the sphere of the supernal palaces found immediately beneath the divine realm.

3. THE PILLAR IN THE PSEUDO-MIDRASH *SEDER GAN `EDEN* AND ITS ZOHARIC PARALLELS

Another important source in which the pillar links the two paradises is a composition referred to by scholars as *Seder Gan `Eden*. Written in the form of a Midrash, this short text addresses the structure of the two paradises. It is part of a larger composition attributed spuriously to Rabbi Eliezer the Great, a famous second-century rabbinic figure. Adolph Jellinek and Gershom Scholem have pointed out that this is yet another title among various pseudepigraphic books composed by the late thirteenth-century Castilian Kabbalist, Rabbi Moses de Leon.[24] As we shall see below, the identification of this author, important as it is in order to situate the work in time and place, is not without its problems.

In the *Seder Gan `Eden*, the concept of the pillar that links the lower paradise to the supernal Eden is conspicuous. The theme occurs several times in this rather short text; I shall highlight here the most important references found in it. In one instance, the column is described as the "median pillar," *ha-`amud ha-'emtza`y*,[25] though it does not play a theosophical role as in the two main layers of the Zohar. In another statement, it spreads from the lower paradise to the seat of divine glory, which is located in the middle of the firmament and is covered by the divine glory; elsewhere it is explicitly identified with the tree of life. [26] This pillar also is described as collecting the tears of God.[27] However, what is much more important for the understanding of some treatments in the Zohar to be mentioned below is the sexual role of this pillar. We read in this text, for example, that insofar as the saints (one of the seven categories of the righteous found in paradise) are concerned:

> All the keys of Paradise are in their hands, and when the pillar that is found in the middle of the garden is moving and singing by itself, the firmament that is over the garden returns. Then they [the saints] advance toward their Creator and come closer to the pillar. And the Man, Clothed by Garments, grasps the four rings of the firmament and the pillar of the firmament knocks the ring that is in the East of the firmament, and [then] all the trees of the garden sing and praise, and then the Glory of the Lord of Israel comes. And the earth illumines from His glory, which is the Garden of Eden. And the category of those saints open first saying "Holy, Holy, Holy."[28]

The occurrence of the verse from Isaiah 6 about the triple sanctus in both the Zohar and the earlier Heikhalot passage strengthens the assumption of a nexus between these texts. Elsewhere in the Zohar the saintly righteous are described as meriting listening to and seeing how:

> The voice of the melody of the firmament...travels by the hand of the Man, Clothed by Garments, and he moves away and the firmament stands and the pillar sings, it ascends and descends, so that the light of the splendor, the light of the pleasantness, is drawn from above within that pillar, and the righteous stand vis-à-vis that light and enjoy it until midnight. It is at midnight that God comes with the righteous to listen to the voice of the turn of the firmament, and the pillar sings and the soil of the garden is elevating, and the righteous are ascending from their mansions toward their Creator, and the entire garden is filled by His glory. At that time, the male and female spirits are copulating, as it was before they had been created. And out of this pleasantness of their desire to see the pleasantness of God, all produce fruit, and from their fruit the spirits of the converts [to Judaism] emerge.[29]

The melody of the firmament is reminiscent of the Pythagorean view of the music of the spheres. Much less conspicuous is the significance of the occurrence of the melody of the pillar.[30] But according to the two passages, there is musical exchange between the firmament and the pillar.

In a careful reading of these two passages, one cannot fail to detect the sexual overtones of the pillar and the firmament. At the end of the second quote, copulation between the spirits is explicitly mentioned, representing the—perhaps lower—reverberation of an event occurring between the pillar and the ring or between the pillar and the firmament. The specific timing corroborates this interpretation, since in the Zohar midnight is considered to be the most propitious moment for intercourse.[31] Moreover, based on widespread Zoharic symbolism, it is possible to infer that the mention of the divinity's filling the earth with its glory hints at the sexual union between the divine potencies of male and female.[32] Therefore, the up-and-down motion of the pillar as well as the occurrence of the verb "knock," makkeh, in the pseudo-Midrash may have phallic and sexual connotations. According to such an interpretation, the masculine power is envisaged as lower than the feminine, which is represented by the firmament. Interestingly enough, the ascent of the souls from one paradise to another by means of the pillar is not mentioned in *Seder Gan `Eden*. Rather, the spirits, *ruḥot,* and in my opinion also the higher souls, *neshamot,* are created as the result of sexual encounters in the supernal worlds, as we shall see immediately below.

The themes found in the two pseudo-Midrashic passages adduced above are repeated with some alterations in a Zoharic passage that is very important to our discussion. We read that:

Because the [higher] souls [*nishmatin*] ascend up to that opening of the firmament, that firmament goes around the garden three times. And out of the voice of pleasantness of the circular movement of that firmament all the souls go out and listen to the pleasantness of that firmament and they see the pillar that causes the ascent of fire, cloud, smoke and incandescent brightness, and they all bow. Then the souls ascend into that opening until they ascend within the circle that is around that point. Then they see what they see, and out of the light and joy of what they see, they ascend and descend, come nearer and [then] go away.[33]

The main difference between this passage and that from *Seder Gan `Eden* is the presence of higher souls rather than the righteous as observers of the *hieros gamos.* Though this difference is not so great (after all, the righteous are already departed), it reflects an attempt by the author to compose a Midrash in the classical Midrashic style, in which the personality is described by its good deeds, as opposed to the Zoharic style, which is a little more medieval, dealing with the fate of the soul alone. It is plausible, however, that the Zohar drew on the medieval *Midrash Konen,* in which souls are described as ascending and descending the tree of life, which may take them to heaven and then even higher to paradise.[34] The tendency toward greater concreteness is also reflected in the change from the term "ring," *taba`at,* in the *Seder Gan `Eden* to "circle," *`iggula',* in the Zoharic version.

4. WORSHIP OF THE PILLAR

In the last passage and other parts of the Zohar, the concept of worship of or bowing before the pillar by the souls of the righteous is introduced.[35] In the *Ra`aya' Meheimna',* a later layer of the Zohar, it is clear that the pillar plays the same role as "the Holy One, Blessed be He," since its relationship with the Shekhinah as its female counterpart reflects the famous dictum: "The Holy One, blessed be He and His Shekhinah."[36] The divine nature of the median pillar is related to discussions in Exodus on the two pillars of fire and cloud, considered to be manifestations of divine guidance, and on the people's bowing before the pillar of cloud (Exodus 33). However, it seems that Zoharic literature follows a trend found in the immediate vicinity of the circle of Kabbalists who composed it—the writing of Rabbi Isaac ben Jacob ha-Kohen.[37]

In another composition belonging to the later layer of the Zohar, *Tiqqunei Zohar*, an entire liturgical segment is related to the median pillar: the six middle prayers of the ʿAmidah and the eighteen benedictions are directed to it. Described also as the king, or the sefirah of Tiferet, the median pillar is described as answering the demands found in that part of the liturgy.[38] Elsewhere in the same composition Moses directs the prayer of the thirteen attributes to the median pillar while standing on a stone, which is the "central point," corresponding to the Shekhinah, or the last sefirah.[39] Not the deceased righteous but the live Moses prays to the median pillar. In summary, unlike the main layer of the Zohar, where the median pillar is a symbol for the sefirah of Yesod, the later layer portrays the pillar as a symbol for the sefirah of Tiferet.

According to other passages in the Zohar, particularly one at the very beginning of the printed book, "the pillar is the foundation, the generator of offspring, the holy limb upon which the entire world dwells."[40] Here the image of the pillar has evident phallic meaning, but this time it is connected to the divine realm in a manner that recalls the quote from the book of the Bahir adduced in chapter two. Thus, we may assume that the image of the pillar recurs in the structure of several realms of reality, and in many of these instances, it has sexual implications. However, I have not found a comprehensive description in the Zohar of the entire spectrum of reality as constituted by the central pillar and the other planes of being that are penetrated and united by it.

According to another composition in Zoharic literature, the soul, if it is found worthy, is given a pass to paradise:[41]

And when it comes to Paradise, there is a pillar there of cloud and brightness, mixed with each other, and smoke around them, "And the Lord will create upon every dwelling place of mount Zion, and upon her assemblies [*Miqra'eah*], cloud and smoke by day; and the brightness of a flaming fire by night." And it [the pillar] is fixed from below up high, to the gates of heaven. And if the soul is worthy to ascend on high, she ascends on that pillar, [but] if she does not merit [it], [then] she remains there and enjoys the goodness that is [descending upon it] from above." And this Paradise is illumining from the supernal light, as Rabbi Yossi said: "I have seen the Paradise which corresponds to the curtain of the terrible ice that is on high, and there is 'the dew of lights' from above. And the soul enjoys the splendor of the *Shehkinah* but is not nourished by it. And if it merits ascending more then it ascends on this pillar until it arrives to the third opening, which is called Zebul. There are many guardians there and they open [the gate] to it and it enters that gate and praises the Holy One, blessed be He, in the supernal temple, and Michael, who is the supernal priest of God, sacrifices this soul...and Michael causes the ascent of the soul until the fourth, fifth and sixth openings and he says before the Master of the Universe: "Happy are Thy sons, the sons of Thy beloved ones, Abraham, Isaac and Jacob, happy is the soul that merits this." Afterwards the souls are caused to ascend to the seventh gate that is called `Aravot*, where the treasures of life are. And the souls of the righteous that reach the seventh gate become servant angels."[42]

This passage is an excerpt of the earliest layer of Zoharic literature known as *Midrash ha-Ne`elam*. It is bizarre, however, that it is quoted by two Kabbalists who were among the first to adduce Zoharic material but who also did not quote from this early layer. Parts of the passage have been copied by Rabbi Menahem Recanati,[43] who never quoted anything from the *Midrash ha-Ne`elam* with the exception of *Midrash Ruth ha-Ne`elam*, and only a few quotes printed as *Midrash ha-Ne`elam* in *Zohar Hadash* are found in the writings of Rabbi David ben Yehudah he-Hasid.[44] The specific origin of these quotes deserves a separate analysis. If the attribution to *Midrash ha-Ne`elam* is correct, this may be the first Zoharic mention of the eschatological pillar; in this context, the terrestrial paradise connects with the heavens, and no higher paradise than the heavens is mentioned.[45] The pillar facilitates the ascent of meritorious souls to a system of seven firmaments, but it is not part of those higher heavens. In this passage, the purpose of the posthumous ascent is the transformation of the soul into a servant angel. The contemplation of the glory of the master and peering to see the *hieros* *gamos*—features appearing in the main bulk of the Zohar, as we shall see below—are absent here.

Midrash ha-Ne`elam provides a clear example of Jewish psychanodia according to Ioan P. Culianu's conceptualization of the term. It deals with ascents to and through a pillar, heavens, gates or openings, but never through planets, as in the traditions discussed above in other chapters. What is interesting here is the combination between two different themes found in late antiquity Jewish texts: psychanodia, on the one hand, and the sacrifice of the soul that occurs in the third heaven, called Zevul, where the supernal temple is found according to some sources, on the other.[46] The combination of the higher pillar's ending in the third heaven and the sacrifice is reminiscent of Eliade's distinction between shamans' actual ascent through the pillar and the more common practice of offering that takes place there.[47]

The last Zoharic text enjoyed special dissemination. It was authored by Rabbi Tzevi Hirsch Kaidanover, an early eighteenth-century Polish rabbi active in Frankfurt au Main. His influential book, *Qav ha-Yashar*, was written first in Hebrew and then translated by the author into Yiddish and by someone else into Ladino.[48]

5. THE PILLAR AS A VEHICLE

We now turn from personal to national eschatology. As seen above, the eschatological pillar is climbed by the souls of the deceased righteous. The Messiah, however, also is described frequently as the righteous.[49] A strongly apocalyptic passage in the main layer of the Zohar describes the emergence of a pillar of fire that spreads downward for forty days and is seen by all nations. After seventy days, the Messiah enters the pillar of fire, where he will be hidden until twelve months after the great apocalyptic battles. This pillar brings him to the firmament in a manner similar to that described in the Zoharic texts discussed above.[50] There he receives the "strength" [*Tuqppa`*] and the "crown of kingship" [`*Ateret Malkhut*][51]; then he returns by means of the same pillar that disappears and comes back after another year. It is quite plausible that the reception of strength reflects the impact of the Bahiric pillar tradition, as discussed in the previous chapter. Afterwards, all nations recognize him as Messiah. It should be pointed out that according to Zoharic symbolism, the Messiah ben Joseph is identified with the tzaddiq and thus with the sefirah of Yesod, which is connected to the median pillar.[52]

In this case, the pillar is not a cosmic column or an *axis mundi* that is constantly fixed in the same place and is used by the ascendant as a type of ladder. Unlike the more widespread view expressed in the Zohar, it is a vehicle that elevates and occultates the Messiah. Additionally, not only do the souls disappear, but also the vehicle itself shares the fate of its transportees. This dynamic pillar is reminiscent of the ascending and descending pillar and the assumption that the Messiah is occultated for a certain period in a supernal palace as described above in *Seder Gan `Eden*.[53]

The Zoharic passage introduces another form of continuum between the two worlds: the pillar of fire. However, the pillar climbed by the presumably dead Messiah, his occultation, then his coronation and return to public activity are not concerned with the structure of the universe or the manner of reconstructing the ontic continuum by a mystical activity. Rather, a dramatic and less explicable process that is much more mythical and hence closer to the style of late apocalyptic Midrashim is described. The ascent and return of a dead Messiah are also reminiscent of the Christological vision of the final eschatological event. What concerns me especially is the quite plausible view that the Messiah mentioned in this passage is the Messiah the son of Joseph, a figure that is depicted in numerous late antiquity and early medieval sources as being killed as part of the apocalyptic scenario and revived by the Messiah the son of David. In any case, this figure resorts to the pillar for his ascension like any of the dead righteous discussed above.

In considering the various descriptions of the pillar in the above passages, one may discern attempts to unify impacts on various senses: music, colors, motion and, according to other contexts not adduced here, scents and aromas. Put together, these events in paradise conspire to induce delight or sensuality through sensuous forms, though their targets are the souls of the righteous rather than their bodies or senses. Paradise is conceived as a synergism of the senses; the depiction of its concreteness is due to the acceptance of Nahmanides's eschatology.

Apparently independent of the Zoharic texts and their sources, we find within the same generation of writers a work by Rabbi Abraham Abulafia describing a vision that brings together the concepts of pillar and redemption. The latter here refers to the individual redemption of the intellectual soul. Rabbi Abulafia combines the two concepts by means of a pun. He interprets the term *mo`ed*, which stands for the date of the redemption in the book of Daniel, as an anagram for `amud, or "pillar." Hence, we are to assume that everything depends on redemption. Furthermore, this term hints at the verb *no'adeti,* "I have encountered," referring to God's revelation to Moses.[54] Thus, major terms for redemption and revelation are connected to each other and to the term pillar.

6. The Pillar as Conductor to the Divine Realm

One of the most fascinating passages dealing with the pillar is found in Zohar I, fol. 219a. After entering the lower paradise, the soul is described as bearing some form of spiritual body.[55] The reception of such a garment is presented in the context of four pillars, only one of which is related to the soul that receives this body. After staying for a while, an angel calls and:

> ...the pillar of the three colors is made available, which is called "dwelling place of mount Zion," as it is written "And the Lord will create upon every dwelling place of mount Zion, and upon her assemblies [*Miqra'eah*], a cloud and smoke by day; and the brightness of a flaming fire by night." The soul ascends on that pillar to the opening [named] *Tzedeq,* in which Zion and Jerusalem are found. If she merits ascending more, its lot and inheritance is fine, to adhere to the body of the King.... If it merits ascending more it receives the glory of the King to refine in the supernal refinement.[56]

In this case the pillar does not just serve as a median to the supernal paradise found in the realm of the palaces, but also allows the meritorious righteous to reach the tenth sefirah, described by the term Tzedeq. This feminine potency is the first divine power attained by the ascending soul of the righteous within the supernal realm. However, even higher is the next attainment, which brings the soul to cleave with or be drawn within the body of the king, the sefirah of Tiferet. This cleaving to, and sometimes integration of the soul within, the body of the king is known in the Zohar.[57] Even higher is another stage at which the soul receives the glory, presumably constituting the most sublime achievement. Indeed, according to another Zoharic passage, the souls of the righteous divest themselves of the garments of the lower paradise and ascend to contemplate the glory of their master, *Yiqara' de-Mareihon,* during special and cyclically recurring moments in time—namely Sabbaths and other festivals.[58]

This sort of contemplation is mentioned often in the Zohar.[59] The assumption is that after climbing the cosmic eschatological pillar, the soul starts the ascent toward the median line within the divine world, which consists of the sefirot Malkhut, Yesod, Tiferet and Keter. The reception of the glory may have something to do with the retrieval of the lost supernal splendor, *Yiqara' 'Ila'ah*, that encompassed Adam and Eve before the original sin.[60]

7. THE PILLAR AND THE JUDGMENT

According to a Zoharic discussion, the eschatological pillar serves not only for the ascent of righteous souls but also as a mechanism that judges all souls: "In the pillar that serves to weigh, within the blowing air, there is a scale on one side, and another scale on the other side. On the one side there are the scales of righteousness, on the other—the scales of deceit. And those scales never stop and the souls ascend and descend, enter and return."[61] There can be no doubt that this is a description of the paradisiacal pillar, which is enriched by the theory of the scales. The mention of blowing air also fits the paradisiacal background.[62] The ascent and descent of and entrance into the pillar exactly reflect other cases in the Zohar concerning the eschatological pillar. How the pillar is integrated with the two scales is a difficult question. In any case, it is clear that not just the souls of the righteous but rather all souls arrive there. Thus, this passage differs from other Zoharic discussions that allow access to the pillar solely to the righteous, but is reminiscent of a view found elsewhere in this book that describes the median pillar as judging the true judgment.[63] It should be mentioned that columns related to the act of judgment as part of the mundane world are known in the Romanian folklore of Moldova.[64]

8. CONTEMPLATING A SUPERNAL SECRET

We return now to the remark found in *Seder Gan 'Eden*, according to which the pillar reaches the seat of glory. Due to the feminine nature of other places touched by the pillar—firmaments, rings, openings—it seems that the supernal seat too has a feminine quality. This also appears in much earlier sources, especially in an influential passage that seems to have inspired descriptions of the atmosphere observed by high souls on high. In Heikhalot literature, we read that:

Each and every day, and each and every moment
When Israel recites Holy before Me,
Teach them and tell them:
Lift your eyes to the firmament,
Corresponding to your house of prayer
When you say before Me: Holy.
Teach them that there is no greater joy
in My world that I have created
But that moment when your eyes are lifted to My eyes
And My eyes are looking into your eyes
When you say before Me: Holy.
because the voice emerging from your mouth
in that moment pushes it away
and ascends before Me like the scent of the aroma.
Bear witness to them
of the testimony you see in Me,
regarding what I do to the features of the face of Jacob,
your father,
which is engraved upon My Seat of Glory,
for when you say before Me, Holy,
I bend down over it, clasp it, embrace it, and kiss it,
and My hands are on its arms, thrice daily,
for you say before Me:
Holy, as it says:
'Holy, Holy, Holy.'[65]

As several scholars have pointed out, this passage has sexual implications; the throne or divine seat has been interpreted as a bride.[66]

The visage of Jacob represents the people of Israel on high. Though there is indeed a projection of the nation on high,[67] I assume that this theological action means something more than propelling the lower onto the higher. Rather, I propose that this projection is related to the search for immortality. Here, as in an important passage found in *BT, Yuma'*, fol. 54ab, the sexual relations between two powers reflect the matrimonial relations between God and Israel.[68] In both cases, this relation is an ancient betrothal that is ensured, and perhaps even renewed, by the performance of rituals in general according to the Talmudic passage or by the mystic's reciting of the sanctus—according to the Heikhalot passage. While the Talmudic discussion deals with the ritual performance of the entire nation and the vision of the two embracing cherubim by the pilgrims to Jerusalem, the Heikhalot text only mentions that mystics can observe the sexual embrace, and I assume that it is their recitation of the sanctus that induces this ability.[69] Read in an intertextual manner, the two passages allow an understanding of the ascent to the divine palace and the observation of sexual relations between God and the image of Jacob as a personal, or at least an elite, attainment of an earlier, more communal right to look upon the cherubim. In both cases, the national moment is conspicuous: the sexual relations are envisioned as emblematic of the ongoing election of Israel. The tenor of the Heikhalot passage and that of the Zohar describing the vision as "they see what they see" do not possess anything ineffable. In both, it is not a mystery that is dealt with but a scene that can be seen and described, if one wants to do so. This is very different from the manner in which Paul depicts his vision of paradise as unutterable. In *Sefer Shi`ur Qomah*, he addresses in detail the anthropomorphic understanding of the scriptures and of Kabbalah in general, and in this context, he briefly discusses the Pardes. He mentions the various reasons for the interdiction to gaze on high and indicates that one of the aspects of the Shekhinah is her "nakedness"—`ervatah, or her genital organ—which is to be covered lest the demonic powers enter there. This, he continues, was the sin of Noah, who uncovered the genitals of the Shekhinah, hinted at by the term `Oholoh, allowing the impure powers to enter. This also is related to the sin of Adam, who was driven by lust to inspect the place where the impure powers attached to the Shekhinah. The sin of the sages who entered the Pardes was that compelled by their lust they cleaved to the place of the impure powers.[70]

9. LATER REPERCUSSIONS OF THE ZOHARIC STANCES

The occurrence of the eschatological understanding of the pillar in late thirteenth-century texts is not isolated in the history of Jewish mysticism. Neither is the approach of the Besht, discussed in the next chapter, a return to a repressed tradition. On the contrary, the fact that the most important references to the pillar occurr within the Zohar sanctified this theme, and numerous Kabbalists returned to it in their writings due to the impact of this canonical book. Since the Zohar's various passages differ concerning the role of the pillar and its place in the various palaces, attempts have been made to systemize these views. The

most important organizational attempt is found in a passage authored
by Rabbi Moses Cordovero and included in a widely known treatise
composed by one of his admirers, Rabbi Abraham Azulai. Describing
the seventh palace, Rabbi Cordovero wrote:

> This palace is only for [the sake of] the ascent of the souls from
> therein on high, namely the ascents of the souls from the lower
> Paradise to the supernal Paradise. And the secret of the ascent is by
> means of the pillar in the middle of Paradise, and this pillar is found
> in the garden of the palace of the Holy of the Holiest. Behold the
> garments do not ascend from the garden to the mansion at all, but
> the soul remains divested from the garment and it adheres to the
> pillar and enters within it, and from within it she will ascend on
> high. And the secret of this pillar from without is the secret of cloud
> and smoke.... And when the time of the ascension arrives, as it is
> written "And the Lord will create upon every dwelling place of
> mount Zion, and upon her assemblies [*Miqra'eah*], [a cloud and
> smoke by day; and the brightness of a flaming fire by night]," she
> comes close to this pillar and is drawn within the pillar, which is
> from without of cloud and smoke so that what is within it will not
> be seen and remembered, and within it there is brightness and light
> of a flame, namely the glory of the mansion, so that the spirits will
> not see the glory of the soul when she ascends. And the pillar has
> within it four mansions that are four colors—white, red, green,
> black—*vis-à-vis* four configurations that are lion, which is white, ox,
> which is red, green and black which are man and eagle, and each
> soul will adhere to the color and configuration, ascends and is linked
> to its aspect. And from here the supernal form starts to purify itself.
> And this pillar stands in the middle of the palace, like that [which is
> found] in the supernal palaces, namely the palaces of *Yetzirah*, a pil-
> lar by means of which they are descending and thrown to the *Yihud*,
> and a pillar by means of which they ascend on high. And in this
> palace there is no station at all but it is made for the ascents of the
> souls. But it is difficult [to assume] that this pillar does not descend
> downward in all the palaces but is found [exclusively] in the seventh
> palace.... But it seems that all the palaces have a link and a path to
> the seventh palace like the *sefirot* that are all linked to the *Binah*.[71]

Though the eschatological role of the pillar is paramount, what is characteristic of the effort made by Rabbi Cordovero is a shift from the pillar as an inter-paradisiacal column to a more comprehensive one that connects the sub-divine and divine realms into a bigger structure. The pillar appears to be closer to an *axis mundi*. More definitive is another of Rabbi Cordovero's passages quoted again by Rabbi Azulai: "This pillar is found in all the palaces, and its secret is the righteous, which is indeed a pillar and it is called everywhere the linkage of the *sefirot*. This is the reason why this pillar is by the way of the linkage between the causatum to its cause. And it is known that the measure of the pillar is like half of the length of the body.... *Yesod* is exactly in the middle of the body, between right and left."[72] Here there is an effort to build a continuous entity that permeates the entire structure of the non-divine world and arrives at the divine realm.

One of the most influential ethical writings composed by Kabbalists, stemming from the school of Rabbi Cordovero, incorporates the Zoharic treatments of the pillar. Rabbi Elijah da Vidas's famous *Reishit Hokhmah* addresses the Zoharic theme in a relatively innovative manner. This Kabbalist describes the perfect man as someone who is detached from this world even when acting in a corporeal manner in it, since his thought is directed solely to the wellbeing of the divinity. The rank of deceased saints:

...is not like that of the other people who merely study the Torah and perform the commandments, whose rank is the lower Paradise. These righteous men ascend on high by means of the pillar that is in the middle of the garden, which is called *Miqra'eah*. On it is said "And the Lord will create upon every dwelling place of mount Zion, and upon her assemblies [*Miqra'eah*], a cloud and smoke by day; and the brightness of a flaming fire by night." And Rashby [Rabbi Shime'on bar Yohai] interpreted it in the *Zohar* as dealing with Paradise, and the pillar is the cloud and the smoke and the brightness. The cloud and the smoke from without, and the brightness from within. What is the reason that the cloud and smoke are from without? It is so that the other righteous men that are in Paradise should not look at those who ascend on high. And *Miqra'eah* are the righteous who prepared their thought in a proper manner. This means that out of their intention during the Torah and prayer, the garment of the soul has been made, so that they will be able to ascend to the supernal Paradise. And it [the garment] is called

Miqra'eah, because they are called and invited to embellish the Divine Presence, and it is said there that when these souls ascend on high they unify all the powers in heaven.[73]

Following hints found in rabbinic literature, *Miqra'eah* is conceived of as related to the righteous.[74] The noun *Miqra'eah* in the Zohar designates the pillar.[75] This is, grammatically speaking, a collective name, which may be translated as "those who are called" or invitees apparently to an assembly, in a manner reminiscent of the pillar *'Adaneiah* mentioned by the anonymous Ashkenazi author above. This collective entity is understood as representing the righteous. However, in this passage we find the pillar identified by a noun that is applied to the select righteous, and later on the same page, the group of *Miqra'eah* is mentioned.[76] We therefore have a certain transference: the pillar is called *Miqra'eah*, the pillar is called righteous, and then righteous men as a whole are called *Miqra'eah*. Though it is speculative to assume that the pillar is just a name for the elite of the righteous, this implication should not be dismissed. If understood in an extreme manner—that the pillar is just a structure comprised of the souls that ascend toward the supernal paradise—the above passage represents an interesting version of the identity of the pillar-righteous: the pillar is less the center of the world or a part of a stable cosmology and more a posthumous collective attainment of the elite. However, even according to a more cautious reading of the text, the understanding of the pillar as a collective entity carves a great role for the human *perfecti*. This passage is deeply influenced by the Zoharic depictions of the pillar, while their sexual aspects have been totally obfuscated.

A younger contemporary and acquaintance of Rabbi da Vidas, the more famous Rabbi Hayyim Vital, addresses the theme of the eschatological pillar several times in his writings. In his commentary on the Bible entitled *Sefer 'Etz ha-Da'at Tov*, he offers the following account:

> The terrestrial paradise is the opening and gateway to ascend though it to the supernal celestial paradise, because corresponding to it are the trees of the pillar [*atzei ha-'amud*] [found] in the middle of the lower paradise, as it is known.... Would [Adam] not sin, he worships God until he would complete his work, and he would ascend to the supernal and principal paradise that was created as a mansion, and the world of souls. Because the terrestrial world is but

a gateway to enter the supernal salon, which is the supernal paradise.[77]

This is an exceptional case in which the two trees in paradise are identified explicitly as the inter-paradisiacal pillar. Following the more popular style of this book, Rabbi Vital does not transport the Zoharic paradisiacal myth to another form of existence, as we shall see below in the case of the more technical and influential *Sefer `Etz Hayyim*.

Late in the eighteenth century, the concept of the pillar was connected to the posthumous ascent by one of the most important Hasidic figures, Rabbi Shneor Zalman of Liady. In his *Tanya*, the most widely read Hasidic book, it is said that:

> All the souls who worshiped God in awe and love, that are hidden in the heart of all Israel, do not ascend thereto but during the Sabbath and the head of the month through the pillar from the lower Paradise to the higher Paradise, which is the World of Creation, designated as the higher Paradise, in order to delight in God and enjoy from the brilliance of the *Shekhinah*. Because there is no joy and delight for the created intellect but in what it intellectualizes and understands and knows and comprehends by his intellect and understanding, what he can understand and comprehend of the light of the Infinity, by means of His Wisdom and Understanding, Blessed be He, which illumine there in the World of Creation. And the reason that those souls merit to ascend higher than the angels...[78]

Here, the supernal paradise represents a place where the infinite light stemming from the higher divine structure, the World of Emanation, is perceived in a realm that is lower, the World of Creation. In a way, the comprehensive divine is attained by a refraction of the infinite into the finite. Interestingly enough, the beatitude of paradise, described in images of light, is interpreted as dealing with processes of cognition. Here we have a fascinating synthesis of the mythical pillar and its architectural paradise with the act of intellection as the acme of postmortem attainment. This nexus between intellectual and ascensional imagery is interesting in that it combines two different realms that competed in medieval works: the Greek noetic vision and the more archaic architectural one.

10. PILLAR, PERFORMANCE AND THE RIGHTEOUS

The relationship between the pillar and the righteous, visible from rabbinic texts onward but more accentuated in Kabbalah, establishes a strong affinity between cosmology and the performance of ritual. Only those elite figures designated as righteous sustain the world, and only their souls climb the paradisiacal pillar post-mortem. This is not a matter of knowing the structure of the world in order to have the capability of using it in a certain moment. Neither is it a gnosis that is salvific because someone attended it. Nor is it solely a transformation of the personality and of the body that turns someone into an expert in ecstasy, as is the case in some forms of Shamanism. According to many schools of theosophical–theurgical Kabbalah, it is the result of accumulative efforts to sustain the world while one is alive that allows one to reach the status of a climber of the pillar in the afterworld. Though these Kabbalists believed in an objective structure of reality, they emphasize the cooperation of humans for its sustenance through a certain set of actions. Sustaining the world has repercussions on the inter-divine structure, and I propose designating these repercussions as theurgical operations, or contributions to the lower world, and their effects as connected to a magical worldview. Though such effects are related to the deeds of living individuals, there are some results of the deeds of the souls of the dead righteous in the paradisiacal situation, as we saw in the case of the intercourse of the spirits, that generate spirits. By and large, the paradisiacal situation is connected much more to forms of psychanodia that allow the souls of the righteous to contemplate the supernal world and the processes taking place there.

From another point of view, according to the above Kabbalists, the performance of the commandments allowing the posthumous ascent of the souls is not an exceptional or extraordinary event in Jewish society, as it is in the case of the shaman. The righteous ideally does what is demanded of all other Jews and, in so doing, does not transcend the *regimen vitae* of his group but performs it *de facto*. According to a Zoharic text, the righteous is described as the pillar of the world and as someone whose prayer is effective.[79]

Let me summarize the different functions the pillar played in the Kabbalistic books we have examined. It is a cosmic pillar upon which the world stands; it is a symbol for a divine power that governs the world; and later on, in Zoharic literature, it fulfills a function in the posthumous eschatology of righteous souls. There is a certain distinction, however, in the way the pillar is understood in late thirteenth-century Castilian Kabbalistic literature. Despite the very significant affinities between *Seder Gan `Eden* and Zoharic literature, the way in which the pillar is understood in the pseudo-Midrash is unique: it is a dynamic pillar that is watched by the souls of the righteous, not a static column that serves as a stairway as in the Zohar. In other words, though the Pseudo-Midrash propagates the view that the pillar mediates between the two paradises, it nevertheless is not eschatological. Simultaneously, I have found no mention of an eschatological pillar in Rabbi Moses de Leon's writings in Hebrew but only references to a cosmic one, even in contexts that address the ascent of the soul.[80] Likewise, the term `*amud 'emtza`y*, which permeates the Zohar in its slightly Aramaicized form, is absent in Rabbi de Leon's Hebrew writings. He makes reference to the median line, *qav 'emtza`y*, the sources of which we shall return to in chapter five, but not—as far as I know—to a median pillar or to the term *heikhal* in the context of the ascent of the soul.

The Zohar resorts to both the cosmic and eschatological pillars (without, however, distinguishing between them) yet differs from the *Seder Gan `Eden* in describing their use. This rather clear-cut distribution problematizes the attempt to offer a homogenized approach to these three types of writings—the Zohar, *Seder Gan `Eden* and de Leon's Hebrew texts—as belonging to the same Kabbalist. It should be mentioned that in at least one case in the Zohar, the existence of two pillars in paradise is assumed.[81]

11. THE TIMING OF POSTHUMOUS PSYCHANODIA

As we saw in one of the quotes from the Zohar, the ascent is accomplished at privileged moments in time: on the Sabbath and on the first day of the Jewish month. If the purpose of the ascent is to contemplate the supernal *hieros gamos*, these days refer in fact to the evenings preceding them. In other words, the ascents of the departed souls to the supernal paradise are performed at night. This observation transforms Zoharic instances of psychanodia into nocturnal events, just as the erotic encounters between the divine powers are imagined to take place at night.[82]

These specific times—the recurrent Sabbath and the first evening of the moon cycle—are categorized as "cyclical time": a precise time that occurs regularly. By referring to these points in time, the authors of the Zohar assume that the departed righteous do not exist in a supernal zone in which time is abolished. Rather, these righteous souls are aware of the natural rhythms of the week and the moon that govern life. As the righteous, they are imagined to have acquired a certain *habitus* during their lives. For the theosophical–theurgical Kabbalists, however, the rhythm in which they live is not merely an astronomical event, a ritual recurrence in human society, but rather the very rhythm of divine life. It is the theosophical processes that are perceived as being paradigmatic, not the astronomical ones.[83] Thus, it is not only the righteous, alive and dead, who participate in the ritual rhythm as articulated by the Jewish calendar, but also the divine powers that constitute it. The cyclical time of the human ritual is propagated within the divine sphere and defines the events in that realm as dynamic. To be sure, this is not a new development in Judaism, since the description of God resting on the day of the Sabbath is constitutive for most Jewish forms of thought. Dynamism is one of the conditions in which the mythical mode of thought emerges as pointed out in a convincing formulation by Ernst Cassirer:

> Only where man ceases to content himself with a static contemplation of the divine, where the divine explicates its existence and nature in time, where the human consciousness takes the step forward from the figure of the gods to the history, the narrative, of the gods—only then have we to do with "myth" in the restricted, specific meaning of the word... Only by his history is the god constituted; only by his history is he singled out from all the innumerable impersonal powers of nature and set over against them as an independent being. Only when the world of the mythical begins as it were to flow, only when it becomes a world not of mere being but of action, can we distinguish individual, independent figures of it. Here it is the specific character of change, of acting and being acted upon, which creates a basis for delimitation and definition.[84]

The mythical sexual events—the descent of the male divine power into the female divine power—attract the souls of the righteous to participate by ascending toward the place where the encounter occurs. A recurrent Kabbalistic stance following from rabbinic statements sees Friday night, which is part of the Sabbath according to the Jewish method of counting, as the propitious time when scholars, or the righteous, are encouraged to have intercourse.[85] Thus, attempting to contemplate the sexual event on high is part of a certain rhythm that allows those souls who alone may see it to ascend upon the pillar between the two paradises.

Since the nexus between time (Sabbath) and space (pillar) is quintessential, it may be interesting to draw attention to a phrase found in early thirteenth-century Kabbalah that brings these two elements together. Rabbi Yehudah ben Yaqar, a Barcelonan authority interested in Kabbalah, addresses the Hagigah cosmological speculations concerning the seven pillars. One pillar stands, in his opinion, for the Sabbath, while the other six represent the days of the week. The Sabbath pillar— `amud ha-Shabbat—is the most perfect one.[86] As Elliot Ginsburg points out, this text may be deciphered theosophically as addressing the relationship between the sefirah of Yesod and the other six lower sefirot.[87] It is also quite plausible that this stance had an impact on the Zoharic discussions mentioned above.[88] Again as Ginsburg notes, the Sabbath was considered to be the center of the days of the week.[89] The centrality of the Sabbath in time is reminiscent, in my opinion, of the centrality of the pillar in space. This affinity between temporal and local centrality is quite evident in one of Rabbi Vital's books.[90]

12. THE MANICHEAN PILLAR OF LIGHT AND GLORY

As pointed out in the previous chapter, despite the many discussions concerning the cosmological pillar, I have not found an eschatological one in early Kabbalah previous to the last decades of thirteenth-century Castile. Scholem assumes that the ascent of the soul into the divine realm by means of a pillar is implicit in the Bahir, and he points out a fascinating parallel to the eschatological pillar found in this early book: the Manichean column of splendor.[91] Due to this perceived affinity, he writes that in the Bahir there is "a Gnostic transfiguration of the talmudic notion [of the righteous]."[92] If Scholem is correct, then the Bahir may have been influenced by Manichaeism and thus could have served as a conduit for or a mediator of the ancient Gnostic term to medieval Kabbalah. I believe that Scholem's insight is very important but unsubstantiated. Nevertheless, in the case of the Zohar, which Scholem does not mention in this context, the situation is different. Scholem presumably conflates the Zoharic stance with that of the Bahir, assuming that in the latter book, souls ascend on an eschatological pillar. However, when we disentangle the two, the historical question changes substantially: the Manichean influence may not be valid, in my opinion, for the earliest forms of Kabbalah that emerged in Provence and Catalunia, but perhaps it is so for a circle of Kabbalists that flowered in Castile much later. An examination of the eschatology cultivated in the Provencal and Catalunian schools demonstrates another type of personal eschatology.[93]

The affinities between the Manichaean and the Zoharic visions of the pillar are as follows:

1. The concept of a pillar that is luminous is found in both the Zohar and in Manicheanism.[94]
2. Both Manichaeans and the circle of the Zohar share the view that a pillar of light or of glory leads souls to paradise.[95] In his copy of Widengren's book on Manichaeism, Scholem remarks that the pillar is parallel to the "pillar in Paradise for the ascent of the soul."[96]
3. The pillar of glory is identical to the perfect man in Manichaean sources.[97] In the Zohar, `amuda' de-'emtza`ita' is related to Adam, as both are symbols of the sefirah of Tiferet.[98]
4. In Manichaean sources, the ascent of the pillar of glory is attributed to the souls of the deceased righteous—tziddiq[99]—as is the case of the tzaddig in the Zohar.[100]
5. According to Saint Ephrem the Syrian's critique of Manichaeism, the Manichaeans worship different parts of their theosophy, including, as he puts it explicitly, the column of glory.[101] As seen above, the Zohar conveys the act of bowing to or worshipping the pillar.[102]
6. The ascent by means of the pillar of glory takes place after the purification of the soul in both Manichaean sources and the Zohar.[103]
7. In the Zohar and in *Seder Gan `Eden*, the pillar occurs in the context of the various firmaments and is conducive to them, especially in the passage attributed to the *Midrash ha-Ne`elam* discussed above. In Manicheanism, the pillar of light is an astronomical entity identical in some ways to the Milky Way.[104]
8. Scholem notes the potential impact of the Zoroastrian theory of the garment that is given to the deceased righteous after death.[105] He also proposes an eleventh-century figure writing in Egypt as the potential source who also might have impacted Zoharic eschatological

theory. It should be pointed out, however, that Manichaeism, as Scholem himself remarks, adopted the already-existing Zoroastrian theory.[106]

9. A historical observation may be added to the perception that the use of the eschatological pillar in the Zohar is unique. It was written, by and large, in Aramaic, a language that was not the normal tool of expression of European Jewry. However, Syriac, an Aramaic language that is one of the many in which Manichean literature has been preserved, presumably was known by Mani himself. Moreover, some decades before the composition of the Zoharic literature, a book written in Syriac was known to Nahmanides: the *Wisdom of Solomon*, an ancient Jewish composition from which he quoted two citations in Syriac using Hebrew characters.[107] This composition may also have been known to Rabbi Joseph Angelet, an early fourteenth-century Kabbalist who wrote in Aramaic and whose connection to Zoharic literature is analyzed by Yehuda Liebes.[108] Is it possible that a Manichean fragment, or a text influenced by Manichaenism, reached some Kabbalists in late thirteenth-century Castile. This may explain why there are divergences between the status of the eschatological pillar in *Seder Gan 'Eden* and the views found in the Zohar, which are absent in the Kabbalistic writings of their contemporaries.[109]

Some years ago, I made the following observation concerning the emergence of the Zohar: "This view of the *Zohar* as the zenith of a certain process taking place over the two decades 1270–1290 is not, however, identical with the view that this work is the exclusive composition of R. Moses de Leon, as assumed by Scholem or Tishby. I believe that older elements, including theosophical views, symbols and perhaps also shorter compositions, were merged into this Kabbalistic oeuvre which heavily benefited from the nascent free symbolism."[110] In recent years, the exclusivity of the role played by Rabbi Moses de Leon in the composition of the Zohar has been challenged. The most important argument is found in detailed and incisive studies by Liebes.[111] More recently, Ronit Meroz has made additional contributions.[112] Liebes explains the diversity of views on the same topic found in the Zohar as reflecting the opinions of different Kabbalists. Recently, he has been even more inclined in his oral discussions than in his printed studies to diminish the role of Rabbi Moses de Leon in the composition of the

Zohar.[113] I hope that the different approaches to the pillar in the circle of the Zohar proposed above contribute another piece of evidence for Liebes's thesis. The materials that might have come to the attention of the authors of the Zohar need further confirmation: does the present scrutiny of a very specific topic point in a more concrete manner in this direction?

Persuading as these points may be *prima facie*, there are nevertheless important differences between the Zoharic and the Manichean issues outlined above—divergences that may problematize direct Manichean influence on the Zohar. First and foremost, the column of light is a purely eschatological vehicle in Manicheanism, which means that the purified souls ascend by the column to the moon and sun without descending back, as in Zoharic views. This is indeed a major discrepancy, but I do not see it as a major obstacle in assuming that some form of Manichean tradition had an impact on some aspects of Zoharic eschatology. In more general terms, there are Enochic elements in Manichaeism, and some of these affinities between the Zoharic and the Manichaean views may reflected common sources.[114] In any case, it seems that if indeed there were Manichaean influences on thirteenth-century Kabbalah, they should be limited to Kabbalists active in the second part of this century and particularly in Castile; these potential influences are not detected in the work of the first generation Kabbalists active in Provence and Catalunia.

In seeking the origins of the Zoharic stance on the eschatological pillar, it is implausible for the time being to assume a developmental understanding of Kabbalistic doctrine on this topic based on the available material in pre-Zoharic Kabbalah. This observation does not mean that numerous other Kabbalistic doctrines of this book did not emerge from an inner evolution of ideas found in earlier Kabbalistic schools. This fact is obvious, in my opinion. The question, however, is what are the sources of other—perhaps few—doctrines that cannot be traced to earlier available sources, as is the case with the eschatological pillar? Based on the examination of the above texts, one can conclude that a linear development of Kabbalah from the main stances of the Bahir does not adequately explain the entire realm of processes that were formative in the constitution of Kabbalah, even for thirteenth-century theosophical Kabbalah. To formulate this more methodologically, attempts to ground Kabbalah, as well as other important cultural phenomena, in historicistic terms sometimes produces interesting explanations, though its application as a general principle may complicate rather than facilitate the understanding of its history.

13. SYMBOLIC INTERPRETATIONS OF ZOHARIC PARADISIACAL ARCHITECTURE

Two interesting metamorphoses of the Zoharic structure are related to the two paradises and the connective eschatological pillar. Ontologically speaking, this structure is found beneath the divine structure of the ten sefirot, and righteous souls are believed to have access to it by means of the pillar. Moreover, time and again, in both the main part of the Zohar and in Rabbi Moses de Leon's writings, the two paradises are depicted as reflecting each other.[115] However, there is a clear distinction between the two and between the entire system of paradises, palaces and firmaments and the divine structure. In the later Zoharic layer, known as *Tiqqunei Zohar* and *Ra`aya' Meheimna'*, there is a clear, though succinct interpretation of the Zoharic stance regarding the inter-paradisiacal pillar as pointing to the sefirotic system. First, an anonymous Kabbalist distinguishes between the paradise of the "Holy One, Blessed be He," on the one hand and the paradise of the archangel Metatron on the other. Then he writes that Eden is the supernal Shekhinah, which is the sefirah of Binah; the tree of life is the median pillar; and the garden is the lower Shekhinah, the sefirah of Malkhut.[116]

Thus we may describe the evolution of the attitude to the pillar in Zoharic literature as a sequence of three different stances. In the first Zoharic layer, namely the allegorical interpretations of some of the first pericopes of Genesis known as *Midrash ha-Ne`elam*, the pillar is absent, as it is in Rabbi de Leon's writings. In the second layer, known as the bulk of the Zohar, there are two different attitudes to the pillar: it is static, serving as a bridge between the two paradises, or it is dynamic, as in the discussion related to the Messiah. In the last layer of the book, the eschatological pillar is transposed into the sefirotic realm.

The next major development in the perception of Zoharic paradise architecture took place in the second half of the sixteenth century in Safed. In Lurianic Kabbalah, though the non-divine structure exists, there is a much more sustained attempt to read the Zoharic texts as symbolically indicating the intra-divine structure. What is eminently paradigmatic is not the supernal paradise, but the higher, sefirotic system. So, for example, we read in the classic of Lurianic Kabbalah, Rabbi Hayyim Vital's *Sefer `Etz Hayyim*:

...and the firmament, because it is the secret of *Da'at*, the twenty-two letters of the Torah are rooted in it, like the lower *Yesod*. And from the supernal dew that flows from the three *mohin* of the *'Attiqa'* [*Qaddisha'*] to the head of *Ze'ir 'Anppin*, from there the twenty-two letters are emanated to the *Da'at*...and from this firmament, that is the secret of *Da'at*, a pillar is emanated, which is the secret of the spinal column, that is descending from the *Da'at*, from its aspect of *Yesod*, that is the central opening, and it emanates until the soil of the garden, which is *Malkhut*, and from there the souls ascend and descend continuously. In it [the pillar] there are the three colors of the rainbow, because the *Yesod* is called rainbow, and it is comprised from *Hesed, Gevurah* [and] *Tiferet*, [which are] the three colors. And, according to the root of the soul, it ascends to one of those colors. During the copulation that takes place during the head of the month and Sabbath, the three lights of *Hesed, Gevurah* and *Tiferet*, [stemming] from the supernal *Da'at*, are revealed, in order to illumine the three colors of that rainbow, which is the pillar. Then the souls ascend on it in the secret of the female waters, to the firmament of the *Da'at* of the Feminine [configuration, *Nuqbba'*]...this pillar is in the middle of the garden and it is the aspect of *Tiferet*, and beneath the Tree of Life that river emerges.[117]

This passage is quite complex, which assumes acquaintance with Lurianic theosophy. The emergence of this complexity created the need to anchor itself in canonical writings, and the Zohar was, for Luria, indubitably one of them. This search for a proof text triggered the reinterpretation of Zoharic paradisiacal mythology in terms of the new theosophy. Unlike the rather simplistic identification of the terms "Eden," "garden" and "median pillar" with diverse parts of the sefirotic realm in the first passage adduced in this section, here the interpretation is much more dynamic and complex.

Let me explicate the main concepts that inform the above discussion: the Da'at is a sefirah that is located between the sefirot of Hokhmah and Binah and is part of the line that connects the highest part of the divine realm to the lower. Like all the sefirot in Lurianic Kabbalah, this sefirah comprises aspects of all the others, including that of Yesod. Thus, the Da'at is conceived of as a firmament from which the pillar descends to the last sefirah, that of Malkhut, understood as a garden, presumably the lower garden of Eden, as in the passage from

Tiqqunei Zohar. The aspects of the three sefirot—Hesed, Gevurah and Tiferet—found within the Da`at are expressed as three lights that illumine the colors found in the rainbow or the pillar. In the last part of the passage, the discussion has to do with the aspect of the firmament found within the last sefirah, Nuqbba', which includes, as mentioned above, aspects of all the other sefirot, including its own firmament that is Da`at. Thus, the relationships found in the higher part of the theosophical system reverberate in its lower plane. The ascents of the souls reach only this lower plane, where they play a role in triggering the sexual relationship between the pillar and the firmament. Unlike the Zoharic narrative of the paradise story, where contemplation is the purpose of the ascent, in the Lurianic interpretation another view is adduced that also can be found in other parts of the Zohar: the souls ascending on high serve as "feminine waters"—as triggers for the sexual union.[118]

By and large, the entire passage is framed by basic Lurianic theosophy, which assumes that the realm of the *'Adam Qadmon*, the cosmic primordial man, tantamount to the ten sefirot is organized by another theosophy that in most of its versions is comprised of five configurations, called *partzufim.*[119] The highest one, *'Arikh 'Anppin*, is a supernal configuration that corresponds to the first sefirah, Keter. *'Abba'*, the father, corresponds to the supernal male power of Hokhmah. *'Imma'*, the mother, corresponds to the feminine Binah. *Ze`ir 'Anppin*, the smaller configuration, comprises the sefirot of Da`at, Hesed, Gevurah, Tiferet, Netzah, Hod and Yesod. Last but not least, *Nuqbba'*, the lower feminine configuration, corresponds to the sefirah of Malkhut. Each of these five configurations comprises an independent system of ten sefirot.[120] This passage mentions all these configurations and describes two different movements: the descent of the dew from the higher divine plane downward and the ascent of the souls upward. Both are related to the pillar: the downward one is explicitly so in the passage under scrutiny; the upward one is implicit, based on the Zoharic eschatological understanding of the pillar. The origin of the Lurianic pentadic series of configurations may be Zoharic or may reflect more closely some forms of post-Zoharic Kabbalah related to the Zohar.[121] In any case, the similarity between this Kabbalistic theosophy and the pentadic series in Manicheanism is astonishing. There also, the hypostasis called the Perfect Man, reminiscent of the Lurianic *'Adam Qadmon*, is constituted by five anthropomorphic configurations.[122] As mentioned above, it is hard to determine exactly when the pentadic configuration entered theosophical kabbalah—with the emergence of the Zohar or only later on, in Lurianic Kabbalah. If it is Zoharic, then the occurrence of the theologoumenon in this literature may be another example of Manichean influence. If it is a Lurianic innovation (which I doubt), it should be seen together with the emergence of the impact of Manicheanism on this type of Kabbalah, which should be added to the Lurianic view of the redemption of the divine sparks from their involvement in a state of mixture, whose affinities to Manicheanism have already drawn the attention of scholars.[123]

14. Concluding Remarks

We have inspected above some instances of posthumous ascent of the soul framed by a spatially structured supernal universe that the soul encounters after death. There are different understandings of the ultimate purpose of this posthumous ascent. One is to be transformed into an angel. Another, which I support, is to contemplate the *hieros gamos*, which would provide a clear example of consonance between cosmogony, in our case a theogony, and the nature of the journey of the soul. The syzygic structure of the sefirotic realm, especially of the eighth and the tenth sefirot, invites a new ideal: the knowledge and the contemplation of the *hieros gamos* by select elite. The ascending souls of the righteous, climbing the paradisiacal pillar, are imagined to be capable of seeing the supernal event in which the male divine potency, envisioned as an intra-divine median pillar, is involved.

The personal eschatological descriptions adduced above are small parts of much longer discussions that do not resort to the image of the pillar and that demand, in my opinion, a more complex understanding of the nature of this literature. Described as theosophy by Scholem, its eschatological aspects require much more investigation.[124] As pointed out by Liebes, the tenor of the Zoharic layer called the *Iddras* has cardinal messianic overtones.[125] Here we addressed this layer only marginally. However, on the grounds of the above analyses, the question may be raised whether or not the bulk of the Zohar includes a significant eschatological message that is original to this composition. The relatively extended length of the two compositions dedicated to the structure of the Heikhalot demonstrate the importance of the aftermath existence in the overall structure of the Zohar. If this proposal is accepted, then we may have to qualify Scholem's assumption that early Kabbalah, namely the pre-Expulsion writings, was interested in cosmology and theosophy but not in Messianism.[126] This stance is incorrect insofar as the ecstatic Kabbalah of Rabbi Abraham Abulafia is concerned.[127] As mentioned above, Liebes has already investigated the deep messianic structure of one of the most "sublime" layers of the Zohar, and its eschatological discussions require even more drastic qualification.

Indeed, the surge of interest in personal eschatology in the second part of the thirteenth century among Jews in Spain has not attracted due scholarly attention. It is the appearance of not only *Seder Gan 'Eden* but also other discussions on paradisiacal structures and process-es that permeate Zoharic literature, in addition to the prominence of paradisiacal topics in Rabbi Moses de Leon's three important Hebrew books: *Sefer Shushan 'Edut, Sefer ha-Nefesh ha-Hakhamah* and *Sefer Mishkan ha-'Edut.*[128] Moreover, the sudden emergence of the impor-tance of various theories of metempsychosis in some important Kabbalistic schools corroborates this interest in personal eschatology. This is conspicuous in the writings of Nahmanides and his Kabbalistic school, Rabbi Moses de Leon, Rabbi Joseph from Hamadan, Rabbi Joseph ben Shalom Ashkenazi, Rabbi Todros Abulafia and, last but not least, in the vast Zoharic literature. Under the impact of these Kabbalists, two others, Rabbi Isaac of Acre and Rabbi Menahem Recanati, adopted this special interest in personal eschatology in the fourteenth century and became much more concerned with it than were the Kabbalists who preceded them.

Paradisiacal overtones are quite explicit in the ecstatic Kabbalah of Rabbi Abraham Abulafia, the titles of which include *The Life of the World to Come, 'Otzar 'Eden Ganuz, Gan Na'ul* and *Sefer ha-Ge'ulah,* the Book of Redemption. Though he conceived himself to be a Messiah, his Kabbalistic system mainly constitutes a path for self-redemption that involves well-elaborated mystical techniques. The accentuation of the eschatological tone in late thirteenth-century Kabbalah in Castile, Italy and Sicily becomes more obvious against the backgrounds of the two types of Kabbalah under discussion here. Rabbi Abraham Abulafia interpreted Maimonides's philosophy in a much more eschatological manner than the Great Eagle would have imagined. The Maimonidean Kabbalist speaks about the possibility of experiencing the world-to-come while alive, while the philosopher would restrict this experience to the posthumous phase.[129] This is also the case, however, when we

examine the manner in which the Zohar appropriated Heikhalot literature. The ascent on high to receive information, as cultivated in that literature, disappeared, as we saw in chapter one. What is conspicuous
now is a post-mortem experience of ascent that is described in the
parts of the Zohar designated as Heikhalot. The introduction of the
theme of the eschatological pillar, absent in Heikhalot literature, is
therefore one small detail that reflects a deeper transformation in attitude toward the ancient mystical texts that took place when the authors
of the Zohar adopted the idea of palaces.

Some of this surge of interest in eschatology has to do with rumors
related to the alleged role of the Mongol tribes as the sword of God, according to some Christian apocalyptic writers, or the Ten Lost Tribes,
according to some some Jews.[130] However, the personal aspects of eschatology, especially those related to the ascent on high, may be connected—at least to a certain extent—to the translations of Arabic
sources. One entitled *Libro della Scalla* that deals with the ascent on
high was written by scholars of King Alfonso Sabio in the immediate
vicinity of the place where the Zoharic literature was composed.[131]
Interestingly enough, the composition of Dante's *Divina Commedia*—
under the impact of Arabic sources, especially *Liber Scalae*, translated
in Romanic languages[132]—may serve as an additional indication of the
renascence of interest in personal eschatology in Christian Europe,
though while Dante's eschatology is concerned with hell as part of the
general economy of *Divina Commedia*, the Zohar is much more concerned with paradise. Caught in the political struggles of his time, including religious animosities, Dante needed a more spacious and color-
ful hell; the Zohar was composed by a minority figure who was much
less concerned with opponents and more focused on the righteous and
their fate in the fully elaborated depiction of paradise. I am not aware
of a single treatise dedicated to the topic of hell in Zoharic literature or
in the Kabbalistic circles active at the end of the thirteenth century,
while a composition like *Seder Gan `Eden* and the two treatises on the
Heikhalot are found in late thirteenth-century Kabbalah.

Thus we may assume that the use of the term "pillar" for the column that links the paradises and for the human entity that unifies the
lower and the celestial worlds may point to a continuum between these
two different types of pillar. If this is the case, such a continuum may
testify to the existence of a more comprehensive column that is much
closer to *axis mundi* visions. In any case, the concept of the median pil-

lar, `amuda' de-'emtza `ita', recurs in *Seder Gan `Eden* and especially the later layers of the Zohar.[133]

To return once again to Culianu's theory of psychanodia as having a distinct nature in ancient Jewish sources that simultaneously avoid discussions about ascension via planets and spheres, as seen in chapter one, there is no significant resort in Kabbalistic sources to the ascent of the soul through the seven planets. This is the case both in the accounts of the living ascents of the soul and the psychanodia of the souls of the deceased righteous.

NOTES

1. See Haviva Pedaya, *Name and Sanctity in the Teaching of Rabbi Isaac the Blind* (in Hebrew) (Jerusalem: The Magnes Press, 2001), pp. 279–80; and Elliot R. Wolfson, "By Way of Truth: Aspects of Nahmanides' Kabbalistic Hermeneutic," *AJS Review* 14:2 (1989): pp. 112–16.
2. See Hillel of Verona, *Tagmulei ha-Nefesh*, ed. Joseph B. Sermoneta (Jerusalem: Israeli Academy of Sciences, 1981), pp. 195–96, where he may refer to Nahmanides, as Sermoneta assumes, and Gershom Scholem, ed., "Two Treatises by R. Moses de Leon," *Qovetz `al Yad* 8:18 (1976): p. 350, n. 164.
3. Jean Delumeau, *Une histoire du Paradis* (Paris: Fayard, 1992).
4. See Shlomo Pines, "Nahmanides on Adam in the Garden of Eden in the Context of Other Interpretations of Genesis, Chapters 2 and 3," in *Exile and Diaspora: Studies in the History of Jewish People Presented to Prof. H. Beinart* (in Hebrew), eds. A. Mirsky, A. Grossman, and Y. Kaplan (Jerusalem: Makhon Ben Zvi, 1988), pp. 159–64; and Amos Funkenstein, "Nahmanides' Symbolical Reading of History," in eds. J. Dan and F. Talmage, *Studies in Jewish Mysticism* (Cambridge, Mass.: Association of Jewish Studies, 1982), pp. 129–50.
5. See Moshe Idel, "*Nishmat 'Eloha*: The Divinity of the Soul in Nahmanides and His School," in *Midrash ha-Hayyim* (in Hebrew), eds. S. Arzi, M. Fachler, and B. Kahana (Tel Aviv: Yediyy`ot 'Aharonot, 2004), pp. 338–81.
6. Louis Ginzberg, *The Legends of the Jews* (Philadelphia: Jewish Publication Society, 1968), vol. V, p. 91, n. 49 on two pillars in the paradise. In *Visio Pauli*, an early medieval Christian apocalypse, the two pillars are inscribed with the names of the righteous; see C. Kappler, et. al, *Apocalypses et voyages dans l'au-dela* (Paris: Le Cerf, 1987), p. 257. On two cosmic pillars having anthropomorphic forms in the Mediterranean in ancient times, see Bernard Goldman, *The Sacred Portal: A Primary Symbol in Ancient Judaic Art* (Lanham: University Press of America, 1986), p. 89.
7. *Midrash Alpha Betot*, chapter 4 in *Batei Midrashot*, eds. S. A. Wertheimer and A. Wertheimer (Jerusalem: Mossad ha-Rav Kook, 1955), vol. II, p. 427.
8. See chapter 2.

9. See the sources collected by Naftali Wieder, *The Judean Scrolls and Karaism* (London: East and West Library, 1962), pp. 39–43.

10. Yehudah Even Shemuel, ed., *Midreshei Ge'ulah* (in Hebrew), 2nd ed. (Jerusalem: Bialik Institute; Tel Aviv: Massada, 1954), pp. 140, 282 and 323.

11. *Zohar Hadash*, fols. 90a–91b.

12. Ibid., fol. 85a.

13. The Hebrew root *PRH* means to hover or float.

14. *Zohar Hadash*, fols. 82d–83a.

15. *Zohar* II, fol. 210a. See also ibid., I, fol. 81a, where the pillar is described as comprising all the colors, and ibid., II, fol. 8a, which provides a similar context but without the pillar. On the pillar and the three lights in *Atharva-Veda* X, 7, 40, see Sergiu Al-George, *Arhaic și Universal: India in conștiinta romineasca* (Bucharest: Editura Herld, n.d.), p. 36; and n. 22 below. The colors of light with no reference to the pillar but rather to the sefirah of Tiferet are mentioned in Hebrew in de Leon's *Sheqel ha-Qodesh*, ed. Charles Mopsik (Los Angeles: Cherub Press, 1996), p. 43. See also the paraphrased text translated into Hebrew in Rabbi Aharon Berakhia of Modena, *Ma'avar Yabboq*, fol. 118b–119a. According to this Zoharic passage, the three colors of the opening, presumably pointing to the vagina, illumine the colors of the phallic pillar. For more on the sexual aspects of the term pillar in the Kabbalah from the circle of the Zohar, see below.

On the supernal palace and the pillar, see below. In the passage quoted, and in all the other discussions following, the term pillar reflects the Hebrew term `amud, which occurs in the Aramaic passages. "Firmament" here is translated as "pillar" in other versions. "Supernal brilliance" is *Ziwwa' 'Ila'ah*. Compare also to *Zohar* I, fol. 162a, where the phrase *Zihara' 'Ila'ah* occurs in the context of the median line that stands for Tiferet or for Yesod, and to *Zohar* II, fol. 149a. See also chapter 1, n. 78, and below, n. 56.

16. *Zohar* II, fol. 211a. See also chapter 5, n. 44.

17. *Zohar* I, fol. 219a.

18. Mircea Eliade, *Shamanism: Archaic Techniques of Ecstasy* (Princeton: Princeton University Press, 1974), p. 265.

19. See Moshe Idel, "The Journey to Paradise: The Metamorphosis of a Motif from Greek Myth to Judaism" (in Hebrew), *Jerusalem Studies in Jewish Folklore* II (1982): pp. 7–12.

20. Compare to Eliade, *Shamanism*, p. 265.

21. See Moshe Idel, "Panim—On Facial Re-Presentations in Jewish Thought: Some Correlational Instances," in *On Interpretation in the Arts*, ed. Nurit Yaari (Tel Aviv: Tel Aviv University, 2000), pp. 21–56.

22. *Zohar* I, fol. 39ab. For mention of the colors in this context, see n. 15 above.

23. Compare to *Zohar* I, fol. 42a.

24. See Jellinek, *Bet ha-Midrasch*, reprint (Jerusalem: Wahrmann Books, 1967), vol. III, pp. xxvi–xxviii and 194–98; Gershom Scholem, "The Sources of the 'Story of Rabbi Gadiel the Infant' in Kabbalistic Literature," reprinted in the collection of his studies, *Explications and Implications* (in Hebrew) (Tel Aviv: `Am `Oved, 1982), pp. 270–83. For a complete French transla-

tion of this text, see Charles Mopsik, trans., *Le Zohar* (Lagrasse: Verdier, 1981–1996), vol. I, pp. 487–498. For the problem emerging from this attribution to de Leon, see below. On this composition, see more recently Reena Zeidman, "Rav Gadiel Ha-Na`ar's Torah in the Afterlife: A Literary Reading of Gan-Eden," *Eleventh World Congress of Jewish Studies*, Division C, (Jerusalem: World Union of Jewish Studies, 1994), vol. II, pp. 9–16.

25. J. D. Eisenstein, ed., *'Otzar ha-Midrashim* (New York: Reznik, 1915), p. 89.

26. Ibid., pp. 85 and 89. For more on the seat of glory, see below.

27. Ibid., p. 87.

28. Ibid., p. 86. On p. 85, there is a somewhat similar situation, but this time it is not an angel but the Messiah that is shaking the firmament by its rings. For a French translation of this passage, see Mopsik, *Le Zohar*, I, p. 491. The concept of the traveling pillar is biblical and is related to the pillars of fire and cloud. However, in the Bible the motion is horizontal; here it is vertical. The "Man Clothed by Garments" is the angel Gabriel. See Eisenstein, *'Otzar ha-Midrashim*, p. 85, and the passage quoted immediately below.

29. Ibid., pp. 85–86. This passage also is printed as an addendum to *Zohar* II, fol. 271b. On the view that the pillar ascends and descends, see Eisenstein, *'Otzar ha-Midrashim*, p. 87. The turn of the firmament also is found in Rabbi Moshe de Leon's *Mishkan `Edut*, but the pillar is not mentioned. On the pleasantness of God, compare to Psalms 90:17, *No`am Adonai*.

30. For a partial parallel to this issue, see *Zohar* III, fol. 170ab.

31. For the probability that the ascent of the soul was imagined in Hasidism to take place at night, see chapter 4.

32. See, for example, *Zohar* I, fol. 67a; Daniel Matt, trans. and comments, *The Zohar*, Pritzker Edition (Palo Alto: Stanford University Press, 2003/2004), vol. I, pp. 393–94; and *Zohar* II, fol. 83a.

33. *Zohar* II, fol. 221b. "Pleasantness" is translated from *Ne`imu*, which is an Aramaic translation of *No`am* found in the passage from *Seder Gan `Eden* quoted above. "Causes" is translated from *de-salqa'*. "Bow," or worship, is translated from *segidin*. See also the passage from *Zohar* II, fol. 210a, above. For the worship of the cosmic pillar, see Al-George, *Arhaic si Universal*, p. 62.

34. Eisenstein, *'Otzar ha-Midrashim*, p. 255.

35. *Zohar* II, fol. 149a.

36. *Zohar* II, fol. 119a. Compare also to ibid., II, fol. 214b; and *Tiqqunei Zohar*, fols. 2b, 9a.

37. See Scholem, *Implications and Explications*, p. 278.

38. *Zohar Hadash*, fol. 99a.

39. Ibid., fol. 100a.

40. *Zohar* I, fol. 3b. See Matt, *The Zohar*, I, p. 19; Mopsik, *Le Zohar*, I, p. 41; and *Zohar* I, fols. 45a, 46a, 67a and 241b.

41. *Pinqas*. See also *Zohar* I, fol. 81b.

42. *Zohar Hadash*, fol. 21a. An interesting parallel to this passage is found in Aramaic in *Zohar* I, fol. 81ab. The texts have several variants in early fourteenth-century sources and in later sources that quote them, but these

changes do not affect our discussion here. The first quote is Isaiah 4:5. The "dew of lights" is widely conceived in the Jewish tradition to be part of the process of the resurrection of the dead. See Ginzberg, *Legends of the Jews*, vol. V, p. 11, n. 22. This theme does not occur in all the versions of this Zoharic passage. Compare with *Zohar* I, fol. 7a; and II, fol. 83a. Also compare to the connection between the dew and the column or pillar of glory in Manichaeism; see Geo Widengren, *Mesopotamian Elements in Manichaeism* (Uppsala-Leipzig: Lundequistska Bokhandeln, 1946), p. 106. On the column of light, see also Ioan Petru Culianu, *Iocari serio, Ştiinta si arta in gîndirea Renaşterii* (Iasi: Polirom, 2003), pp. 172–73.

This text may be corrupted, since—unlike indicated here—in most Midrashic discussions, the soul is described as nourished from the splendor of the Shekhinah. On Michael's sacrificing of souls, see *BT, Hagigah*, fol. 12b.; and *Zohar* I, fol. 81a. According to *Seder Gan `Eden*, p. 88, the souls of the righteous are sacrificed in the seventh heaven, a clear discrepancy between the Pseudo-Midrash and the Zohar. Compare also to the thirteenth-century magical–theosophical treatise, *Sidrei de-Shimmusha' Rabba'*, printed by Gershom Scholem in *Devils, Demons, and Souls: Essays in Demonology* (in Hebrew), ed. Esther Liebes (Jerusalem: Makhon ben-Tzvi, 2004), p. 123. For a stance similar to that portrayed in the excerpted passage on the angelization of the souls of the righteous, see *Ascension of Isaiah* 9:30/31; and Himmelfarb, *Ascent to Heaven*, pp. 56–57.

43. *Commentary on the Torah* (Jerusalem: 1961), fol. 16c; see also Moshe Idel, *R. Menahem Recanati, the Kabbalist* (in Hebrew) (Jerusalem and Tel Aviv: Schocken Books, 1998), vol. I, p. 102.

44. Rabbi David ben Yehudah he-Hasid, *Mar'ot ha-Zove'ot*, ed. Daniel Matt (Chico, Cal.: Scholars Press, 1982), pp. 267–68.

45. This stance is reminiscent of a view found in a late Midrash entitled *Midrash Konen*, printed in Eisenstein, *'Otzar ha-Midrashim*, p. 256, where souls ascend and descend on the tree of life from heaven to paradise. However, there is no pillar mentioned in this quite interesting cosmogonical text.

46. Especially *BT, Hagigah*, fol. 12b.

47. Eliade, *Shamanism*, p. 265.

48. Rabbi Tzevi Hirsch Kaidanover, *Qav ha-Yashar*, chapter 16, (Vilnius, 1865), fols. 32b–33a.

49. See Yehuda Liebes, "The Messiah of the Zohar," in *The Messianic Idea in Israel* (in Hebrew) (Jerusalem: Israeli Academy for Sciences, 1982), p. 114, n. 118; and p. 206, n. 406.

50. *Zohar* II, fol. 7b. It should be mentioned that the disappearance of the Messiah and his return is reminiscent of Moses's ascent to the mount of Sinai for a period of time and his return. For the nexus between the ascents and descents of these two figures, see the interesting passage by Rabbi Hayyim Vital, translated and discussed by Gershom Scholem, *Sabbatai Sevi: The Mystical Messiah*, trans. R. J. Z. Werblowsky (Princeton: Princeton University Press, 1973), p. 53.

51. On the Messiah's diadem, see also *Zohar* III, fols. 164b and 196b.

52. See *Zohar Hadash*, fol. 88b. See also Moshe Idel, "Types of Redemptive Activities in Middle Ages," in *Messianism and Eschatology* (in Hebrew), ed. Z. Baras (Jerusalem: Merkaz Shazar, 1984), p. 267.

53. See Scholem, *Implications and Explications*, p. 276; and Haviva Pedaya, *Vision and Speech: Models of Revelatory Experience in Jewish Mysticism* (in Hebrew) (Los Angeles: The Cherub Press, 2002), pp. 216–17.

54. See *Sefer Sitrei Torah*, Ms. Paris BN 774, fol. 153ab.

55. See also *Zohar* I, fols. 7a and 38b; II, fol. 150a; and III, fol. 11a; and Franz Cumont, *Lux Perpetua* (Paris: Geuthner, 1947), pp. 429–30.

56. *Zohar* I, fol. 219a. Compare to *Zohar* I, fol. 216a, where there is an important parallel, though the theme of the pillar does not occur. For an annotated translation, see Mopsik, *Le Zohar*, IV, p. 68. For the affinity between the pillar—*stupa*—and the king in the Buddhist tradition, see John Irwin, "The Axial Symbolism in the Early Stupa: An Exegesis," in *The Stupa: Its Religious, Historical and Architectural Significance*, ed. Anna Libera Dallapicola in collaboration with Stephanie Zinge-Ave Lallemant (Wiesbaden: Franz Steiner Verlag, 1980), p. 24. The quote is Isaiah 4:5. "The glory" is translated from *Yiqara'*; see also n. 15 above.

57. See, for example, *Zohar* I, fols. 216a, 217b.

58. See, for example, *Zohar* I, fol. 38b; and II, fol. 156b.

59. See, for example, *Zohar* I, fol. 38b.

60. See *Midrash ha-Ne'elam* on the Song of Songs, in *Zohar Hadash*, fol. 69ab. See also *Midrash ha-Ne'elam* on the book of Ruth, in ibid., fol. 90c.

61. *Zohar* II, fol. 95b (*Sabba' de-Mishpatim*). On this passage, see Yehuda Liebes, *Sections of the Zohar Lexicon* (in Hebrew) (Ph.D. diss., Hebrew University, Jerusalem, 1976), pp. 327–335. Liebes, *Sections of the Zohar Lexicon*, pp. 331–32. "Scale" is translated from *tiqla'*; this is a polisemic and quite obscure—though nevertheless important—term in the Zohar; see idib., pp. 327–35. I hope to deal elsewhere with the possible affinities between some of its meanings and Manichaean matters related to the pillar of glory. For some of the other meanings of this term, see Matt, *The Zohar*, II, pp. 83–84, nn. 634–35. On the two scales, see also *Zohar* II, fol. 252a.

62. Liebes, *Sections of the Zohar Lexicon*, p. 332, adduces a lengthy list of the occurrence of similar phrases related to paradise.

63. *Zohar* II, fols. 117ab and 118a.

64. Romulus Vulcanescu, *Coloana Cerului* (Bucharest: Editura Academiei, 1972), pp. 112–13.

65. Peter Schaefer, ed., *Synopse zur Hekhalot-Literatur* (Tuebingen: J. C. B. Mohr, 1981), paras. 163–64. See also idem, *The Hidden and Manifest God*, trans. Aubrey Pomerance (Albany: State University of New York Press, 1992), pp. 46 and 119. The translation of the second part of this passage generally follows Elliot R. Wolfson, *Through a Speculum that Shines: Vision and Imagination in Medieval Jewish Mysticism* (Princeton: Princeton University Press, 1994), pp. 101–02; idem, *Along the Path* (Albany: State University of New York Press, 1995), pp. 25–26 and the pertinent footnotes; David J. Halperin, *Faces of the Chariot* (Tuebingen: J.C.B. Mohr, 1987), pp. 286–88 and 441; Moshe Idel, "On the Trisagion and the

Contemplation of the Merkavah" (in Hebrew), in *From Qumran to Cairo: Studies in the History of Prayer*, ed. Joseph Tabori (Jerusalem: Orhot Press, 1999), pp. 7–15. "Bear witness to them" is according to Ms. Munchen 22. "Holy, as it says" is Isaiah 6:3.

66. See also Erich Neumann, *The Great Mother: An Analysis of the Archetype*, trans. Ralph Manheim (New York: Bollingen Series, 1955), pp. 98–100; and Yehuda Liebes, *On Sabbateaism and Its Kabbalah: Collected Essays* (in Hebrew) (Jerusalem: Mossad Bialik, 1995), p. 195. See the bibliography adduced by Daniel Abrams, *Sexual Symbolism and Merkavah Speculation in Medieval Germany: A Study of the Sod ha-Egoz Texts* (Tuebingen: J. C. B. Mohr Siebeck, 1997), pp. 50–51 and n. 35; de Leon, *Sheqel ha-Qodesh*, p. 74; and Abraham Elqayam, *The Mystery of Faith in the Writings of Nathan of Gaza* (in Hebrew) (Ph.D. diss., Hebrew University, Jerusalem, 1993), pp. 294–95, n. 327.

67. Peter Schaefer, *The Hidden and Manifest God*, trans. Aubrey Pomerance (Albany: State University of New York, 1992), p. 46, n. 149.

68. See Gershom Scholem, *On the Mystical Shape of the Godhead* (New York: Schocken Books, 1991), pp. 111–12.

69. Compare to Ira Chernus, "The Pilgrimage to the Merkavah: An Interpretation of Early Jewish Mysticism," *JSJT* VI:1–2 (1987): pp. 1–35. See also, however, Wolfson, *Through a Speculum*, p. 101.

70. *Shi'ur Qomah* (Jerusalem, 1979), fol. 64ab. Cordovero mentions the *qelippah*, which is attached to imperfect people who cannot contemplate the supernal forms, again in the context of those who entered Pardes.

71. Rabbi Moshe Cordovero, *'Elimah Rabbati*, Ms. New York, JTS Mic. 2174, Tamar 3, chapter 31, pp. 232–33, copied in Rabbi Abraham Azulai's *Hesed le-'Avraham*, Fifth Well, Nahar 50, fol. 41cd. The many affinities between Cordoverian material and Azulai's book, which was printed and became quite influential, are analyzed in detail by Brakha Sack, "The Sources of *Sefer Hesed le-Avraham* by R. Abraham Azulai" (in Hebrew), *Qyriat Sefer* 56 (1981): pp. 164–75. See also Azulai's *'Or ha-Hammah*, I, fol. 36a, on *Zohar* I, fol. 39b, where the colors are understood to point to the four letters of the Tetragrammaton and to four anthropomorphic configurations.

The quote in this passage is Isaiah 4:5. The palaces of *Yetzirah* are the palaces of the third of the four cosmic worlds according to many Kabbalistic cosmologies. "Thrown" is translated from *Nizraqot*. It seems that the term *Yihud* describes the union between the two lower sefirot here. "Station" is translated from *Mador*—a place where souls stay for a while. An important passage dealing with the ascent of souls by the pipeline by which its individual influx descends, which bears all the signs of Rabbi Cordovero's thought, is found in the work of an early seventeenth-century Kabbalist, Rabbi Isaskhar Ber ben Petahyyiah Moshe, *Sefer Pithei Yah* (Prague, 1609), fol. 5a. This author resorts also to the image of ladder in this context.

72. *'Or ha-Hammah*, I, fol. 38a, citing Rabbi Cordovero.

73. Chapter 4: The Gates of Holiness, in *Reishit Hokhmah ha-Shalem*, ed. C. J. Waldman (Jerusalem: 'Or ha-Mussar, 1984), vol. II, pp. 53–54. A paraphrase of this passage, without mention of the source, is found in Rabbi

Aharon Berakhiah of Modena, *Sefer Ma`avar Yabboq*, fols. 118b–119a. The quote in this passage is Isaiah 4:5.

74. See *BT, Babba Batra'*, fol. 75a; and Rabbi Todros ben Joseph Abulafia, *Sha`ar ha-Razim* (in Hebrew), ed. Michal Kushnir Oron (Jerusalem: Bialik Institute, 1989), p. 85.

75. *Zohar* I, fol. 219a.

76. Da Vidas, *Reishit Hokhmah*, vol. II, pp. 53–54; see also p. 60.

77. Rabbi Hayyim Vital, `Etz ha-Da`at Tov, reprint (Jerusalem: Moznayyim, 1985), p. 129. "Because the terrestrial world is but a gateway to enter the supernal salon" reflects `Avot 4:16.

78. *Tanya*, I, chapter 39.

79. *Zohar* I, fol. 43a.

80. See, for example, Rabbi Moshe de Leon, *The Book of the Pomegranate*, ed. Elliot R. Wolfson (Atlanta: The Scholars Press, 1988), pp. 373–74; and *Sefer Mishkan ha-`Edut*, Ms. Cambridge, Add. 1500, fol. 50a.

81. *Zohar* II, fol. 130b.

82. See the rich material collected and analyzed in Elliot Ginsburg, *The Sabbath in the Classical Kabbalah* (Albany: State University of New York Press, 1989), pp. 101–21. It should be pointed out that Muhammad's *mi`raj* also took place at night.

83. See Moshe Idel, "Some Forms of Order in Kabbalah," *Daat* 50–52 (2003): pp. xxxi–lviii.

84. Ernst Cassirer, *The Philosophy of Symbolic Forms* (New Haven: Yale University Press, 1971), vol. 2, pp. 104–05.

85. See Isaiah Tishby, *The Wisdom of the Zohar: An Anthology of Texts*, trans. D. Goldstein (London and Washington: Littman Library, 1991), vol. III, pp. 1223–24; Ginsburg, *The Sabbath*, pp. 289–95; and Elliot R. Wolfson, "Eunuchs Who Keep the Sabbath: Becoming Male and the Ascetic Ideal in Thirteenth-Century Jewish Mysticism," in *Becoming Male in the Middle Ages*, eds. J. J. Cohen and B. Wheeler (New York: Taylor & Francis, Inc., 1997), pp. 172–74.

86. Rabbi Yehudah ben Yaqar, *Perush ha-Tefillot va-ha-Berakhot*, ed. Shmuel Yerushalmi (Jerusalem: Me'orei Israel, 1979), vol. I, pp. 110–11.

87. Ginsburg, *Sabbath*, pp. 151–52, n. 88.

88. See ibid.; and the material referred to in chapter 2, section 6.

89. Ginsburg, *Sabbath*, pp. 85–92 and 155–57.

90. Rabbi Hayyim Vital, *Sefer `Etz ha-Da`at Tov*, fol. 15cd.

91. See Gershom Scholem, *Origins of the Kabbalah*, ed. R. Z. J. Werblowsky, trans. A. Arkush (Philadelphia: Jewish Publication Society and Princeton University Press, 1987), p. 153. See also chapter 2, section 3.

92. Scholem, *Origins of the Kabbalah*, pp. 152–53.

93. See Moshe Idel, "In the Light of Life: An Inquiry in Kabbalistic Eschatology" (in Hebrew), in *Sanctity of Life and Martyrdom: Studies in Memory of Amir Yekutiel*, eds. I. M. Gafni and A. Ravitzky (Jerusalem: Merkaz Shazar, 1992), pp. 191–212.

94. Geo Widengren, *The Great Vohu Manah and the Apostle of God: Studies in Iranian and Manichaean Religion* (Leipzig: Uppsala, 1945), pp. 13–15;

Gedaliahu Guy Stroumsa, *Savoir et Salut* (Paris: Le Cerf, 1992), pp. 267–68; and Ioan P. Couliano, *The Tree of Gnosis*, trans. Hillary Wiener and Ioan P. Couliano (San Francisco: Harper, 1992), pp. 172–73.

95. See Widengren, *Great Vohu Manah*, pp. 13 and 33.

96. Ibid., p. 33.

97. Ibid., pp. 14–15. See *Kephalaia* 35:9, discussed in Manfred Heuser, "The Manichaean Myth according to Coptic Sources," in *Studies in Manichaean Literature and Art*, eds. Manferd Heuser and Hans-Joachim Klimkeit (Leiden: Brill, 1998), pp. 42–43.

98. For the identification of `amuda de-'emtza`ita' with Adam, see *Zohar* I, fol. 28a, a passage belonging to the later stratum called *Ra`aya' Meheimna*; and II, 169b.

99. See Widengren, *Great Vohu Manah*, p. 14.

100. See especially the text translated by Widengren, ibid., p. 13, where there is a cluster of themes reminiscent of Kabbalah; the column is also the living tree and is related to righteousness.

101. See A. V. Williams Jackson, *Researches in Manichaeism* (New York: Columbia University Press, 1932), p. 303.

102. See *Zohar* II, fol. 149a.

103. Widengren, *Great Vohu Manah*, passim.

104. See Williams Jackson, *Researches on Manichaeism*, p. 13. On the importance of astronomy in Manichaeism, see Ioan P. Coulianu, "The Counterfeit Spirit in Manichaeism," in *Manichaica Selecta: Studies Presented to Professor Julien Ries*, eds. Alois van Tongerloo and Soren Giversen (Lovanii: Manichaean Studies, 1991), pp. 53–58.

105. Compare to Scholem, *On the Mystical Shape*, pp. 264–65.

106. Ibid., pp. 315–16, n. 30.

107. On this issue see Alexander Marx, "An Aramaic Fragment of the Wisdom of Solomon," *Journal of Biblical Literature* 40 (1921): pp. 57–69. See also Daniel Abrams, *The "Book of Illumination" of R. Jacob ben Jacob Hacohen* (in Hebrew) (Ph.D. diss., New York University, New York, 1993), pp. 216–17. The impact of this book on *Midrash ha-Ne`elam* was the topic of a debate between R. J. Z. Werblowsky on the one hand and Samuel Belkin and Joshua Finkel on the other. See the latters' "The Alexandrian Tradition and the *Midrash ha-Ne`elam*," in *The Leo Jung Jubilee Volume*, eds. Menahem M. Kasher, Norman Lamm, and Leonard Rosenfeld (New York: Shulsinger, 5722/1962), pp. 79–90, where all bibliographical references on this debate are listed.

108. Yehuda Liebes, *Studies in the Zohar* (Albany: State University of New York Press, 1993), pp. 86, 109, 134, 178, 195, 197–98, 207, 224 and 225.

109. For the emergence of the notion of the mixture between good and evil reminiscent of Manichaeism in an earlier circle of Castilian Kabbalists, see Moshe Idel, "The Interpretations on the Incest Interdictions in Early Kabbalah" (in Hebrew), *Kabbalah* 12 (2004): pp. 149–53.

110. Moshe Idel, *Kabbalah: New Perspectives* (New Haven: Yale University Press, 1988), p. 380, n. 66.

111. For a short form of these studies translated into English, see Liebes, *Studies in the Zohar*, pp. 85–138.

112. Ronit Meroz, "Zoharic Narratives and Their Adaptations," *Hispania Judaica Bulletin* 3 (5760/2000): pp. 3–63; and her forthcoming book, *The Rose and the Scent* (in Hebrew) (Jerusalem: Mossad Bialik).

113. See also Pedaya, *Nahmanides*, p. 464, n. 83.

114. See John C. Reeves, "An Enochic Motif in Manichaean Tradition," in Tongerloo and Giversen, *Manichaica Selecta*, pp. 295–98; and idem, *Jewish Lore in Manichaean Cosmogony* (Cincinnati: HUC Press, 1992), especially p. 179, n. 28. The earlier bibliography on Jewish sources of some Manichaean views is adduced in this monograph. See especially Gedalyahu G. Stroumsa, *Another Seed: Studies in Gnostic Theology* (Leiden: Brill, 1984), pp. 156–63.

115. Yael Nadav, "La eschatologia de R. Moshe de Leon" (in Hebrew), *Tesoro de los judios sefardies* II (5719/1959), pp. 69–76.

116. See *Zohar* I, fol. 27a.

117. Rabbi Hayyim Vital, *Sefer 'Etz Hayyim* (Warsaw, 1891), Gate 43, chapter 3, II, fol. 96b. On the supernal dew, see above, n. 42. For the role of the *Nous* in Manichaeism as the source from which lower messengers emanate, see Widengren, *Great Vohu Manah*, pp. 20, ff.

118. See Elliot R. Wolfson, *Circle in the Square* (Albany: State University of New York Press, 1995), pp. 110–15; and idem, "Weeping, Death and Spiritual Ascent in Sixteenth-Century Jewish Mysticism," in *Death, Ecstasy, and Other Worldly Journeys*, eds. J. J. Collins and Michael Fishbane (Albany: State University of New York Press, 1995), p. 237, n. 22.

119. See Lawrence Fine, *Physician of the Soul, Healer of the Cosmos: Isaac Luria and His Kabbalistic Fellowship* (Palo Alto: Stanford University Press, 2003), pp. 138–41; and Gershom Scholem, *Major Trends in Jewish Mysticism* (New York: Schocken Books, 1967), pp. 269–70.

120. Fine, *Physician of the Soul*, p. 139.

121. The answer depends on the manner in which the anthropomorphic structures in the theosophies of the Zohar and of Rabbi David ben Yehudah he-Hasid are understood, an issue that cannot be addressed here. See Liebes, *Studies in the Zohar*, pp. 223–24, n. 293.

122. On the great importance of the pentads in Manichaenism, see Ioan P. Couliano, "The Counterfeit Spirit in Manichaeism," in Tongerloo and Giversen, *Manichaica Selecta*, pp. 53–58. See also idem, *Tree of Gnosis*, pp. 173 and 175–76; and Jackson, *Researches in Manichaeism*, pp. 296–313.

123. See Scholem, *Major Trends*, pp. 269, 280; and Isaiah Tishby, "Gnostic Doctrines in Sixteenth-Century Jewish Mysticism," *Journal of Jewish Studies* VI (1955): pp. 146–52. Interestingly enough, Tishby—writing years after the publication of Scholem's *Major Trends*—does not find it necessary to mention his master's explicit references to the possible impact of Manichaenism.

124. See Scholem, *Major Trends*, pp. 205–43.

125. Liebes, *Studies in the Zohar*, pp. 1–84.

126. Gershom Scholem, *The Messianic Idea in Judaism* (New York: Schocken Books, 1972), p. 39.

127. See Moshe Idel, *Messianic Mystics* (New Haven: Yale University Press, 1998), pp. 58–125.

128. See Scholem, "Two Treatises," pp. 348–61.

129. See Moshe Idel, "Abulafia's Secrets of the Guide: A Linguistic Turn," in *Perspectives on Jewish Thought and Mysticism*, eds. A. Ivri, E. R. Wolfson, and A. Arkush (Amsterdam: Harwood Academic Publishers, 1998), pp. 292–96.

130. See Idel, *Messianic Mystics*, pp. 8, 81 and 124.

131. On the importance of the geographical proximity between the Alfonsine and Kaballistic renaissances in Castile, see Moshe Idel, "On European Cultural Renaissances and Jewish Mysticism" (forthcoming). See also idem, "The Concept of the Torah in Heikhalot Literature and Its Metamorphoses in Kabbalah" (in Hebrew), *Jerusalem Studies in Jewish Thought* 1 (1981): pp. 46–47, n. 68.

132. See Miguel Asin Palacios, *La Escatologia Musulmana en la Divina Comedia*, 2nd ed. (Madrid: Hisperion, 1984); E. Cerulli, *Il "Libro' de la Scalla" e la questione dele fonti arabo-spagnole della Divina Commedia* (Vatican City: Biblioteca Apostolica Vaticana, 1949); idem, *Nuove ricerche sul "Libro della Scalla" e la cognoscenza dell'Islam in occidente* (Vatican City: Biblioteca Apostolica Vaticana, 1972), especially pp. 12–13; and Geo Widengren, *Muhammad, the apostle of God, and his ascension* (Wiesbaden: Lundequistska bokhandeln Uppsala, 1955), pp. 11–112. On the possibility that Jewish material stemming from Heikhalot literature influenced *Libro della Scala*, see Salo W. Baron, *A Social and Religious History of the Jews* (New York: Columbia University Press, 1958), vol. VIII, p. 285, n. 23; and Ioan P. Couliano, *Experiences de l'extase: Extase, Ascension et recit visionaire de l'Hellenisme au Moyen Age* (Paris: Payot, 1984), pp. 164–72. See also David J. Halperin, "Hekhalot and Mi'raj: Observations on the heavenly journey in Judaism and Islam," in Collins and Fishbane, *Death, Ecstasy*, pp. 269–88.

133. See the Hebrew text identified by Efrayyim Gottlieb as belonging to the author of the two later layers of the Zoharic literature, printed in his *The Hebrew Writings of the Author of Tiqqunei Zohar and Ra'aya Mehemna* (Jerusalem: Israel Academy of Sciences and Humanities, 2003), p. 92, where the Hebrew form `amud ha-'emtza'y occurs. Unlike the recurrence of the Aramaic phrase for median pillar in the Aramaic writings, in the Hebrew ones—which in my opinion are earlier—see ibid., Introduction, pp. 23–29; it occurs only one time.

CHAPTER 4:

Psychanodia and Metamorphoses of Pillars in Eighteenth-Century Hasidism

1. THE BESHT AND THE EPISTLE OF THE ASCENT OF THE SOUL

Eighteenth-century Hasidism, a major form of Jewish mysticism, preserves a peculiarly interesting version of the ascent on high. Its founding master was Rabbi Israel ben Eliezer (1699–1760), better known as the Besht, the acronym of the Hebrew words *Ba'al Shem Tov*, the "Possessor of the Good Name." According to some texts, he performed several ascents of the soul on high.[1] As seen in the preceding chapters, this practice is by no means unknown to the period between the emergence of Heikhalot literature and the middle of the eighteenth century. In the span of a millennium and then some that separates these two types of Jewish literature, many mystics are described as ascending on high. The affinity between the older and the Hasidic material is obvious not only in instances of ascent on high but also in the manner of study cultivated by the Besht.[2] It seems that despite the major impact of Kabbalistic literature on Hasidism, some aspects of this movement recycled and even reemphasized late antiquity material.

The Besht is described by a mid-nineteenth-century Hasidic master as someone whose "soul was ascending and body remained as a still as a mineral, and he spoke with the Messiah and with the Faithful Shepherd and they gave answers to his questions, and he was an expert in matters of the Account of the Creation and in the Account of the Chariot, and in the entire Torah."[3] Here, as in ancient Jewish literature, the ascent on high is connected to famous esoteric topics of the two accounts.[4] Thus, the Besht is envisaged by his much later follower as an expert on matters of ancient Jewish mysticism, which include the performance of ascents on high. Indeed, the ascent on high to converse with the Messiah is found in Heikhalot literature.[5] Some may argue against the authenticity of using a mid-nineteenth-century passage to better understand mid-eighteenth-century experiences. But the above text combines the ascent on high to speak with the Messiah and the experience of the Besht in matters concerning the two accounts and the Torah.

The Besht describes his alleged ascent on high in a passage from a famous epistle attributed to him and addressed to his brother-in-law, Rabbi Gershon of Kosov.[6] In the Besht's epistle, it is written, *inter alia*:

> On *Rosh ha-Shanah* of the year 5507 (1746), I performed an incantation for the ascent of the soul, known to you. And in that vision I saw wondrous things, which I had never seen until then from the day that I became spiritually aware. And it is impossible to relate and to tell what I saw and learned in that ascent hither, even in private. But when I returned to the lower Paradise, I saw the souls of living and of dead persons, both of those with whom I was acquainted and of those with whom I was not acquainted...numberless, in a to-and-fro movement, ascending from one world to the other through the pillar known to adepts in esoteric matters.... And I asked my teacher and master that he come with me, as it is a great danger to go and ascend to the supernal worlds, whence I had never ascended since I acquired awareness, and these were mighty ascents. So I ascended degree after degree, until I entered the palace of the Messiah.[7]

From the opening statement it is evident that this enterprise is not a unique event but a practice both cultivated by the Besht on prior occasions and known to his brother-in-law. Another 1750 ascension of this figure is introduced by the phrase: "and on *Rosh ha-Shanah* of 5510 I performed an ascent of the soul, as is known."[8] Again, the founder of Hasidism mentions that his experience is not an idiosyncratic one, unparalleled by anything known in his entourage, but rather familiar at least in some close circles. According to the epistle, the Besht practiced this ascent several times beforehand, meaning that we may date the first instance of such an event around 1740. In both cases, the ascension of the Besht's soul took place on the eve of the New Year. Is this occasion an especially propitious moment for predicting the future? There seems to be a pattern in the occurrence of revelatory events in connection with Jewish holidays.[9] The Jewish New Year in particular is connected to eschatological revelations in some medieval sources.[10]

In the following, we once again are given the impression that the Besht does not address a new theme but rather elaborates upon a topic known to the addressee:

I asked the Messiah: When do you come? And he answered: You will know [the time] which is when your doctrine will be revealed in public and it will be disclosed to the world, and "your fountains will well outside," what I have taught you and you apprehended, and also they will be able to perform the unifications and the ascents [of the soul] as you do, and then the shells will be abolished, and then there will be a time of good-will and redemption. And this [answer] surprised me, and I was deeply sorrowful because of the length of time when this will be possible; however, from what I have learned there, the three things, which are remedies and three divine names, it is easy to learn and to explain. [Then] my mind was calmed and I thought that it is possible for my contemporaries to attain this degree and aspect by these [practices], as I do, namely to be able to accomplish the ascents of souls, and they will be able to study and become like me.[11]

From the perspectivistic point of view, we witness here a conjugation between the shamanic element and the eschatological one. This is quite an exceptional mixture if judged from the perspective of an Eliadean description of the archaic–universal structure of religion, which is considered a non-eschatological religiosity. Indeed, on the one hand, this passage deals with a more concrete type of pillar: one that is seen by a live human being, though not by his group. On the other hand, it is deeply concerned with eschatology—not the Zoharic personal type, but rather that concerning the fate of the nation. It is crucial to the topic of this book to emphasize the attempt to reinterpret ideal Judaism as permeated by ascents of the soul: the Messiah claims that he will come when the technique for ascents of the soul is disseminated.

This psychanodic interpretation of Judaism represents the culmination of a vector mentioned earlier: the continuously increasing importance of apotheotic traditions in Jewish mysticism, beginning with ancient Enochic literature.[12] The meaningful development of Jewish mysticism is related to a growing interest in the various avatars of Enoch. It is therefore no surprise that one of the biblical figures that becomes a paragon for Hasidism, beginning with the traditions attributed to the Besht himself, is none other than the mystical figure of Enoch as a modest cobbler who reached the supreme religious attainment for his devotion.[13]

The above passage has been the subject of many learned analyses and of a small polemic among scholars of Hasidism, the thrust of which is the divergence between a more messianic reading of the text, ushered by Ben-Zion Dinur and elaborated critically by Isaiah Tishby, and a less messianic one, found in Gershom Scholem's writings.[14] However, despite the interest expressed by these scholars in this short but rich epistle, many of its details remain unexamined. Eagerness to demonstrate the importance of the text for the messianic nature of Hasidism, on the one hand, or its irrelevance to the other concept of Hasidism as neutralizing Messianism, on the other, has resulted in the neglect of some components of the text that may contribute to the effort to settle this controversy. The analysis below will attempt to show that at least some details in the Besht's passage describe his activity in concurrence with the way medical magicians were portrayed in his lifetime.

2. The Besht as an Iatromant

In his study on ecstatic experiences, Ioan P. Culianu refers to some ancient experts by the Greek term *iatromant*—a medicineman who is capable of ecstatic experiences.[15] It seems that this description also fits the Besht. Let me start with the term *segullot*, or remedies, the medical aspect of which occurs together with the divine names. This term is used in a historical document that describes the Besht first as a Kabbalist and shortly thereafter as *Doktor* and *Balsem* (or *Balszam*).[16] Indeed, this latter pair of words seems to be widely used in descriptions of similar persons. In the magical writing *Mif'alot 'Elohim* attributed to Rabbi Yo'el ben Naftali Katz, a famous seventeenth-century magus, for example, the Besht is described as the "master of a [magical] name," a quote from the "writings of the Kabbalists" that address medical astrology, where it is written that astrological details "are necessary both to the master of the name and to the doctor."[17] Therefore, this pair of words in the Besht's revelation is relevant to the practice of the founder of Hasidism. However, despite this parallelism, the mention of the divine names together with *segullot* is reminiscent of the introduction to *Shimmushei Torah* referred to below. This is a matter not only of precise linguistic but also contextual similarity: in both cases, the ascent on high is mentioned. Like Moses, the Besht ascended on high and received names and remedies.

This similarity is not the only one between the introduction to *Shimmushei Torah* and the Besht's epistle. Let us inspect the possible meaning of the phrase, "your fountain will well outside," which occurs in the passage quoted above. Its source is a biblical verse (Proverbs 5:16), and it may refer to the dissemination of the Besht's teachings. Nevertheless, this metaphorical understanding does not fully exhaust the meaning of this phrase. In a description of the Besht, again found in the writing of Rabbi Isaac Aiziq Safrin of Komarno, it is said, *inter alia*, that the wonders of the Besht were "heard from the days of the Tannaites...and a small word of his was a fountain of wisdom, a true principle for [the understanding of] all the writings of our master Isaac Luria...and he had comprehensions of the ascent of the soul, and ascent to the *Pardes*, the real comprehension of Rabbi Akiva and his companions."[18] This comparison of the Besht with the Tannaitic figures, either as wonder-workers or as mystics, is relevant. The ascent to the Pardes, the mystical orchard, is explicitly mentioned, and it seems that it was formative—at least to the Rabbi of Komarno—in understanding the extraordinary figure of the Besht. The use of *ma`ayan hokhmah* in the epistle, however, is also illuminating. This phrase is the title of several Kabbalistic books, but especially pertinent to our context is that it also designates the introduction to *Sefer Shimmushei ha-Torah*, in which the divine names and the remedies are revealed to Moses. Moreover, it appears in a treatise from Heikhalot literature, the so-called Hebrew Enoch, in which it stands for a mythical entity found in the supernal world.[19] Related phrases are found in a variety of rabbinic sources to indicate exceptional creativity.[20] However, it seems that the occurrence of *ma`ayan hokhmah* in the Besht's epistle, used in the context of the ascent on high, may reveal an affinity with late antiquity texts in which this topic is important. What is the significance of the Rabbi of Komarno's assumption that one "small word" of the Besht may serve as a clue to Lurianic Kabbalah? Again, this may be part of the exaggerated hagiography that surrounds the historical figure of the Besht. However, when comparing this description to the epistle, it seems that the divine names may be good candidates for the "small word" that is the important clue to Lurianic thought.

The power of remedies—apparently popular magical recipes—and the divine names are nothing new then. The Besht's recourse to these topics in his epistle can be viewed from a dual perspective. They could indicate an unconscious attempt by the Besht to enhance his reputation as a doctor whose magical techniques were either revealed from above or at least recommended by the highest authority. Or the Besht may have resorted to a theme found in an authoritative text, *Shimmushei Torah,* which mentions these techniques as having been revealed to no authority other than Moses. By dint of these two possibilities, the dissemination of the lore or knowledge of the Besht has eschatological significance: people will be able to heal themselves as well as to perform ascents on high as the Besht has. The reproduction of the attainment of the Besht is tantamount to redemption. Thus, we should pay attention to the content of the eschaton described here: it will consist of a change in nature, but it is human nature that will be healed, rather than a dramatic shift in history.

The healing of the body and the perfection of the soul by its ascent on high is the definition of the eschaton. Thus, it seems that Dinur's, Tishby's and more recently Mor Altschuler's emphasis on hints of historical and apocalyptic eschatology is not corroborated. Scholem's attempt to dispel the presence of eschatological content altogether, however, is also insufficient: the Messiah is addressed by the Besht, and the former indeed is imagined to offer a scheme for further historical development. This is a non-historical, non-political and non-geographical eschatology, but it is eschatology nonetheless as understood within the main parameters of the Besht's activity. The spiritual experience of the ascension and the well-being of the body achieved by magical means, according to the epistle, can be attained in the lifetime of the Besht by the very few, and the messianic time is envisaged not as the result of the advent or the activity of the redeemer but rather as an accumulative achievement of individuals. Phenomenologically speaking, this view of Messianism is reminiscent of that of Rabbi Abraham Abulafia, who believed that the dissemination of his ecstatic Kabbalah, based on combinations of letters and divine names, would enable the whole nation to reach a spiritual state, which is tantamount to a certain vision of Messianism.[21]

3. On Shamanism in the Carpathian Mountains

The origins of the Hasidic movement are related to the so-called revelation of the Besht, or the disclosure of his "real" nature. Before his revelation, he spent time in the northern part of the Carpathian Mountains. It was there, according to legend, that the Besht shifted from years of solitude to more open and intensively public activity.[22] The se-

cret mystical path known to the Besht and to his companions was kept
secret from the masses.

The techniques of the Besht at this time, according to his epistle,
were related explicitly to ascents of the soul. In the Yiddish version of
the legend that is quoted above, the Besht's utter concentration of thought
is described as being out of this world.[23] Such ecstatic or trance-like experiences were related to a certain way of life: *hitbodedut* and *hanhagah*
on the one hand and a certain type of *Yihudim* on the other.[24] The *hanhagah*, or the *regimen vitae*, of the Besht is mentioned in a book by his
acquaintance, Rabbi Meir Margoliot, as if it were an articulated issue.[25]
I propose that these mystical practices can be traced to earlier Jewish
sources, but the Besht's emphases on the ascent on high and on mystical states of consciousness deserve further consideration. The first-per-
son account of the ascent of the soul is a relatively rare phenomenon in
Jewish mysticism; a confession that contains not only the name of the
person but also the precise date is uncharacteristic of the reports on ascensions with which I am familiar before the time of the Besht.

Interestingly enough, ecstatic practices in which the soul is described as leaving the body for several hours, during which oracular
dreams were experienced, were known on the Moldavian side of the
Carpathian Mountains.[26] Though this is indubitably a very ancient
Eurasian practice (as analyzed by Carlo Ginzburg[27]), it may be relevant
for our discussion to highlight evidence concerning the practice in the
region of Bacau around the year 1648 as related by a Catholic friar,
Marcus Bandinus. This author mentions the *incantatores*, a term reminiscent of the term "incantation" used in the quote from the Besht's
epistle above.[28] Indeed, the Hebrew expression for performing an incantation for the ascent of the soul, *hashba`at `aliyyat neshamah*, is absent from all Jewish literature prior to the Besht. While ancient ecstatic
practices generally were not received positively in Christian Europe, in
this particular area alone the *incantatores* and *incantatrices* were highly
regarded and, according to Bandinus's formulations, were considered
to be similar to the *doctores subtilissimi et sanctissimi* in Italy.[29] Moreover,
ecstatic practices were not restricted to the few but were open to everyone.[30] The assumption is that this was not a Rumanian practice but one
brought from Asia by a tribe of Magyars, known as Czangos, who
stopped in the Moldavian Carpathians.[31]

Thus, less than a century before the revelation of the Besht, in the immediate vicinity of the place where the founder of Hasidism spent his time in solitude, ecstatic practices similar to his ascent to heaven were known and performed by Gentiles. These practices have nothing to do with Jewish sources but stem from Eurasian religious heritage. However, as I have pointed out in prior discussions, practices similar to those of the Besht are also apparent in earlier types of Jewish mysticism, some of which presumably were formulated in areas remote from the Eurasian zone.

What therefore is the significance of the coexistence of similar practices in practically the same period and geographical area? There is no simple answer to this question. Detailed descriptions and analyses of Jewish mystical techniques have not yet been undertaken. A preliminary hypothesis is that, though the Besht's and his contemporaries' ascents of the soul caused a resurgence of a Jewish mystical practice that had been in existence for centuries according to literary sources, this practice experienced particular impetus precisely in the Carpathian region. In other words, one aspect of nascent Hasidism—the ascent of the soul—can be attributed to the consonance between Jewish mystical traditions found in much earlier sources as well as mystical–magical practices in vogue in the geographical area from which Hasidism emerged.[32]

4. The Besht and the Eschatological Pillar

It seems that as late as the second half of the eighteenth century, the ascent on high *in spiritu* was not just the patrimony of the founder of Hasidism. This topic recurs in at least two contemporary texts from Eastern Europe. Rabbi Yehiel Mikhal, the Maggid—or the preacher—of Zlotchov, an acquaintance of the Besht, was reported to sleep only for a few reasons, one of which was to create the opportunity to ascend to the firmament.[33] This technique was known and reportedly practiced, though not very highly appreciated, by the great opponent of Hasidism, Rabbi Elijah, the Gaon of Vilnius.[34] It seems that in matters of religion, there are both changes and continuities in the emergence of similar phenomena in both the eighteenth-century Carpathian region and the Lithuanian town of Vilnius, and late antiquity Israel. In an early nineteenth-century legend describing the final teachings of the Besht, a mysterious pillar is mentioned—quite a natural topic to be discussed in a *contemplatio morti*. According to this legend, the pillar is a column that connects the lower and the higher paradises, and by means of it, souls of the dead ascend from one to the other.[35] This is no doubt a clear case of posthumous psychanodia, the Kabbalistic sources of which have been described above and which the Besht could have adopted. In some, particularly those of the late thirteenth century, the terms *no`am* and *ne`imu*, translated as "pleasantness," recur in the context of the pillar or the column. In the legend related to the Besht, he spoke about the column, addressing those present in the last hours of his life: "he described what it was like in the world of the souls, and he interpreted the order of worship. He told them to recite [the verse] 'Let the pleasantness of the Lord our God be upon us.'"[36] According to another Hasidic source authored by the Besht himself during one of the most important phases of his visionary activity, he not only saw the pillar ascended by the souls of both the living and the dead to the supernal worlds but also encountered the Messiah. In the *Epistle of the Ascent of the Soul,* in a passage already quoted above in a more extensive manner, he writes: "When I returned to the lower Paradise, I saw the souls of living and of dead persons, both of those with whom I was acquainted and of those with whom I was not acquainted...numberless, in a to-and-fro movement, ascending from one world to the other through the pillar known to adepts in esoteric matters."[37]

The Hebrew term used in the two sources related to the Besht and translated as pillar is `*Amud.* Thus, the resort to the pillar by souls of both living and dead persons in ascending to higher realms is quite obvious, and presumably the Besht imagined that he himself had done so while alive. In any case, it is clear here, as in the legend, that psychanodia is a matter of some form of hidden knowledge. Nevertheless, esoteric as it may be, this type of knowledge was available to and used by the Besht and a few of his contemporaries. During the mid-nineteenth century, there was a revival of interest in spiritual ascent. In some writings by Rabbi Isaac Judah Yehiel Safrin of Komarno, Rabbi Israel's ascents are mentioned and elaborated upon far more frequently than in the Hasidic writings of the preceding hundred years. Rabbi Israel is portrayed as attaining spiritual perfection, and he mentions, *inter alia,* "the ascents of the soul and ascents to Pardes" and "the apprehensions of Rabbi Akiva and his companions."[38] The affinity between ascent of the soul and ascent to the Merkavah or to the Pardes story is self-evident. The connection between the two is also apparent in Rabbi Safrin's book *Heikal ha-Berakhah,* in which the journey of the four who entered Pardes is described as a celestial ascent, taking place after one strips oneself of corporeality and uncleanness.[39] In comparison to the ancient discussion of the Pardes journey, in which the ascent seems to take place *in corpore*, Rabbi Safrin's account is of a spiritual experience. Moreover, according to this Hasidic master, even Moses's ascent to receive the Torah was an ascent of soul. In his voluminous *Commentary on the Zohar*, Rabbi Safrin interprets Moses's abstention from food and drink for forty days in a manner reminiscent of the description of the mid-thirteenth-century Rabbi Michael the Angel, discussed above in chapter one. The body of Moses, he states, "was thrown in the cloud with but little vitality, as it is for all those who practice ascents of the soul, such as our master Rabbi Israel the Besht, and others like him. [But] their body is thrown down like a stone for only a short hour or two, no more; however, Moses's body was thrown down for forty days and [the vitality] returned to it after forty days, and he was [again] alive."[40]

Moses was thus the incomparable master of ascents of the soul, as he sustained his mystical experience for an uncommonly long period, yet nevertheless returned to life.[41] This cataleptic understanding of Moses has been attributed explicitly to the Besht himself. Thus, even the receiving of the Torah is seen as accomplished with the help of this mystical technique, and Rabbi Isaac Safrin of Komarno himself practiced it. In his mystical diary, he confesses that: "I performed a *yihud* and linked myself with the soul of our divine master, Isaac Luria. And from this union I was overcome by sleep, and I saw several souls, until I was overwhelmed by awe and fear and trembling, as was my custom. And from this it seemed that I shall rise to greatness. And I ascended further and I saw Rabbi [Abraham] Joshua-Heschel...and I awoke."[42] This experience is closely related to that of the Besht. However, it is rare for a later mystic to confess that he seemingly employed this technique in a regular manner in order to communicate with the souls of the dead. At any rate, as late as 1845—the date of this experience—the ancient practice still was considered viable. Despite the fact that so many Kabbalists addressed the topic of the pillar as related to both the structure of the world and to the eschatological experience of the soul, none described his own experience as related to climbing or watching the pillar. From this point of view, it seems that the Besht's description of his experience represents a unique example of the interiorization and absorption of the cosmo-theological worldview of the Kabbalistic tradition. Among the Jewish mystics who resorted to the more personal use of the pillar, it is the Besht who may be described in shamanic terms, an issue to which we shall return below in much greater detail. To formulate this statement differently, if the theoretical framework was provided by the theosophical–theurgical Kabbalistic tradition, it was, to the best of my knowledge, only in Polish Hasidism that a nexus between this cosmic framework and a confession of a historically identifiable figure was established. Thus, Rabbi Shimeon bar Yohai, as he was portrayed by the medieval book of the Zohar, and the Besht, both seminal figures to the entire history of Jewish mysticism, allegedly resorted to the archaic method of ascending by means of the pillar at the center of the world in order to reach the supernal realm either while alive or post-mortem.

Due to the attenuation of the role of the theosophical components of the mystical systems of Hasidism, ecstatic techniques and mystical ideals together with magical aspects came more easily to the fore. Hasidic forms of mysticism, certainly those belonging to what I call the mystical–magical model, should be understood within the context of fluctuations occurring within the basic motifs, themes and models of Jewish mysticism as a whole. Without a more comprehensive understanding of all the mystical possibilities inherent in the literary corpora that constitute Jewish mysticism, descriptions of Hasidism as mysticism are more inclined to be historical reductions of the immediately preceding to the seemingly similar. Thus, a panoramic approach to Jewish mysticism, and especially to Hasidism, is required for a more accurate understanding of the processes related to the various encounters between models on the one hand and historical circumstances on the other.

While emphasizing the vital contributions of earlier stages of Jewish mysticism to the better elucidation of Hasidic spiritual physiognomy, we should not remain solely within the perimeters of Jewish mysticism and history but rather make comparisons with pertinent phenomena in European occultism, such as its intellectualistic propensities, and with the concrete aspects of general religious categories such as Shamanism. To paraphrase a recent definition of the Sufi philosophy of illumination, Hasidism is a unique synthesis of primordial themes and concepts, traditions as old and primal as those of the paleolithic age and as late and refined as those of Renaissance and early modern religiosity.[43]

It seems to me that by contemplating Hasidism only from the refined, namely the mystical, facet, without paying due attention to its primal, magical aspect, modern scholarship offers a unilateral and somewhat distorted picture of the latest phase of Jewish mysticism. Hasidism is a religious modality that combines both preaxial and axial traits,[44] and it seems that awareness of this synthesis is decisive to an understanding of its dissemination to the masses and its attraction for elites. To a great degree, the tzaddiq in Hasidism functions in a way that is reminiscent of the description of the shaman: "[T]he society becomes the shaman's collective patient.... [T]he shaman mediates with the sacred; he heals and is the ritual mediator in his dual sacred and social role."[45] However, though some Hasidic righteous may have been magicians, they also resorted to axial conceptualizations of religion that are indebted to Greek intellectualistic traditions and their medieval and premodern Jewish reverberations. By emphasizing the mixed phenomenological nature of Hasidism, I hope to escape the spiritualized approach to this type of religion found in scholarly writings like those of the schools of Martin Buber and Scholem, while simultaneously avoiding adherence to the apotheosis of the archaic mode found in Eliade's work. Though rural in many important ways, in its elite forms, premodern Hasidism also possesses a decisive axial dimension.

So, for example, according to an early nineteenth-century description of the early Hasidic masters found in *Be'er Moshe* by Rabbi Moshe Eliaqum Beri'ah, son of the Maggid of Kuznitz, the tzaddiq is satisfied only when he is:

> Actually annihilated out of the strength of the union with God, Blessed be He, by his dedication to God...as I have seen some of my teachers and masters...especially my teacher, the holy Rabbi, the man of God... Rabbi Meshullam Zusha, who was totally divesting himself from this world when he ascended in order to cleave to God, to such an extent that he was actually close to annihilating his existence. Thus it was necessary that he should swear an oath and donations that his soul will remain in him.[46]

Inhabitants of Kuznitz, a town in Poland, both Rabbi Moshe Beri'ah and his father were much more interested in unitive experiences than simple ascensions on high.

5. The Tzaddiq as the Present Pillar in Hasidism

The cosmic and the eschatological pillars are considered to be part of the very structure of the world, and as such, their existence is basically independent of what happens in this world. Indeed, as seen in some cases, beginning from *BT, Yumma*, in the book of Bahir and in their repercussions, there are some affinities between the human righteous and the subsistence of the world or of the status of the pillar. However, the assumption is that no specific figure in a given historical period is the pillar of the world. Human figures are symbols of divine powers that are pillars, particularly Joseph in the Zohar, but this does not mean that the authors of the Zohar thought that Joseph was the pillar during his lifetime. Eighteenth-century Hasidism added its own interpretation to the tzaddiq, however, emphasizing the utmost importance of his role in the present and to his group of followers. Less concerned with Zoharic cosmic pillars or intra-divine interpretations of the Lurianic eschatological pillar, the Hasidic masters were interested in strengthening the role played by present figures and thus applied the general descriptions of the pillar in Kabbalah to living persons.[47] This tendency is conspicuous from the first generation of Hasidic masters. Rabbi Menahem Nahum of Chernobyl, an interesting Hasidic author active in the second half of the eighteenth century, wrote that:

Our sages, blessed be their memory, said in the tractate *Ta`aniyyot*, "there is one pillar in the world, from the earth to the firmament, and they counted *tzaddiq*".... "There is one pillar in the world and it is called *tzaddiq*" because the *tzaddiq* is one because of the name of union that he unites himself with all the degrees, which are from earth to firmament, which means from the materiality, which is the aspect of *Tav*, the end of the degrees, until the firmament which is the supernal degree, the aspect of *'aleph*, and this is the reason why he is called *tzaddiq*...and he grasps heaven and earth, because he comprises all the degrees and grasps heaven and earth. And this is the reason that he is called *tzaddiq*, the foundation of the world, which is like the building that stands on its foundation. And when someone wants to elevate it, then it is elevated because of the foundation, and by its means the entire building is being elevated, because it is built on that foundation that is the *tzaddiq*, when he is linking himself to all the degrees. Then, when he ascends on high, he elevates himself together with all the degrees, like the parable of the foundation and the building.[48]

This theory recurs immediately afterwards in various formulations.[49] Though a pillar, the righteous is also an active and dynamic entity. The cosmic pillar is an allegory here; what is of particular importance is that it is interpreted as the unification of the central pillar of the building with all parts of that building. The cosmic pillar is less an Atlas-like sustaining column or that upon which the world is suspended, but more a sort of spinal column that brings together all parts of the organism. The righteous is described as the all, *kol*, in a manner that refers unmistakably to both the Bahir and its reverberation in the Zohar.[50] The holistic approach to reality as bound by the righteous is illustrated through the first and last letters of the Hebrew alphabet, the alpha and the omega, in a manner reminiscent of the vision of Christ at the beginning of the *Revelation of John*. According to Rabbi Menahem Nahum, the holism of the righteous is a matter of both comprising everything like a microcosm and uniting everything by his activity.[51] As we learn from another discussion in the same book, Rabbi Menahem Nahum draws upon the view of his teacher, presumably Rabbi Dov Baer of Medziretch, known as the Great Maggid, who seems to be the one who contrived the formula; while he attributes it to the wrong tractate in the *Gemara'*, he interprets it in a similar manner.[52] It is in this interpretation that the reference to the letters as the mode of activity of the righteous is mentioned and the holistic approach, which describes the righteous as "all," is applied.

Rabbi Menahem Nahum's use of the parable of the building and its foundation is perhaps one of the most architecturally inspired reworkings of the statements in the Hagigah and Bahir discussions. However, he is interested in neither architectural details nor their masonic significance or the paradisiacal architecture referred to by so many Kabbalists, including Luria. Rather, the Hasidic master is concerned here and in other places with placing emphasis on the role of language in the operation of the world.

Last but not least, in Rabbi Menahem Nahum's book, the tzaddiq is believed to unify and elevate not only the entire realm of existence but also souls.[53] He himself plays the role of the pillar, though there is no mention of the eschatological pillar in this book. Furthermore, the iatromantic understanding of the tzaddiq is elucidated through the description of the righteous as healer.[54] In any case, in many forms of Hasidism the ascent on high is considered part of the nature of man rather than an extraordinary or exceptional event. So, for example, we read that the Besht is very easily able to cause the ascent of his soul.[55] In Rabbi Levi Isaac of Berditchev's *Qedushat Levi*—an influential book written by an important master at the end of the eighteenth and early nineteenth centuries—we read that: "Despite the fact that man is dwelling here below, on earth, by the virtue of his deeds he merits walking all his days in the supernal worlds, especially during the Holy Sabbath, because the holiness of the Sabbath is so great that man cleaves to the supernal holiness. Thus we find that man returns to his root during Sabbath.... During Sabbath man returns to the supernal worlds in his thought, out of the great luminosity and holiness of Sabbath."[56]

That which was considered the special achievement of the Besht was accepted two generations later as the very nature of man; psychanodia was believed to be a normal experience. At the end of the quote, however, this psychanodia is transformed into a nousanodia, in line with the medieval emphasis on the adhesion of thought rather than the ascent on high. Just as psychanodia was considered an ideal to be taught to everyone in the epistle of the Besht, so too the ability to walk on high was considered a possibility open not only to mystics in Rabbi Levi Isaac's view. Rabbi Menahem Nahum also assumed that the members of his community would become part of the body of the mystical–magical Messiah during some moments in the Sabbath liturgy.

6. HASIDIC SEMANTICS

The above discussions, as well as many other modern analyses, demonstrate that neither a symbolic nor a theosophical but rather an experiential approach, dealing with spiritual life in the present, is evident in Hasidism. In some descriptions of the righteous, an active obligation is imposed on an elite that is called explicitly by the name *tzaddiqim*. Though language dealing with psychanodic and nousanodic elevation recurs in Hasidic literature, some of these expressions are nothing more than metaphorical, or what may be described as "up-words and phrases."[57]

Somewhat reminiscent of Renaissance views, such as those of Marsilio Ficino and Pico della Mirandola, in which man binds the universe, Hasidism attributes a cosmic dimension to human activity.[58] However, the Hasidic master played a greater role as a "pontific" figure in the general economy of the universe, especially in the relationship between God and his community of followers. And while the Renaissance theories of man were never translated into a social praxis, with an elite active in history that constructed a comprehensive way of life for an entire group, this is exactly what happened in Polish Hasidism. As seen above, the Besht and his followers in the Hasidic elite combined a search for personal perfection with the imparting of blessings and power to the members of his group. Thus, the architectural and geometrical *imaginaire* intended to describe the supernal realms in literatures written by and intended for elites was less appropriate for expressing the role of the elite figure in the society he created or had to sustain. The problem of cohesion became much more important, and this new function of the righteous is reflected in the perception of the pillar as something more than that of Atlas, cosmologically sustaining the world, or that which represents an intra-divine power. Rabbi Menahem Nahum's descriptions, though utilizing images that are traditional in Jewish mysticism, convey a message that is different from the Kabbalistic visions of the righteous.

While Kabbalistic literature is concerned with the two main roles, the eschatological and the cosmological, in Hasidism, the experiential dimension of the pillar function becomes much more conspicuous. The righteous is not found under this world, like Atlas, or in the upper world as a divine power, Yesod, as in theosophical Kabbalah, but rather predominantly within this world. He does not just sustain and/or nourish it, or serve as a pontific figure for the elevation of souls and prayers, but also ensures the very ontological cohesion of the universe.

7. SOME METHODOLOGICAL ISSUES RELATED TO THE BESHT'S EPISTLE

The Besht was described years ago in scholarship as a shaman.[59] The surge of archaic themes in Kabbalah since the late thirteenth century, after centuries of rabbinic creativity and immediately following the peak of Jewish philosophy represented by Maimonidean thought, invites a more general reflection on the dynamics of Judaism and on the way this faith has been portrayed in widespread accounts of the history of religion. First and foremost, what are the historical sources of this surge? As pointed out above, the concept of the cosmic pillar is detected in

Kabbalah and pre-Zohar Jewish cosmogonical sources. However, what is absent in these sources is the shamanic flight or the column as the locus of psychanodia undertaken while alive. Although I have no textual answer to it, posing this question is necessary in order to highlight the inadequacy of simplistic descriptions of Judaism as a religious phenomenon. The Jewish mystics mentioned above theoretically and sometime practically accepted shamanic themes long after the allegedly dominant historical elements of Judaism came to the fore. Following Zoharic imagery of the column on the one hand and the importance of the ascent of the soul on the other, the Besht compiled a sort of synthesis that did not simply remain a matter of interpretation but rather was necessary for the nourishment of a major spiritual enterprise. Geographically and historically removed from literary sources that provided such synthesis, the Besht was inspired to adopt them to address psychological and sociological needs, which may have differed from those that nourished the acceptance and elaboration of the same themes in late thirteenth-century Spain.

Let us now turn to some methodological questions related to the epistle quoted above. It is a rather variegated and multifaceted document, and its interpretation involves many aspects, including its versions, its historicity—namely whether or not it was written by the Besht—and its reliability.[60] I would like to focus here on the affinity of the passages quoted above to the apocalyptic genre. In his definition of the latter, John J. Collins asserts that: "Apocalypse is a genre of revelatory literature with a narrative framework, in which a revelation is mediated by an otherworldly being to a human recipient, disclosing a transcendental reality which is both temporal, insofar as it envisages eschatological salvation, and spatial insofar as it involves another, supernatural world."[61] The Messiah is both a mediating and a revelatory being who discloses in the celestial paradise the secrets of the end. From this point of view, the epistle of the Besht meets the parameters proposed by Collins. However, as mentioned above, salvation in our case is not realized on a precisely given date on which the advent of the redeemer occurs but is an evolving state during which both the mystical ascents of the soul and the magical aspects of the mystical–magical model mentioned above are disseminated to larger audiences. "Eschatological salvation" here is the gradual implementation of the two aspects of this model. Thus, historical as the concern of the Besht may be, it is neither eschatological in the national, geographical or temporal sense of finding a precise date for the advent of the Messiah nor totally divorced from history, as some forms of mysticism, such as the Hindu case, may be. His ascent is much more in the vein of Heikhalot literature, where a conversation with a supernal power concerns the plight of the community or its leaders.

Pointing out either the literary or the conceptual affinities between the ancient Jewish texts and the Hasidic passage in my opinion should be more than a philological enterprise to pinpoint the precise source of the phrases in a certain text. If the above affinities are meaningful, this nexus may indicate that philological links represent a more phenomenological similarity. The ascent on high as portrayed by the Besht may owe much not only to medieval and Renaissance Jewish texts but also to ancient ones. What are the implications of such a claim to the more general picture of Jewish mysticism? Its historical organization, what I propose calling "external history," is just one way to approach the treatment of the mystical material.[62] While suggesting the importance of the immediate environment of the Carpathian Mountains, I do not intend to obliterate the influence of earlier Jewish traditions. In fact, I propose that, since the Middle Ages, all available accounts dealing with living ascents of the soul, as adduced in chapter one and the present analysis, originate with Ashkenazi figures active in France, Germany and Eastern Europe. Rabbi Isaac Luria was of Ashkenazi descent. Some early Ashkenazi figures propagated the ascensional elements found in Heikhalot literature, which was also the case of the Besht.[63] The *Epistle of the Ascent of the Soul*, therefore, may be described as an encounter between two different traditions: the ancient Jewish traditions and shamanic elements lingering in the Carpathians. In the next chapter, we will turn to another tradition that was in vogue among Spanish elites in the Middle Ages that had an impact on some Renaissance views.

Notes

1. See, for example, the passage of Yaakow Kaidaner, *Sippurim Nora'im* (in Hebrew), ed. Gedalyah Nigal (Jerusalem: Carmel, 1992), pp. 36–37. On the figure of the Besht, see Moshe Rosman, *Founder of Hasidism: A Quest for the Historical Ba`al Shem Tov* (Berkeley, Los Angeles, London: California University Press, 1996); and Immanuel Etkes, *Ba`al Hashem, The Besht: Magic, Mysticism, Leadership* (in Hebrew) (Jerusalem: The Zalman Shazar Center, 2000).

2. See Moshe Idel, *Hasidism: Between Ecstasy and Magic* (Albany: State University of New York Press, 1995), pp. 171–76.

3. Adduced from a manuscript of Rabbi Isaac Aizik Safrin of Komarno in Rabbi Shimeon Menahem Mendel's collection, *Ba`al Shem Tov* (Lodge, 1938), vol. I, p. 18. "Mineral" in Hebrew is *Domem*. See also Moshe Idel, *Kabbalah: New Perspectives* (New Haven: Yale University Press, 1988), p. 95, where a Hasidic description of Moses in a cataleptic situation is analyzed. "The Faithful Shepherd" refers to Rabbi Shimeon bar Yohai, the alleged author of the Zohar, as he was described in the later layers of this book entitled *Ra`aya Meheimna* and *Tiqqunei Zohar*.

4. This is the case at least in the Babylonian Talmudic text in *Hagigah*, fol. 15b.

5. See the text printed in Yehudah Even Shmuel, *Midreshei Ge'ulah* (Jerusalem: Mossad Bialik-Massada, 1954), p. 73.

6. I have had the opportunity to deal with this succinctly elsewhere; see Moshe Idel; *Kabbalah: New Perspectives*, p. 94; Ioan P. Couliano, *Out of this World: Otherworldly Journeys from Gilgamesh to Albert Einstein* (Boston and London: Shambhala, 1991), p. 186; Idel, *Hasidism*, pp. 79–80; and idem, *Messianic Mystics*, (New Haven: Yale University Press, 1998), pp. 213–20. This, however, is an appropriate occasion to address this passage from a much broader perspective and to discuss issues that I did not engage in my early analyses.

7. See the version printed at the end of J. Mondshine, ed., *Shivehei ha-Besht*, Koretz version, pp. 235–36. "My teacher and master" plausibly refers to Ahijah the Shilonite. On this prophet as a mystical mentor, see Yehuda Liebes, "The Messiah of the Zohar" (in Hebrew), in *The Messianic Idea in Israel*, ed. S. Reem (Jerusalem: Israel Academy of Science and Humanities, 1982), p. 113, n. 114; and Jonathan Meir, "Ahijah the Shilonite as the Spiritual Guide of the Ba`al Shem Tov" (in Hebrew), *Mishlav* 30 (1997): pp. 33–49. "Degree after degree" is commonplace in Hasidic literature when describing the ascent from one rank to another. See chapter 1, n. 105.

8. Mondshine, *Shivehei ha-Besht*, p. 237.

9. See Gershom Scholem, *Origins of the Kabbalah*, ed. R. Z. J. Werblowsky, trans. A. Arkush (Philadelphia: Jewish Publishing Society and Princeton University Press, 1987), pp. 240–41.

10. See Moshe Idel, *Messianic Mystics*, pp. 21, 45, 82–84, 213, 220, 246 and 289.

11. See Joshua Mondshine, ed., *Sefer Migdal `Oz* (Kevar Habad: Makhon Lubawitch, 1980), p. 124. "They" who will be able to perform ascents of the soul refers to the people of Israel. "The shells will be abolished" is a Lurianic description of the time of the redemption. "My contemporaries" is translated from *'Anshei giliy*. This term is understood in a restrictive sense as the members of the circle of the Besht by Emanuel Etkes, "Hasidism as a Movement: The First Stage," in *Hasidism: Continuity or Innovation?*, ed. Bezalel Safran (Cambridge: Harvard University Press, 1988), p. 17. This understanding is reinforced by a similar situation related by the Besht. In the Yiddish version of the *Praises of the Besht*, he asks his *hechste leit*, the highest among his people, to keep his special mystical practice secret as

long as he is alive. See Abraham Ya`ari, "Two Basic Editions of *Shivhei ha-Besht*" (in Hebrew), *Qiryat Sefer* 39 (1964): p. 552. The Yiddish version uses a Hebrew term for mystical practice, *hanhagah*. For more on this term, see below, n. 23. In the passage printed by Mondshine and translated here, the phrase *'Anshei giliy* does not appear, but *'Anshei seggulah*, or "eminent people," is used instead. See, however, the remark of Mondshine, *Migdal 'Oz*, p. 124, n. 10.

12. Moshe Idel, "Adam and Enoch According to St. Ephrem the Syrian," *Kabbalah* 6 (2001): pp. 183–205; and idem, "Enoch is Metatron," *Immanuel* 24/25 (1990): pp. 220–40.

13. Moshe Idel, "Enoch, the Mystical Cobbler" (in Hebrew), *Kabbalah* 5 (2000): pp. 265–86.

14. See Ben-Zion Dinur, *Be-Mifneh ha-Dorot* (in Hebrew) (Jerusalem: Bialik Institute, 1955), pp. 181–84; Isaiah Tishby, *Studies in Kabbalah and Its Branches* (in Hebrew) (Jerusalem: Magnes Press, 1993), vol. II, pp. 503–07; and Gershom Scholem, *The Messianic Idea in Israel* (New York: Schocken Books, 1972), pp. 182–84. On Scholem's side, see R. J. Z. Werblowsky, "Mysticism and messianism: The case of Hasidism," in *Man and His Salvation: Essays in Memory of S. G. F. Brandon*, eds. Eric J. Sharpe and John R. Hinnells (Manchester: Manchester University Press, 1973), pp. 305–14; and Rivka Schatz Uffenheimer, *Hasidism as Mysticism: Quietistic Elements in Eighteenth-Century Hasidic Thought*, trans. Jonathan Chipman (Princeton: Princeton University Press; Jerusalem: The Magnes Press, 1993). The neutralization of Messianism in Hasidism has already been advocated implicitly by Martin Buber's vision of Hasidism. For another approach to the topic, see Idel, *Messianic Mystics*, pp. 212–47. For more on this polemic, see also D. Ben Amos and J. R. Mintz, trans., *In Praise of the Baal Shem Tov* (London: Aronson, Northvale, 1993), p. 57; Mendel Piekarz, *Studies in Braslav Hasidism* (in Hebrew) (Jerusalem: Bialik Institute, 1972), p. 66; Liebes, "The Messiah of the Zohar," pp. 113–14; Etkes, "Hasidism as a Movement," pp. 16–17; Steven Katz, "Models, Modeling and Mystical Training," *Religion* 12 (1982): p. 259; Abraham Rubinstein, "The Mentor of the Besht and the Writings from which He Studied" (in Hebrew), *Tarbiz* 48 (1978–79): pp. 146–58; Gedaliah Nigal, *Magic, Mysticism and Hasidism* (in Hebrew) (Tel Aviv: Y. Golan, 1992), p. 30; and, more recently, Mor Altshuler, *The Messianic Secret of Hasidism* (in Hebrew) (Haifa: Haifa University Press, 2002), pp. 23–29.

15. Ioan P. Couliano, *Experiences de l'extase: Extase, ascension et recit visionaire de l'Hellenisme au Moyen Age* (Paris: Payot, 1984), pp. 25–43; and idem, *Out of this World*, pp. 114–53. On the assumption that the iatromant is a type found in the Mediterranean area and includes biblical figures like Elijah and Elisha, see ibid., p. 133, following Cristiano Grotanelli.

16. See the document printed and analyzed by Murray J. Rosman, "Miedzyboz and Rabbi Israel Baal Shem Tov," in *Essential Papers on Hasidism*, ed. G. D. Hundert (New York: University of New York Press, 1991), p. 217.

17. Rabbi Yo'el ben Naftali Katz, *Mif alot 'Elohim* (Zolkiew, 1865), no pagination, under the rubric *Kokhavim*.

18. Rabbi Isaac Aiziq Safrin of Komarno, *Notzer Hesed* (Jerusalem, 1982), p. 131. "Fountain of wisdom" is translated from *Ma`ayan hokhmah*.

19. See Ms. Oxford-Bodleiana 1748, fol. 28a; and Hugo Odeberg's edition of *3 Enoch or the Hebrew Book of Enoch*, reprinted (New York: Ktav, 1973), p. 16, where the "well of all the secrets of the Torah and the secrets of the wisdom" is mentioned. The history of the supernal well of wisdom from early Qumran [Dead Sea] literature to modern Judaism still awaits extensive analysis.

20. See Alon Goshen Gottstein, "Rabbi Eleazar ben `Arakh: Symbol and Reality," in *Jews and Judaism during the Period of the Second Temple, of the Mishnah and of the Talmud* (in Hebrew), eds. A. Offenheimer, I. Gafni, and M. Stern (Jerusalem: Zalman Shazar Center, 1993), pp. 173–97.

21. See Idel, *Messianic Mystics*, pp. 65–77.

22. See Shimeon Dubnov, *The History of Hasidism* (in Hebrew) (Tel Aviv: Devir, 1967), p. 46.

23. See Rosman, *Founder of Hasidism*, pp. 191, 193–94 and 205–08.

24. Idel, *Hasidism*, p. 163.

25. Rabbi Meir Margoliot, *Sod Yakhin u-Vo`az* (Jerusalem, 1990), p. 41; see also the additions to *Keter Shem Tov*, fols. 113a–114b. An interesting passage, printed in the name of Rabbi Aharon of Zhitomir, an early nineteenth-century Hasidic master, in Rabbi Yehoshu`a Abraham ben Yisrael's *Ge'ulat Yisrael* (Amsterdam, 1821), fol. 17c, deals with some of the elements mentioned above as part of an allegedly secret tradition stemming from Ahijah the Shilonite and transmitted to the Besht, then to the Great Maggid and Rabbi Levi Isaac of Berditchev. See also Idel, *Hasidism*, pp. 176–77.

26. See Mircea Eliade, *Zalmoxis: The Vanishing God*, trans. W. R. Trask (Chicago: The University of Chicago Press, 1972), pp. 191–94. It should be mentioned that these *incantatores* are described as if dead for several hours, after which they return to their senses in a manner reminiscent of the description of Rabbi Michael the Angel discussed in chapter 1 section 2 and below, n. 40.

27. Carlo Ginsburg, *Ecstasies: Deciphering the Witches' Sabbat*, trans. Raymond Rosenthal (New York: Pantheon, 1991); see also Coulianu, *Out of this World*, pp. 47–49.

28. V. A. Ureche, *Codex Bandinus: Memoriu asupra scrierei lui Bandinus dela 1646* (Bucharest: Analele Academiei Romane, 1895), pp. 154 and clvii–clviii. This passage is referred to by Eliade, *Zalmoxis*, pp. 191–94; and Ginzburg, *Ecstasies*, pp. 188, 189, 194 and 199.

29. Eliade, *Zalmoxis*, pp. 191–92. According to Eliade, the phenomenon of incantatores is unknown in Romania outside the Moldavian Carpathians. See ibid., p. 194.

30. Ibid., pp. 191 and 193.

31. Ibid., p. 194.

32. I attribute the emergence not of Hasidism as a movement but only of the emphasis on the ascent on high to this consonance.

33. See, in the collection of material related to Rabbi Yehiel Mikhal compiled later, *Mayyim Rabim* (Brooklyn: Nehmad, 1979), p. 140. This statement reinforces the nexus between night and the ascent of the soul, an affinity that we have seen in the context of the Zoharic material. The Besht himself has been attributed an oneiric technique of answering questions. See Gershom Scholem, "Two Early Testimonies on Groups of Hasidim and the Besht" (in Hebrew), in *The Jacob Nahum ha-Levi Epstein Festschrift* (Jerusalem: The Magnes Press, 1949), p. 240, n. 40; and Dubnov, *History of Hasidism*, p. 485. Compare, however, to the view of Haviva Pedaya, "The Baal Shem Tov, Rabbi Jacob Joseph of Polonoye and the Great Maggid" (in Hebrew), *Daat* 45 (2000): p. 53, n. 114, who claims that there is no evidence for the nexus between the ascent of the soul and sleep or dreams.

34. See Rabbi Hayyim of Volozhin's introduction to his master's *Commentary on Sifra' di-Tzeni'uta'* (Vilna, 1891), translated in R.J. Zwi Werblowsky, *Joseph Karo: Lawyer and Mystic* (Philadelphia: Jewish Publication Society, 1977), pp. 311–16.

35. See Ben-Amos and Mintz, *In Praise of the Baal Shem Tov*, p. 257.

36. Ibid. The quote is Psalms 90:17.

37. Mondshein, *Shivehei ha-Besht*, p. 237.

38. Rabbi Isaac Aiziq Safrin of Komarno, *Notzer Hesed*, p. 131.

39. See *Heikhal ha-Berakhah* I, fol. 31a.

40. *Zohar Hai* 3, fol. 129d. See also n. 25. Compare Exodus 24:18 and the Lurianic view of Moses's ascent adduced by Gershom Scholem, *Sabbatai Sevi, the Mystical Messiah*, trans. R. J. Z. Werblowsky (Princeton: Princeton University Press, 1973), p. 53. This is similar to cataleptic symptoms related in some cases to iatromants. See Couliano, *Out of This World*, p. 132. For experiences reminiscent of death in Shamanism, see Eliade, *Shamanism*, pp. 33, 64, 214–15 and 288; and Morton Smith, *Clement of Alexandria and A Secret Gospel of Mark* (Cambridge: Harvard University Press, 1973), pp. 242–43.

41. See Philo's allegorization of Moses as the soul ascending to heaven as analyzed by Allan Segal, "Heavenly Ascent in Hellenic Judaism, Early Christianity, and Their Environment," *Aufstieg und Niedergang der romischen Welt*, II, Principat, vol. 23, 2 (Berlin: Gruyter, 1980), p. 1358.

42. Rabbi Isaac Safrin of Komarno, *Megillat Setarim*, ed. Naftali ben Menahem (Jerusalem: Mossad ha-Rav Kook, 1944), pp. 15–16; and Morris M. Faierstein, ed., trans. and intro., *Jewish Mystical Autobiographies: Book of Vision and Book of Secrets* (New York: Paulist Press, 1999), pp. 281–82. Being "overcome by sleep" is again an indication that the practice took place at night. See also Hayyim's introduction to *Commentary on Sifra' di-Tzeni'uta'*.

43. See Hossein Ziai, "Beyond Philosophy: Suhrawardi's Illuminationist Path to Wisdom," in *Myth and Philosophy*, eds. F. E. Reynolds and D. Tracy (Albany: State University of New York Press, 1990), p. 220.

44. See the series of studies edited by Shmuel N. Eisenstadt, *The Origin and Diversity of Axial Age Civilizations* (Albany: State University of New York Press, 1986); and Ewert H. Cousins, *The Christ of the 21th Century* (Rock-

port: Element, 1992), who speaks about a second axial period in the future that will comprise the two different forms of religiosity.

45. Compare to Bartolome, quoted in Lawrence Sullivan, *Icanchu's Drum* (New York: MacMillan, 1988), p. 422. See also Gustav Mensching's interesting remark on the relationship between magic and communal life as part of a coherent vision of reality in his *Structures and Patterns of Religion*, trans. H. F. Klimkeit and V. Srinivara Sarma (Delhi: Banarsidass, 1976), p. 10.

46. Rabbi Qalonimus Qalman Epstein of Cracow, *Ma'or va-Shemesh* (Warsaw, 1902), IV, fol. 8. This story also recurs in Rabbi Nathan Neta` ha-Kohen of Kalbiel, *Sefer Botzina' Qaddisha'* (Brooklyn, 1984), fol. 12b. Compare also the description of the ecstatic state by Rabbi Moshe Eliaqum's father, the famous Rabbi Israel, the Maggid of Kuznitz, in his son's *Da`at Moshe*, (Jerusalem, 1987), fol. 73a. For the ecstatic proclivities of Rabbi Meshullam Zusha of Hanipoli, see also the stories about him in, for example, Martin Buber, *Tales of Hasidim: The Early Masters*, trans. Olga Marx (New York: Schocken Books, 1964), pp. 236, 243, 249 and 252. "Close to annihilating his existence" is translated from *Qarov lehitbattel bi-metziy'ut*. This phrase also occurs in *Be'er Moshe* (Tel Aviv, 1944), fols. 9b and 85c. See also Rabbi Qalonimus Qalman Epstein of Cracow, *Ma'or va-Shemesh* (Warsaw, 1902), IV, fols. 25d–26a.

47. The scholarly literature on the concept of tzaddiq in Hasidism is vast. In English see, especially, Gershom Scholem, *On the Mystical Shape of the Godhead* (New York: Schocken Books, 1991), pp. 120–39; Arthur Green, "The Zaddiq as Axis Mundi in Later Judaism," *Journal of the American Academy of Religion* XLV:3 (1977): pp. 327–47; idem, "Typologies of Leadership and the Hasidic Zaddiq," in *Jewish Spirituality*, ed. Arthur Green (New York: Crossroad, 1987), vol. II, pp. 127–56; Ada Rapoport-Albert, "God and the Zaddik as the two Focal Points of Hasidic Worship," *History of Religions* 18 (1979), pp. 296–325; Joel Orent, "The Transcendent Person," *Judaism* 9 (1960), pp. 235–52; and Idel, *Hasidism*, pp. 189–206.

48. Rabbi Menahem Nahum of Chernobyl, *Me'or `Einayyim* (Jerusalem, 1960), pp. 10–11. The first quote seems to be a mistake; I am unfamiliar of any other such formulation in Rabbinic sources. It seems that the phrase is influenced by *Sefer ha-Bahir*. Elsewhere, the Hasidic author demonstrates familiarity with the Hagigah statement, which he quotes in a manner close to this citation. See the discussion on this issue below. The tzaddiq as foundation of the world appears as early as *Zohar* II, fol. 116a.

49. Rabbi Menahem Nahum, *Me'or `Einayyim*, pp. 11–12. See also Scholem, *On the Mystical Shape*, pp. 134–36.

50. See chapter 2, n. 28, and *Zohar* I, fol. 17a; II, fol. 116a.

51. Nahum, *Me'or `Einayyim*, p. 248.

52. Ibid., p. 248.

53. Ibid., pp. 105–06 and 149.

54. See the text translated in Arthur. I. Green, *Menahem Nahum of Chernobyl: Upright Practices, The Light of Eyes* (New York: The Paulist Press, 1982), pp. 156–57.

55. See the manuscript text of Rabbi Isaac Aiziq of Komarno, printed in *Ba`al Shem Tov* I, pp. 17–18.
56. Rabbi Levi Isaac of Berditchev, *Qedushat Levi* (Jerusalem, 1993), Bereshit, fol. 5a.
57. See the discussion of Marganitha Laski, *Ecstasy in Secular and Religious Experience* (Los Angeles: Jeremy P. Tarcher, 1990), p. 496. For more on ascensional language, see Gilbert Durand, *Les structures anthropologiques de l'imaginaire* (Paris: Dunod, 1992), pp. 138–62. For examples of such phrases, see Idel, *Hasidism*, p. 117; and Rachel Elior, *The Paradoxical Ascent to God*, trans. Jeffrey Green (Albany: State University of New York Press, 1993).
58. For some Arabic and Jewish medieval antecedents of the Renaissance visions of man, see Moshe Idel, "The Anthropology of Yohanan Alemanno: Sources and Influences," in *Topoi* 7 (1988): p. 201–10 and in *Annali di storia dell'esegesi* 7 (1990): pp. 93–112.
59. See Idel, *Hasidism*, pp. 75, 214, 218, 225, and 289, n. 185; and Rosman, *Founder of Hasidism*, pp. 13–14.
60. On the versions of the epistle, see Rosman, *Founder of Hasidism*, pp. 97–113; and Etkes, *Ba`al Hashem*, pp. 292–309.
61. See J. J. Collins, "Introduction: Toward the Morphology of a Genre," in *Apocalypse: The Morphology of a Genre*, ed. J. J. Collins, *Semeia* 14 (1979), p. 9; and Ioan P. Couliano, *Psychanodia I: A Survey of the Evidence Concerning the Ascension of the Soul and its Relevance* (Leiden: Brill, 1983), p. 5.
62. Idel, *Kabbalah: New Perspectives*, p. XIII.
63. For my assumption that the Ashkenazi traditions were a conduit for mystical techniques, see Idel, *Kabbalah: New Perspectives*, pp. 102–03.

CHAPTER 5

The Neoplatonic Path for Dead Souls: Medieval Philosophy, Kabbalah and Renaissance

1. THE UNIVERSAL SOUL AND MEDIAN LINE IN ARABIC TEXTS

In this chapter, another image for the manner in which pure souls ascend on high posthumously will be explored as elucidated in some Arabic sources and then in Kabbalah. An important study by Alexander Altmann serves as the basis for this analysis. Most importantly, discussions in additional sources described here will be compared to the concept of the median pillar.

The Kabbalistic schools that I refer to as theosophical–theurgical, the main representation of which is the book of the Zohar, in many cases adopted architectural strategies to describe the divine system. Geometrical images also recur in these writings, particularly the circle and the center. Others depict the emergence of the world from a point that becomes a line, a plane or a space.[1] Finally, the chain of being, the rungs of which represent either the entire range of or, according to many Kabbalists, only the sefirotic system of reality also emerges.[2] An issue that cannot be dealt with here is if these images are metaphors or if they convey something fundamental to understanding the specificity of a type of theology.

In the material previously discussed in this study, there is little reticence about using architectural, sexual or geometrical imagery, but this is not the case in medieval philosophical theologies. Medieval thinkers adopted belief systems that envisioned the divine reality as spiritual, and images are scant and cautious in their works. Hence, great dissonance occurs between the majority of Kabbalistic theosophies on the one hand and philosophical and minority Kabbalistic theologies on the other. The dominant status of the latter demonstrates the attempt to create a synthesis with the former, meaning that theosophical discussions also resort to images, applying a metaphorical approach.[3] In philosophical discourses, images are used when their appropriateness is strongly qualified; they often relate to scientific models or to the *imagi-*

naire of the sacred scriptures of the religion under scrutiny by the philosopher. Such interaction between philosophy and scriptural religion took place in all three major monotheistic religions, but this broad topic is beyond our scope here. Following the lead of Altmann's important study,[4] we shall examine the interactions between the biblical image of the ladder observed by Jacob in his Bethel dream and philosophical cosmologies. My assumption is that Neoplatonic discussions in which a ladder is mentioned left some vestiges on Kabbalistic writings and on later developments in Renaissance thought.

The philosophical concept that fulfills the connective function in Neoplatonic cosmology is the universal or cosmic soul.[5] After the emergence of the cosmic intellect, the universal soul emanates nature, or the visible reality, and mediates between the intellectual and the corporeal worlds. Particular human souls are simply parts of the universal soul, extensions that are one with the cosmic soul. As such, human souls may return to their supernal source. Thus, the universal soul is not just a celestial transcendental entity but possesses immanence within the corporeal world. Detached neither from the universal intellect nor from nature and the corporeal world, the universal soul serves as the intermediary emanation between the two and is especially relevant to the events taking place in this world. In a discussion of Plotin, the ascent of the body by its contact with the soul is described as being "ennobled and raised in the scale of being as made participant in life."[6]

One of the most influential sources for a Muslim appropriation of this view is found in the Ismailiyah collection of epistles entitled *Ihwan al-Safa*, the Epistle of the Sincere Brethern:

> We have explained in one of our epistles that the forces of the Universal Soul [*al-nafs al-kuliya*], when coming-to-be, immediately penetrate to the bottom of the bodies from the highest level of the [all-] encompassing sphere down to the center of the earth. Having penetrated the spheres, the stars, the elements [*al-arkan*] and places of birth, and having reached the center of the earth as the utmost extension of their limit and as their farthest extreme, they then turn in reverse direction toward the [all-] encompassing [sphere], and this is the "Ascent" [*al-mi`raj*] and the "Arousing" [*al-ba`th*] and the great "Resurrection" [*al-qiyama*]. Consider now, my brother, how thy soul should depart from this world to that place, for it is one of those forces that were dispersed from the Universal Soul, which

penetrates the world. It had already reached the center [of the earth] and had departed from, and escaped, existence in minerals, plants and animals. It had already passed the ill-directed path [*al-sirat al-mankus*] and the crooked path [*al-sirat al-Muqawwas*] but is now on the straight path [*sirat muqawwas*], the last of the grades of hell, that is in the form of humanity. Once it has safely passed this [road], it enters paradise by one of its portals, that is [it enters] the angelic form which thou acquires by pious acts beautiful qualities of character, sound opinions, and true gnosis.[7]

Three sets of imagery are formative in this passage: (1) the geometrical, which serves the (2) ascensional, of Neoplatonic extraction, which represents the (3) spiritual interpretation of the traditional Muslim terminology of "paradise," "ascent" and "straight line." Muslim religious terminology is conspicuous and receives its meaning from cosmology as shaped in pagan Neoplatonism. In this context, the concept of ascent, so important in Neoplatonism, is imposed on the Muslim concept of the ascent of Muhammad. However, it is no longer the mythical soar of the founder of religion that is involved here but the general ascent of righteous souls from one level of reality to another. This ascent is understood in relative terms: any elevation metaphorically represents an entrance to a certain type of paradise. Elsewhere in the same epistle it is said that: "The paradise of the vegetative soul is the form of animality; the paradise of the animal soul is the form of humanity; and the paradise of the soul of the human form is the angelic form.... And the 'Arousing' is the alerting [*intibadh*] of the souls from the sleep of indifference and the slumber of ignorance.... And the 'Resurrection' is the rising of the soul from its grave which is the body."[8]

In another passage from the epistle, the relationship between the universal soul and the corporeal world is described as follows: "This Universal Soul is the spirit of the world as we have exposed it in the treatise where we said that the world is a great man. Nature is the act of this Universal Soul. The four elements are the matter, which serve as its support. The spheres and the stars are like its organs, and the minerals, plants and animals are the objects which it makes to move."[9] What is pertinent to our subsequent discussion is the distinction found here between the universal soul and nature, which is part of classical Neoplatonic cosmology.

As pointed out by Altmann, these passages influenced another

Neoplatonic treatise, a book entitled *Kitab al-Hada'iq*, the Book of the Imaginary Circles, by Ibn al-Sid al-Batalyawsi, an Andalusian Muslim thinker (1052– 1127). This book was translated at least three times into Hebrew and substantially influenced Jewish medieval and Renaissance thought, which will be discussed below.[10] Describing the universal soul, al-Batalyawsi wrote:

> The rank [*martaba*] of this Soul, according to the philosophers who admit it, is below the horizon ['*ufq*] of the Agent Intellect, and the Intellect encompasses it on all its sides, and it [the Universal Soul] encompasses the globe of the spheres. It has, according to what they assume, two circles [*da'iratani*] and a straight line [*khatt mustaqim*], and the first circle is contiguous with the [all-] encompassing sphere, the latter being its [the Universal Soul's] supernal limit. The second circle is the lowest limit, and its place is the center of the earth. This is an approximate way of speaking [*taqrib*], for intelligible substances cannot be described by the attributes of place and the six directions. They [the philosophers who admit the existence of the Universal Soul] hold that between its supernal limit and its lowest limit there is a line [*khatt*] that connects [the two circles], which they call "the ladder of the ascensions" [*sullam al-ma'arij*]. It causes [divine] inspiration to reach pure individual souls, and on it descend [the angels] and ascend the purified spirits to the supernal world. They [the philosophers] discourse on it [the Universal Soul] at length. We have, however, limited ourselves to this resume, since our purpose in this book is different from theirs.[11]

It seems that the Arabic thinker distinguishes between "pure individual souls," which receive inspiration while they are alive as the result of a descent but are found here below, and the "purified spirits" who enter the world of spirituality after death. This distinction is new with al-Batalyawsi; his source, the *Epistles of Ikhwan al-Safa*, mentions only the purified spirits of the dead. While the descending vector deals with the living *perfecti*, the ascending one deals with the deceased. No doubt, the Neoplatonic concepts of *reversio* and *processio* are imposed on the ascent of Muhammad and the resurrection of the body, and prophesy is interpreted in terms of the Neoplatonic *processio*.

The use of geometrical metaphors is important. The number of concentric circles depends upon how many intellectual circles there are:

ten, corresponding to the ten separate intellects, plus two; or three—the intellectual, the spiritual and the corporeal. This picture is similar to a widespread image in the Middle Ages: the concentric spheres that have the earth as their center. Another geometrical image is added to this picture, however; between the centers of the intellectual and the corporeal circles, a straight line is found that serves as the trajectory for the ascent of the soul and the descent of inspiration. I believe that the concentric circles are understood not as existing on a flat horizon, but as possessing a form of hierarchy, and that the line represents not a horizontal but rather a vertical image. This spatial reading of the geometrical picture is strengthened by the mention of the six dimensions. The line presumably is not identical to the universal soul but is found in its very middle. This vertical reading is necessary due to the occurrence of both the term "ascent" and the Qur'anic image of the ladder.

The geometrical line of the metaphor represents the way in which living persons behave in a straight manner in accordance with the Qur'anic imperative. Given the existence of the expression *sirat al-mustaqim* in the Qur'an, which has an ethical meaning, al-Batalyawsi sought a geometrical figure that would combine a specific manner of behavior and retribution by means of ascending to the celestial world, the latter imagined within the framework of a Neoplatonic structure. The meaning of this line may be connected with an assumption widespread in Neoplatonism that the individual soul is not separated from the universal one, but remains connected to it.[12]

The strong Neoplatonic proclivities of this treatise, the author notwithstanding, also are influenced by medieval Neoaristotelian notions, the most conspicuous of which is the agent intellect as the last of the ten separate intellects. Discussions about the soul, important as they may be, are sublated from the philosophical point of view by the emphasis on the attainments of the human intellect.[13]

2. THE MEDIAN LINE IN KABBALAH

Al-Batalyawsi's conical picture of two circles and a connecting line is reminiscent of the inter-paradisiacal descriptions of the pillar that begins from a lower center and arrives at a higher center. This seems to be a simple coincidence; it is difficult to prove any direct impact by the Muslim thinker on the Zohar. Much more plausible, however, is the possibility that the metaphysical view of the straight line influenced some thirteenth- and fourteenth-century Kabbalists. Rabbi Moses de Leon and, earlier, Nahmanides envisioned the median line, *ha-qav ha-'emtza`y*, as identical to the sefirah of Tiferet.[14] In various descriptions of the way in which this divine power operates, it emerges either as the center of a circle, the circumference of which is comprised of the other six lower sefirot, or as the middle of a line. The median line consists of the sefirot that are believed to be the center of the sefirotic realm divided among the left, center and right pillars or lines. These divine powers are Malkhut, Yesod and Keter, to which other sefirot are sometimes added: Binah, Hokhmah and, more rarely, Da`at.

Nahmanides's contemporary and perhaps compatriot, Rabbi Joseph ben Shmuel, understood the meaning of the median lines as pointing to the line that emerges from Keter and ends in the last sefirah in a manner reminiscent of David Neumark's vision of the median pillar.[15] Rabbi Jacob ben Sheshet uses the term *qav ha-mishor* in a similar manner,[16] while his contemporary Rabbi Azriel of Gerona resorts to the phrase *qav ha-yosher*.[17] Rabbi Bahya ben Asher, following Nahmanides as he does in many other cases, equates the term "median line" to Tiferet.[18] Elsewhere, however, the median line is identified with Joseph and thus to Yesod.[19] While most of Rabbi Bahya's discussions deal with descending creative moments, it is possible to find in at least one case a view according to which souls ascend upward within the sefirotic system by means of the median line.[20]

Early Kabbalistic discussions of the median line are much more theosophical; the "practical" or experiential implications of its existence are not elaborated. In other words, the median line is not projected on historical or present figures. In the last decades of the thirteenth century, however, a change is discerned in the way in which the Kabbalists treated this topic. As pointed out by Altmann, Rabbi de Leon's treatise *She'elot u-Teshuvot* contains the following appropriation of al-Batalyawsi's view:

> This is the mystical meaning thereof: Even as Jacob broke down the fence of those oppressive confines and ascended by way of the ladder in a straight line [*ve-`alah derekh ha-sullam be-qav ha-mishor*]...so did his son, Joseph the Righteous.... Thus the Father and his Son *waw* and the outdrawing [*meshekh*] of the *waw* [the *waw* itself being the symbol of the sefirah *Tif'eret*] [Jacob] and its "outdrawing" or direct emanation in a straight line being the symbol of the *sefirah Yesod*

[Joseph] ascended [`alah] and attached themselves by way of the straight line [`al derekh qav ha-yashar], the "middle bar" [ha-beriah ha-tikhon], to [the highest sefirah called] Supernal Crown [Keter `Elyon], after their souls had departed and when they betook themselves to the eternal life [le-hayyei `ad].[21]

As proposed by Altmann, the Muslim thinker may indeed have influenced Rabbi de Leon's view. Terminologically speaking, Rabbi de Leon no doubt drew on one of the translations of the *Book of Imaginary Circles*. However, an important shift from the original conceptual scheme occurs. A Neoplatonic thinker, al-Batalyawsi allows the posthumous ascent of the soul to the cosmic or universal soul to reach no higher than the agent intellect. Here, as pointed out by Altmann, the soul ascends to the highest level in the sefirotic realm, according to Rabbi de Leon. [22] Moreover, I believe that the descriptions of both Jacob and Joseph refer to living persons and not to the souls of deceased righteous that ascend on high. In any case, Rabbi de Leon's work provides the first instance of the conceptual union of Jacob's ladder with the straight line, unlike the Muslim understanding of the ladder as that of Muhammad.

What is most relevant is the discrepancy between this text and the Zohar. As previously discussed, according to the bulk of the Zohar, the soul of the righteous ascends only to the sefirah of Tiferet.[23] Therefore, the difference between the Zohar and Rabbi de Leon's text is not only a matter of terminology, of median pillar versus median line, but also of concepts: in Rabbi de Leon's work, the ladder is mentioned in connection with the median line, while this is not the case in Zoharic eschatology on the median pillar.

While the Catalan and Castilian Kabbalists, like Rabbi Bahya or Rabbi de Leon, for example, never visited Jerusalem, Nahmanides did. This fact produces another range of possibilities that are less symbolic and more "realistic," less reflective and more active. According to Nahmanides, "[w]hoever prays in Jerusalem is regarded as if he prays before the Throne of Glory, for it is the gateway of heaven, open to hear the prayer of Israel, as it is said, that is the gateway to heaven."[24] He recited the following prayer over the ruins of Jerusalem:

> Our feet stood inside your gates, O Jerusalem,
> The house of the Lord and the gateway of heaven,

> Jerusalem built up, a city knit together
> With that above it.[25]

We see here a combination of Bethel images from the Bible with material from Jerusalem. In Genesis 28, Jacob is described as follows:

11 When he reached a certain place, he stopped for the night because the sun had set. Taking one of the stones there, he put it under his head and lay down to sleep.

12 He had a dream in which he saw a ladder resting on the earth, with its top reaching to heaven, and the angels of God were ascending and descending on it.

13 There above it stood the LORD, and he said: "I am the LORD, the God of your father Abraham and the God of Isaac. I will give you and your descendants the land on which you are lying.

14 Your descendants will be like the dust of the earth, and you will spread out to the west and to the east, to the north and to the south. All peoples on earth will be blessed through you and your offspring.

15 I am with you and will watch over you wherever you go, and I will bring you back to this land. I will not leave you until I have done what I have promised you.

Though the biblical verses have nothing to do with Jerusalem, they have been interpreted as pointing to the center of the world as understood by a religious ideology that locates the holy city there. Nahmanides, a faithful rabbi, Kabbalist and follower of an earlier Midrashic understanding of the *axis mundi*, seems to be the first medieval Jewish mystic who not only spoke about the importance of the city but also visited it and expressed his emotions upon viewing the tribulations caused by the conquest of the Mongols in 1267. He did not attenuate the concreteness of the city as corresponding to the gates of heaven or offer a philosophical interpretation of its meaning, despite the fact that he resorted to the median line in describing the sefirah of Tiferet. Though he may have been acquainted with al-Batalyawsi, Nahmanides did not adopt his theory.

A conspicuous example of Jewish interpretation of al-Batalyawsi's view is found in Nahmanides's school. Rabbi Bahya ben Asher, a late thirteenth- and early fourteenth-century Kabbalist, never visited

Jerusalem but wrote about Moses's request to enter the land of Israel before his death:

> [B]ecause he has already comprehended the supernal median line [*ha-qav ha-'emtza`y shel ma`alah*] he asked [God] that he will see by the sense of sight the mundane median line, in order to comprehend that which corresponds to it...since you have granted me with the knowledge by which I have received the supernal central point, might your grace multiply so that I may see the good land, which is the central point of the lower [world] [and] the good mountain, which is Jerusalem, which is the central point of the good land, and the Levanon, which is the Temple, which is the central point of the "good mountain"...because since He has taught him and caused him to understand the supernal, by means of the eye of the intellect, it is incumbent that He should not conceal from him the lower one, but he should merit to come there to see it in order to add a merit upon his other merits by the fulfillment of the commandments which depend upon it, and from the lower [center] his soul should ascend to the supernal [center].[26]

Crucial to understanding Rabbi Bahya's view is the fact that Moses is granted a spiritual perception of the supernal Jerusalem; the town is described as the center of the sefirotic world. It is only toward the end of his life that Moses sees the corporeal Jerusalem, and the physical experience seems to be secondary to a contemplative process, the role of which is to enable him to perform commandments that cannot be fulfilled outside the perimeter of the land of Israel or possibly of Jerusalem alone. Insofar as Jerusalem is mentioned in the context of a spiritual meditation, it is part of a continuum that stretches to the higher Jerusalem that is part of *ascensio spiriti* but not a symbolic reading of a text or a decoding of the meaning of the lower city. Though manifestly influenced by the Neoplatonic vision of Al-Batalyawsi, Rabbi Bahya does not reduce the lower city to a symbol but retains some form of concreteness.

For a better understanding of the lower and supernal Jerusalem, let me dwell upon the most probable source of this passage. Elsewhere Rabbi Bahya speaks about the correspondence between the lower and the supernal temple, the latter being the place from which the souls descend to our world and to which by means of a path and a trajectory they return to its origin in God.[27] This passage is rather similar to that concerning Moses quoted above. Elsewhere, when speaking of Jacob's death, Rabbi Bahya mentions a "paved [or straight] path" by which the soul returns to God.[28] Based on these texts, I have no doubt that the lower point, or the mundane Jerusalem, and the supernal Jerusalem, symbolized by the supernal point, constitute Kabbalistic adaptations of the human soul, which is the center of the lower world, and the cosmic soul, which is the center of the spiritual world. Moreover, a lengthy verbatim quote as well as a shorter one, apparently translated into Hebrew by Rabbi Bahya himself from the *Book of the Imaginary Circles*, appear elsewhere in the same book.[29] As Altmann convincingly shows, this twelfth-century Neoplatonic world, composed by a Muslim Andalusian philosopher, deeply influenced thirteenth-century and even later Kabbalah; Rabbi Bahya's texts are yet another example of this significant impact.[30]

What is considerably different in Rabbi Bahya's work from that of the Muslim thinker is the occurrence of two parallel median lines, inferior and superior.[31] But both Arab and Jewish philosophers, as asserted by Rabbi Bahya, assumed that a spiritual eye could apprehend the divine world.[32] Thus, the supernal Jerusalem contemplated by Moses independently from the lower Jerusalem is a Kabbalistic adaptation of a crucial Neoplatonic concept: the cosmic soul. When seen in this manner, the supernal Jerusalem, conceived by a Kabbalist as identical to the last divine manifestation, can be apprehended directly, without the mediation of the literary symbol or of the concrete city. In other words, the synthetic path that leads from the lower to the higher, from the symbolic to the significant, is far from being the only way open for an understanding of the sefirotic realm. The spiritual eye ensures direct vision of the divine power designated by the term "supernal Jerusalem," a cognitive process that may ignore the concrete, which is nevertheless important to the fulfillment of the religious ritual. In any case, Moses's ascent to the supernal Jerusalem as described above constitutes an interesting example of the impact of the Islamic view of Muhammad's nocturnal *mi'raj*, which took place in Jerusalem according to Muslim legend.[33]

A final question about the last quote concerns whether or not Moses, the seer of the supernal Jerusalem, represents a *sui generis* case. Was the paragon of the prophets an idiosyncratic figure, and was his attainment considered exceptional to the extent that the above passage is relevant solely for his unique personality? In my opinion, based on the unearthing of Rabbi Bahya's Neoplatonic philosophical sources, this seems relatively implausible. I believe that many, though not all, of the diaspora Kabbalists who had seen Jerusalem only, perhaps, in their spiritual eye would have happily embraced the possibility of expanding Moses's achievement to their own time. In any case, the assumption is that Moses wished to go to Jerusalem to die there, as the city was viewed as the starting point of the ladder that ensures the ascent of the soul. Moreover, in addition to the Muslim Neoplatonic tradition mentioned above, this reflects a well-known custom of traveling to the land of Israel to die.

Another Kabbalistic school is connected to a mysterious book entitled *Sefer ha-Temunah* or *Sefer ha-Temunot*. The date and the place of its composition, as well as its author, require further in-depth investigation. Scholem first thought that it belonged to early Kabbalah, and later, to the late thirteenth century; he also believed it was written in Gerona.[34] A more plausible assumption is that this book as well as other writings of its school were composed sometime in the second half of the fourteenth century in the Byzantine Empire.[35] Altmann discerned the impact of al-Batalyawsi's work on commentary in this book and, following Scholem, was inclined to date a certain passage that will be dealt with later in our analysis at the end of the thirteenth century. However, it seems that the time of origin of the subsequent texts should be postponed by at least half a century.

In *Sefer ha-Temunah*, a cryptic sentence asserts that the last sefirah commanded that:

> ...a palace should be built for her, namely a sanctuary for her holiness, sanctified and inscribed with all the inscriptions of the supernal sanctuary, and of the supernal of the supernal, and by all the topics found in her, and the soul and the heart, in order to descend and dwell there from the supernal sanctuary to the lower one. And all the members of her house descend and ascend by Her means from the supernal gateway to the lower gateway, from the supernal temple to the lower one, and from the lower one to the higher one.[36]

The anonymous commentator on this passage describes the manner in which the descent and the ascent take place: "a path and a ladder have been made from the supernal to the lower temple."[37] However, what is even more important is the identification of the members of the house who ascend and descend. According to another passage by the same commentator and addressed previously by Altmann, not only the path and the ladder but also the souls are mentioned explicitly:

> And the supernal angels ascend to that Image, and this Image symbolizes [romezet] the order of emanation which contains the supernal Sanctuary [miqdash 'elyon]. Our Father Jacob, who saw the ladder ["the subject-matter of the ladder," 'inyan ha-sullam] in his dream, knew that even as there is a Sanctuary in the [world of] emanation above, so there is a Sanctuary below, for it is written: "and this is the gate of heaven." And from the Upper Sanctuary to the one below there is a kind of ladder [ke-min sullam], that is to say, a well-known path [derekh 'ehad yadu'a], which leads from Sanctuary to Sanctuary, and on this path the angels ascend and descend, and so likewise do the souls."[38]

Thus, there can be little doubt that the commentator was acquainted with al-Batalyawsi's eschatology, but I also believe that it can be found in the work that was being commented upon. Early in the book of the commentary cited above, it is rather cryptically written that the last sefirah is called "ocean,"

> ..."and the living soul is his name" [and] "'Elohim Hayyim" and "behold the angels of the Lord are ascending and descending on it" and each and every one of them receives its mission and the righteous understood this in his dream and he knew that there is a supernal Image on high and corresponding to it there is [one] below. And there are emissaries that ascend from their place to the supernal Image, and on the ladder they are descending below to the lower [Image] since the Shekhinah does not descend lower than ten.[39]

A cardinal point is the description of Shekhinah as a living soul, which corresponds to the cryptic phrase found later in the same book: "they ascend and descend by Her means." Therefore, like al-Batalyawsi's universal soul, the Shekhinah also serves as the conduit for the souls and angels here.

The connection between al-Batalyawsi and late thirteenth-century Kabbalah was not just a matter of Rabbi de Leon's adaptation of some elements from the work of the Muslim author. Here the Rabbi Bahya, who added the assumption that the ladder connects the supernal and the lower Jerusalem as well as the temples, presents an even more significant case of al-Batalyawsi's influence. The association of the Bethel ladder with the *axis culti* of Jerusalem and the temple certainly was not new to the Kabbalists; this juxtaposition occurs explicitly in the work of the famous eleventh-century commentator Rabbi Shlomo Yitzhaqi, known as Rashi, and in Rabbi Bahya's and Nahmanides's treatments of Jacob's dream.[40] Both follow a much earlier series of attempts to identify the Bethel revelation and cosmology with Jerusalem cosmology.[41] However, common to both Rabbi Bahya's work and *Sefer ha-Temunah* is the occurrence of the term "path," *derekh*, in referring to the ladder, which indicates not so much the descending but the ascending, eschatological factor.[42] Thus, we may assume that the circle of the *Sefer ha-Temunah* drew from some traditions found in the circle of Nahmanides's followers.[43]

The reverberation of the eschatological concept of the ladder occurs in a late sixteenth-century writing of one of the most important Kabbalists. Discussing the famous ladder dream of Jacob, Rabbi Hayyim Vital wrote that the experience of the patriarch was not a prophecy, since prophecy did not exist at the time. When in paradise, however, the soul is shown a prophetic dream in which she sees that the worlds are connected to each other by means of a ladder:

[A] ladder connects all the worlds...and the ladder that is fixed on earth, in the paradise on earth, because souls are ascending from there, through that ladder, about which it is said, "And the Lord will create upon every dwelling place of Mount Zion, etc.," as it is mentioned in the *Zohar*, pericope *Wa-Yaqhel*. And the head of the ladder and of that pillar reaches heaven, the heaven of heavens, that are known as *'Aravot*, where there is the treasure of souls, and there is the presence of God, blessed be He. And this is the reason why it is written that "God stands on it, and the angels of the Lord ascend and descend on the ladder." Namely in order to cause the descent of the born souls into this world, and the ascent of the souls of the deceased to the next world.[44]

Some lines later, the pillar is described as linking the terrestrial and the supernal paradises, and the passage from the Zohar mentioned above is again referenced.[45] Therefore, the supernal paradise, the divine presence and `Aravot may be synonyms for the superior end of the pillar.

Al-Batalyawsi's vision, which connects the image of the ladder with the ascent of dead souls, is united with the Zoharic theory of the ascent by a pillar. At the beginning of the quote, however, the ladder plays the role of a connective power, bringing together not only the two paradises but also all the worlds. It is plausible to surmise that, in the vein of other discussions found in Lurianic Kabbalah that are also concerned with extra-divine entities, this indicates something more comprehensive and more cosmic than the inter-paradisiacal nexus. Interestingly, the unborn soul is shown the cosmic connection of the worlds by means of the ladder. This is apparently a form of knowledge that is supposed to be forgotten in the manner of Platonic anamnesis, as is the case with knowledge of the Torah in some rabbinic sources.[46]

Sacred geography is projected on high, and its symbols are elaborated according to rules that govern interactions between theosophical themes—sefirot, median lines, correspondences between higher and lower entities—and literary entities, such as names found in the sacred scriptures. Thus a spiritual realm is created on high that projects its own meaning upon the understanding of geography on low. With the emergence of such "enriched geography" created by historical circumstances of privation, this spiritual surplus invites more action than contemplation. The symbol becomes less important in the presence of the center of power, and its place is occupied by religious action performed in the concrete center of holiness. Spirituality as represented by Rabbi Bahya, emphasizing the symbolic modality, seems to be characteristic of the absence of the sacred place that is fraught with energy. The living encounter with the sacred center as the result of direct contact with the *axis mundi*, is provoked in the cases of Nahmanides's and Rabbi Vital's more activist religious mentalities. Life in Jerusalem, according to Rabbi Bahya's passage, provides the opportunity to perform the commandments and finally to ascend to high. Thus, the symbolic modes of cognition of the transcendent and of its perception by the "eye of the intellect" are secondary to the mythical life of ascent. The primordial axis, based as it is upon the geographical center and actual presence, was the founding form of perception of Jerusalem, while symbolical interpretations that gravitate around absence implicitly attenuated mythical aspects, as the intellectual perception sometimes did. In other words, in the case of the term "Jerusalem," as in others in Kabbalah, the symbolic mode sometimes attenuates the strength of the mythical elements, as do the ecstatic or intellectual components.[47] Thus, the mythical aspects of Jerusalem are anchored in much earlier traditions of the double city that connect the high and the low by the *axis mundi*. While the concepts related to the mythical axis gravitate around the concept of power, those related to the ecstatic and the intellectual involve an inner life that to a certain extent may substitute for the importance of external factors. The strong light of sacrality could be dimmed by the symbolic mode, which is easier when Jerusalem is remote and practically unattainable. It seems that the symbolic mode can be understood as an exilic modality of interpretation of the mythical elements in the biblical and rabbinic concepts of Jerusalem as the place where the divine directly bestows his power.

3. AL-BATALYAWSI, YOHANAN ALEMANNO AND PICO DELLA MIRANDOLA

The substantial impact of al-Batalyawsi's book on medieval thought, revealed by the penetrating analysis of David Kaufmann and strengthened by Altmann's study, did not stop with the Middle Ages. In fact, this book also influenced some major Jewish Renaissance figures, as evidenced in Don Isaac Abravanel's *Commentary on the Pentateuch* and, in my opinion, in his son's *Dialoghi d'Amore*.[48] Both quoted the *Book of Imaginary Circles* in Italy after been expelled from Spain. Some decades earlier, the Florentine Rabbi Moses ben Yoav demonstrated acquaintance with this book in his sermons, which are extant in a manuscript.[49] However, it seems that the Renaissance author who was especially fond of this book was Rabbi Yohanan ben Isaac Alemanno, born in Mantua and active for many years in Florence. Kaufmann has duly recognized this fact, and other instances of appropriations of views from this book are found in Rabbi Alemanno's voluminous writings.[50]

A version of al-Batalyawsi's passage, named *'Einei ha-'Edah*, occurs in Rabbi Alemanno's incomplete *Commentary on the Pentateuch*:

The Universal Soul named the World Soul is hovering upon the waters, that is the *hyle*, which is easily influenced by it [the Universal Soul] like flowing water which can easily receive a form and [also] lose it. And it [the Universal Soul] is encompassed by the world of the Intellect and encompasses the world of Matter. It [the Universal Soul] is not within it [the world of Matter] but [it is] with it. And it is said: "God created" [namely] the World Soul which gives nature [*teva`*] to every [material] body, according to the preparation of its mixture. And when it [the body] puts away its form, the [World] soul gives it another form, according to its preparation. And it [the World Soul] is always with the matter in order to stir it to [received forms] lest it will be without them. It [the Universal Soul] is common to all the souls. And through it, because it cleaves to the intellectual world, the angels descend in order to direct the world, and the subtle spirits and souls ascend to the supernal world, and it [the Universal Soul] is a ladder upon which they are ascending and descending.[51]

Rabbi Alemanno changes al-Batalyawsi's text at two points pertinent to our discussion. First, he seems to be the only author to use al-Batalyawsi's passage together with the term "nature." Yet this term does not mean the universal soul, which is represented by the simile of a ladder, but rather the soul's activity as the source of the forms received by the *hyle* and therefore of the nature of all things. Nevertheless, in an earlier work of Rabbi Alemanno's, we find the following sentence: "and it is named the Soul of the World and the Universal Soul and the generating nature."[52] The strong distinction between nature and universal soul from Neoplatonic sources was sometimes attenuated by Christian authors in the first part of the twelfth century, but I hardly believe that Rabbi Alemanno was acquainted with those sources, which were criticized by the Church.[53]

Second Rabbi Alemanno viewed the universal soul as *natura naturans* and generated things as *natura naturata*. This stance is found neither in the *Epistles of the Sincere Brethern* nor in al-Batalyawsi. The ladder can be interpreted properly in Rabbi Alemanno's works as a simile not only for the universal soul, as al-Batalyawsi explicitly conceived it, but also presumably of nature and its descending powers. This is a slight shift from the Neoplatonic vision of nature as the result of the acts of the universal soul or nature as matter in relation to it; here both active nature and the universal soul are identified. In Rabbi Alemanno's version, the souls and the spirits ascend on the ladder, and the distinction between the dead and the living, so carefully pointed out in al-Batalyawsi, is glossed over. Moreover, unlike al-Batalyawsi's view, which asserts that the soul can attain only the agent intellect, according to Rabbi Alemanno, the human soul can reach God, as we shall see in Pico's *Oratio de Dignitate Hominis*. Al-Batalyawsi.[54] In an earlier work written around 1498, a quasi-pantheistic stance connects the entire world by the power of love that permeates everything. In Rabbi Alemanno's introduction to the commentary on the Song of Songs, he writes:

> But the divine spirit is circulating around and around, from Him and toward Him as it is well-exposed in al-Batalyawsi's *Book of Imaginary Circles*. And if you want to know who is making this low despised entity to ascend on high and who is making the supernal entity to descend here below, behold who is the possessor of the might, the force and the strength to do it? It is the desire [*hesheq*] mentioned by the prophets when they said: "Only the Lord desired in thy fathers to love them," and said that "because he has set his desire in me, therefore I shall deliver him."[55]

Rabbi Alemanno, though acquainted with numerous Kabbalistic books, was nevertheless close to the medieval and Renaissance forms of philosophy. He was much less concerned with the mythical architecture of the Zohar mentioned above, and he adopted many philosophical stances that attenuated even the few mythical views to which he resorted. His use of al-Batalyawsi is just one of numerous examples for this synthetic stance.

The famous student of Rabbi Alemanno, the young Count Giovanni Pico della Mirandola, describes the purge of the soul by moral philosophy, *princeps concordiae*, in his *Oratio de Dignitate Hominis*:

> Yet this will not be enough if we wish to be companions of the angels going up and down on Jacob's ladder, unless we have first been well fitted and instructed to be promoted duly from step to step, to stray nowhere from the stairway, and to engage in the alternate comings and goings. Once we have achieved this by the art of discourse or reasoning, then inspired by the cherubic spirit, using philosophy through the steps of the ladder, that is, of nature, and penetrating all things from center to center, we shall sometimes descend, with titanic force rending the unity like Osiris into many parts, and we shall sometimes ascend, with the force of Phoebus, collecting the parts like the limbs of Osiris into a unity, until, resting at last in the bosom of the Father, who is above the ladder, we shall be made perfect with the felicity of theology.[56]

The subject of this passage is the ascent of the human soul to God. In order to be able to complete this ascent, the soul has to be pure since only purified souls are allowed to climb on the ladder. [57] Pico's concept of this ladder is nature; with its help we can penetrate all things from center to center. The meaning of this phrase is not self-evident; it seems to indicate that the bottom of the ladder is the center of one circle, while its summit is the center of another. But what do these circles or centers represent? Pico does not supply an answer, and one cannot be found in the various editions and translations of the *Oratio*. It seems that the source of Pico's ladder motif, which could be al-Batalyawsi's passage from the *Book of Imaginary Circles*, might provide a clue.

There are certainly differences between the two works. First, al-Batalyawsi regards the universal soul as a ladder between earth and the agent intellect; for Pico, the ladder is an allegory for nature. Second, al-Batalyawsi believes that the spirits of the dead, when pure, can ascend to the intellect, while Pico describes the souls of living men who attempt to reach God. These differences notwithstanding, the similarities between the two are obvious. Both al-Batalyawsi and Pico use the simile of a ladder extending between two centers or circles. Both describe purified souls ascending on this ladder. And finally, evidence of the presence of al-Batalyawsi's book in Florence goes beyond Rabbi Alemanno's references to a passage from it. The manuscript of a Hebrew translation of this book is preserved in the Medici Library in Florence, and as mentioned above, an earlier, mid-fifteenth-century Florentine rabbi referred to this book in his sermons. [58]

I would like to mention here Origen's famous passage in *Contra Celsum* (VI: 21–22), which includes an alchemical description of the seven rungs of Jacob's ladder and mentions two celestial circles, all in the context of the descent of the souls and their return upward. [59] This striking similarity notwithstanding, it seems to me unlikely that Origen's text might be Pico's source for three reasons: (1) the two circles in Origen's work are both celestial, whereas Pico speaks of the sublunar realm; (2) Pico, like Rabbi Alemanno, considers the ladder as nature, whereas Origen, or Celsus, associates the ladder with seven metals; and (3) Origen deals with the ascent and descent of souls when they die or are born, respectively, while Pico—and Rabbi Alemanno—view the ladder as a simile for a psychanodial process undertaken by the soul while still alive.

To summarize, a ladder linking two centers upon which souls ascend occurs both in Pico's *Oratio* and in al-Batalyawsi's book, but the description of this ladder as nature upon which living souls ascend is shared only by Rabbi Alemanno and Pico. The latter's *Oratio* was written in 1486; Rabbi Alemanno's above-mentioned works were written after 1499. A conclusion based on these dates, however, would be misleading. The influence of Pico's interpretation of al-Batalyawsi's text on Rabbi Alemanno is hardly probable, since (1) Rabbi Alemanno had first-hand knowledge of the Hebrew version of al-Batalyawsi's book and quoted from it extensively, sometimes attributing it mistakenly to Ptolemeus,[60] while Pico never mentioned al-Batalyawsi or his work; (2) Rabbi Alemanno's text is closer to the Hebrew version of al-Batalyawsi's passage than Pico's text; and (3) Rabbi Alemanno was Pico's teacher.[61] The assumption that Rabbi Alemanno influenced Pico before the period in which he wrote his *Oratio* seems to be the most reasonable conclusion based on the material discussed above; this implies an encounter between these persons at least two years before the date we are sure they met: 1488.[62] Antedating the first meeting of Pico and Rabbi Alemanno is of great importance to the study of Pico's works written between 1486 and 1488, which were his most influential onces. This would imply that, in addition to Flavius Mithridates and Elijah del Medigo, Pico had a third teacher, at least from 1486.[63] This conclusion strengthens the great significance of Rabbi Alemanno's writings, even if they were composed later, to the understanding of Pico's thought.[64]

It is also worthwhile to scrutinize the final part of the text quoted from the *Oratio*. According to Pico, the two movements on the ladder are the descent, which means the rending of the unity in order to produce the many, and the ascent, which stands for the collecting of the many into their original unity. The two motions indicate differing types of contemplation used by the human soul to attain its final perfection and peace.[65] Rabbi Alemanno refers to the simile of the ladder in order to define the function of geometry and astronomy as steps by which one can ascend to heaven, but this text seems to be a gloss. It is reasonable, therefore, to interpret the ascent and descent as two speculative ways of knowledge—as synthesis and analysis.[66] If this is indeed Pico's perception of the biblical phrase regarding the angels who ascend and descend upon the ladder, then he shared it with some Jewish texts. As indicated previously, in Rabbi Samuel ibn Tibbon, the "ascending and descending angels" are, therefore, also equated with the philosopher's

use of synthetic and analytical methods.[67] It is quite improbable that
Pico innovated such a peculiar interpretation of the ladder without being
influenced by an already existing Jewish view.[68] In addition to Rabbi
Alemanno, Pico could have been aware of Rabbi Bahya's passage, since
the Renaissance thinker was acquainted with at least parts of the Kabbalist's *Commentary on the Pentateuch*.[69]

We may compare the closing sentences of the quoted text by Pico
with one of his theses: "Anyone who thinks deeply about the fourfold
constitution of things—first the unity and stability of remaining, second
procession, third reversion, fourth beatific reunion—will see that the
letter *beth* works first with the first letter, medially with the middle letter and last with the last letters."[70] The combinatory practice found in
Pico's thesis has been described by Chaim Wirszubski, who detected
the precise Kabbalistic source of this passage.[71] At least three of the
four states parallel the various stages described in the *Oratio: processio* is
the ascent, *reversio* is the descent, and *reunio* is the state of peace and
perfection in the bosom of the Father. It is possible that even the first
state (*mansio*) is alluded to in a reference to God standing on the summit of the ladder. This correspondence between the *Oratio* and one of
the theses, to which the *Oratio* serves as an introduction, strengthens
Edgar Wind's perception of the passage in the *Oratio* as influenced by
Proclus.[72] Moreover, as Wirszubski has shown, the first three states alluded to in the thesis are Latin renderings of Proclus's three main concepts.[73] It seems, therefore, that Pico not only used the medieval Judeo-
Arabic view of Jacob's ladder as exposed by Rabbi Alemanno, but also
added a novel element to it: it is seen as a figure for the Neoplatonic
concepts he found in Marsilio Ficino's translations. To these layers,
Pico applied the mythical explanation of the descent as the division of
Osiris into his limbs, and the ascent figures as their collection.[74]

The late Professor Altmann kindly drew my attention to a remarkable Neoplatonic interpretation of Dionysos's dismemberment found in
Macrobius's *In Somnium Scipionis* (I: 12, 11), which could indeed have
had an impact on Pico:

> [M]embers of the Orphic sect believe that the material mind is rep-
> resented by Bacchus himself, who, born of a single parent, is divided
> into separate parts. In their sacred rites they portray him as being
> torn to pieces at the hand of angry Titans and arising again from his
> buried limbs alive and sound, their reason being that *nous* or Mind,

by offering its undivided substance to be divided and again by returning from its divided state to the indivisible, both fulfills its worldly
functions and does not forsake its sacred nature.[75]

Pico may have studied this passage in the 1472 edition of
Macrobius's works printed in Venice and transferred the philosophical
interpretation of the myth of Dionysos to that of Osiris.[76]

4. The Ladder, *Natura* and *Aurea Catena*

In the previous sections, it is evident that the split between the cosmological and the eschatological paths, as found in the Zohar, is not paral-
leled in the views expressed by the Muslim Neoplatonic thinker or by
the Kabbalists who followed him. The integration of the two functions
of the straight line lost importance from the early sixteenth century,
and the dominance of the cosmological became increasingly evident,
obfuscating the eschatological function of both the line and the ladder.
This phenomenon was associated with Homer's golden chain as interpreted by later thinkers and found in the Neoplatonic tradition.[77]

In considering Jacob's ladder, Johann Reuchlin's *De Arte Cabalistica*
represents the view of a Kabbalist named Simon who addresses his in-
terlocutors: "For our frailty we fall short of the good which is called
God, and cannot climb there except with steps and ladders. You cus-
tomarily refer to the Homeric chain. We Jews look to the holy scripture
and talk about the ladder our father Jacob saw, from the highest heaven
stretching down to earth, like a cord or rope of gold thrown down to us
from heaven, a visual line penetrating deep within nature."[78] *Prima facie*,
Reuchlin's text seems to be independent from Pico's perception of Jacob's
ladder, but such a conclusion may be premature. In his *Heptaplus*, Pico
asserts that Moses alluded to Homer's *catena aurea* without any specific indication of exactly where such a concept is dealt with.[79] Pico's
views in *Oratio* and *Heptaplus* seem to be combined by Giovanni Nessi,
a Florentine defender of Savonarola. In his *Oraculum de Novo Saeculo*
published in 1497, he explicitly compares the "aurea cathena" with
Christian theologians' views that one could ascent to heaven by means
of Jacob's ladder.[80] Here, Homer's *catena aurea* is closely related to
Jacob's ladder, and they are connected to the study of theology as the
supreme goal as Pico asserts in his *Oratio*.

What is new in Reuchlin's passage is the addition of the golden cable to the visual line. These two motifs seem to represent the almost verbatim use of a Pseudo-Dionysian simile found in his book *Divine Names*; we find a discussion in III:1 on how one can rise to God: "Let us then elevate our very selves by our prayers to the higher ascent of the Divine and good rays—as if a luminous chain suspended from the celestial and reaching down hither, we, by ever clutching this upwards... are carried upwards to the higher splendors of the luminous rays."[81] Presumably under the influence of Pico's identification of the ladder with nature, Reuchlin added the detail that the rays pervade nature. The occurrence of Pseudo-Dionysius in Reuchlin's discussion seems to be a deliberate choice; he incorporates "ancient" Christian theology with the biblical ladder and the Homeric chain, evidently on the assumption of *philosophia perennis* that is hinted at in Pico's view of Jacob's ladder.[82] But Reuchlin apparently intended to achieve more than this; the quoted passage from *De Arte Cabalistica* is part of the speech of a Kabbalist, and the author may have intentionally used a Christian source for this speech in order to achieve the tacit agreement of Kabbalah with Pseudo-Dionysius. In any case, the third image occurring in Reuchlin's passage, the *linea visualis*, seems to indicate an acquaintance with al-Batalyawsi's text or one of its reverberations, the most plausible of which is Rabbi Bahya's passage dealt with above. The occurrence of natures, *naturas*, may express Rabbi Alemanno's naturalistic understanding of the philosophical text. Regardless, it is obvious that Reuchlin was fond of the image of the ladder, as evidenced in other places in the same book.[83]

In another famous symposium by persons of different religions, Jean Bodin's *Colloquium Heptapleomeres*, we find the following text: "Senamus: 'What then will happen to Plato who, in accordance with the opinion of Homer, represents a golden chain let down by Jupiter from heaven'... Salomon: I think the Homeric chain is nothing other than the ladder represented in the nocturnal vision of Jacob the Patriarch. God was at the top of the ladder, and angels descended from the top of heaven to the earth and then ascended again to heaven."[84] As in Reuchlin's text, a Jew points out the similarity between Jacob's ladder and Homer's (and Plato's) *aurea catena*. The passages dealt with earlier in this section represent attempts to bring together Jewish and Greek topics as part of what can be described as a *philosophia perennis*. These are theologically-oriented discourses in which the concept of a natural chain of being nevertheless is inserted in the framework of a biblical topic.

While these Christian authors followed Pico and represent, indirectly, a continuation of a medieval ontology based on strong hierarchies, a significant change is discernible at the end of the sixteenth century. According to Giordano Bruno, God is latent in nature, and a hierarchical structure is implied in the metaphor of the ladder. In his *Expulsion of the Triumphant Beast*, he writes:

> Because just as Divinity descends in a certain manner, to the extent that one communicates with Nature, so one ascends to Divinity through Nature, just as by means of a life resplendent in natural things one rises to the life that presides over them.... I see how those wise men, through these means had the power to make intimate, affable, and friendly toward themselves, the gods who, by means of cries they sent forth through statues, gave these wise men advice, doctrines, divinations, and superhuman institutions; whence with magic and divine rites they rose to the height of divinity by means of the same ladder of Nature by which Divinity descends even to the lowest things in order to communicate herself.[85]

It seems that Osiris's dismemberment and the collection of his limbs as the ascent, which occurs in Pico's *Oratio*, are presented here as a simile for God's descent into nature and man's ascent to God. Both events take place through one and the same ladder—the "ladder of nature." This term, which is used by both Pico and Bruno, is valuable evidence of the former's influence on the latter. But while Osiris is mentioned in Pico, Bruno fails to use this name in his works. Nevertheless, Osiris is alluded to in a very subtle way. The quoted passage is found in a dialogue between Momus and Isis, and the whole purpose of Bruno's work is to praise the ancient Egyptian religion, which is considered by the author to be the ultimate source of Judaism.[86] Bruno describes the ancient religion of Egypt in terms explicitly influenced by *Asclepius*, the well-known oration of *Corpus Hermeticum*.[87] From the Hermetic source, Bruno adopts the magical view evident in the quotation and uses it, *inter alia*, in his interpretation of Pico's ladder of nature. For Bruno, the perfection of man necessitates his possession of magic powers that can be acquired through the proper use of various elements of nature, which is defined by Bruno in these words: "natura est deus in rebus"— nature is God in things.[88] Bruno alludes to rites that are methods by which the divine powers inherent in nature can be used.[89]

Rather than adopting Pico's divine ascent through the study of philosophy and theology, which also was accepted by Nessi and Reuchlin, Bruno proposes magical methods that aim not only to unity the soul with God but also (and primarily) to extend human powers. While Pico's thought operates in a field of two extremities linked by intermediaries hinted at by the ladder simile, Bruno's use of the term *scala della natura* is entirely metaphoric. For Pico, the universe is reminiscent of the medieval stratification of planes of being, and the ascent is interpreted as being much more substantial. Bruno in another work writes that: "just as [in the case of] the two extremities, as it is said about the extremities of the ladder of nature, one contemplates not two principles but one, not two entities but one, not two contraries which are different but one and the same that concords. The altitude is the profundity, the abyss is the inaccessible light, darkness is clarity, the great is the small, the confused is the distinct."[90] Bruno explicitly blurs the distinction between God and nature and changes the simile of the ladder into a metaphor alluding to the variegated aspects of nature. This tendency is obvious when the text quoted above from Bruno's *Spaccio* is compared to a passage in *De la Causa*: "I would like to remark that the very same ladder by means of which nature descends in order to produce things is that which the intellect uses in order to know them. Each of them proceeds from unity to unity, passing through the multiplicity of the intermediaries."[91] Bruno changes the word "God" in *Spaccio* into "natura." God, who sits at the summit of the ladder, becomes identical to the ladder itself. The metaphor stands now for the mere—and, according to Bruno, only apparent—transition from unity to plurality. The ladder is referred to elsewhere in the same work as *scala de lo essere*—the scale of being, including everything that exists.[92] I wonder if, in addition to the concept of the ladder, and thus a linear picture, some form of circle is not hinted at here.

In an even more significant passage found in his treatise on natural magic, Bruno describes the procession and the return of everything from and to God, which serves as an explanation of the more succinct passage adduced above:

[T]he magicians are considering as an axiom, to keep under their eyes in all their operations, that God is converting into gods, the gods into celestial bodies or astral bodies, which are in turn embodied divinities, those astral bodies [convert] in demons which are the lovers and the inhabitants of the astral bodies, one of which being is earth. Demons [turn] into elements, elements into mixtures, mixtures into feeling in soul, soul into any living being. This is the descent of the ladder. Immediately the living being ascends by the soul to the feeling, the feeling by mixtures, the mixtures by elements, and by it into demons, by them in astral bodies, by those in embodied gods or ethereal and corporeal substances, by them in the soul of the world or the spirit of the world and finally by means of it to the contemplation of the most simple unity, the best and maximal incorporeality, absolute and self-sufficient. Thus just as from God the descent is by means of the world to the living being, so also the ascent of the living being to God is by means of the world. He is at the peak of the ladder as pure act, active potency, [and] purest light. At the basis of the ladder, which is matter, the darkness, the pure passive potency which can become everything below, just as God can do all the things on high.[93]

The most recent editor and translator of the book from which this passage is quoted pointed out the biblical source of the last part of the citation: Genesis 28:12.[94] Various suggestions on possible Renaissance sources for this text, particularly Marsilio Ficino and Cornelius Agrippa of Nettesheim, as important as they are to some aspects of the passage, do not include references to the ladder image that is so crucial to Bruno's discussion. As in earlier passages, the ladder of nature here is a metaphor for a certain type of chain of being. The question hence may be posed: to what extent was Bruno aware of the Jewish or Arabic discussions analyzed above? The Nolan thinker was acquainted with Kabbalistic ideas, as he mentions Kabbalah twice in his *De Magia Naturali*.[95]

Influenced by Bruno's works, Friedrich von Schelling presents the Italian thinker's ideas in a dialogue called *Bruno, oder ueber das gottliche und naturliche Princip der Dinge*. The dialogue ends with the following speech by Bruno:

Diesem folgend werden wir erst in der absoluten Gleichheit des Wesens und der Form die Art erkennen, wie sowohl Endliches als Unendliches aus Inneren hervorquillt, und das eine nothwendig und ewig bei dem andern ist und wie jener einfache Strahl der vom Absoluten ausgeht und es selbst ist, in Differenz und Indifferenz,

Endliches und Unendliches getrennt erscheine, begreifen, die Art
aber der Trennung und der Einheit fur jeden Punkt der Universums
genau bestimmen und dieses his dahin verfolgen wo jener absolute
Einheitspunkt in die zwei Relativen getrennt escheint, und in dem
einen den Quellpunkt der reellen und naturlichen, in dem andern
der ideellen und der gottlichen Welt erkennen, und mit jener zwar
die Menschwerdung Gottes von Ewigkeit, mit dieser die nothwendi-
ge Gottwerdung des Menschen seien, und indem wir auf dieser
geistigen Leiter frei und ohne widerstand auf und ab uns bewegen,
jetzt herabsteigend die Einheit des gottlichen und naturlichen
Princips getrennt, jetzt ihm aufsteigend und alles wieder aufldsend
in das Eine, die Natur in Gott, Gott aber in der Natur sehen.[96]

As Edgar Wind has pointed out, Schelling seems to use both Bruno's
De la Causa and Pico's *Oratio*.[97] But the last sentence can be understood better when compared to Bruno's views in *Spaccio*, since only
there is nature described as God in things. The ladder of nature of Pico
and Bruno changed into a spiritual ladder, preserving only the epistemological facet of the simile, whereas its ontological dimension was
completely blurred.

5. Some Conclusions

It is fascinating to see how the biblical figure of the ladder, which describes how the world is governed by means of angels, developed in different intellectual milieus. On the one hand, this form of connectivity
became an eschatological experience, as evident in Heikhalot literature,
in early Islam Qur'an and in some forms of philosophy and Kabbalah.
On the other hand, from the Renaissance a strong emphasis was placed
on the naturalistic understanding of the ladder as a result of the graft-
ing of the Greek Neoplatonic mode of thought on the ladder image
stemming from the Bible. With the ascent of the Greek element in the
Renaissance period, the naturalistic tendency became more and more
accentuated. A shift initiated by the surge of Greek thought during this
period produced, *de facto*, an inversion of the medieval vision of philosophy as the handmaiden of theology.[98] Now, it is theology, represented
by Jacob's ladder, that is conceived of as the handmaiden of philosophy,
represented by nature. The ladder of nature therefore embodies the do-
mestication of the mythical and miraculous biblical worldview by re-

sorting to more stable schemes, which become the object of scientific studies. Bruno hints at looking at nature in order to contemplate the divine in a manner reminiscent of medieval views. Eschatology moves to the background, and even cosmology becomes decreasingly important, while a static type of ontological concatenation of factors moves to the forefront. Though Bruno indeed accentuates the importance of magic and its roots in dynamic concatenation, the primary European development followed other directions. A more stable vision of nature reduced the importance of magic and left even less room for personal eschatology as represented by the ascent to another spiritual part of reality.

In summary, the ladder motif metamorphosed from its philosophical interpretation by Arab philosophers, to its slight transformation by a Jewish author, who apparently influenced his Christian student (Pico) and thence a series of Renaissance writers, to the naturalistic turn given it by Bruno. This is only one minor example of how the encounter between Jewish and Christian theologians in the Renaissance period stimulated western thought.[99] With the Renaissance, however, another trend becomes more and more discernible. It seems probable that the frequent usage of the term "scale of nature" in English poetry influenced Adam ha-Kohen Levensohn, a Jewish poet of the Enlightenment period, who wrote a lengthy poem on Jacob's ladder as the ladder of nature: *Sullam ha-teva`*. This poem serves as an introduction to the Hebrew summary of J. H. Bernardin de Saint-Pierre's *L'Harmonie de la Nature*[100] written by Joseph Herzberg of Mohilev and printed under the same name *Sullam ha-Teva`* in Vilnius in 1850.[101] Ultimately stemming from the encounter between Greek philosophy and biblical thought, the result of which was shaped by thinkers like Pico and Bruno, it penetrated Jewish thought and informed the title of the Hebrew poem mentioned above.

Let me attempt to distinguish the two lines of development that may be discerned from the above discussions. The emergence of the eschatological understanding of the pillar in medieval Spain became a more experiential issue in mid-eighteenth-century Eastern Europe, as we learned in the previous chapter from the Besht's *Epistle of the Ascent of the Soul*. The eschatological and mystical elements were enhanced in the Hasidic epistle in comparison to what we found in the Zohar and in the Safedian interpretations of this book. At the same time, the importance of the pillar theme was not accepted by fifteenth- and sixteenth-century Kabbalists in Italy, and natural elements became more evident in this cultural center and in the reverberations of more philosophical interpretations, especially since the Renaissance. This was partially due to certain reluctance toward the Zohar in the period between 1470 and 1558 in Italy.[102] Both Jewish philosophers and Kabbalists were inclined toward philosophy, and Christian Kabbalists, many of whom were active in or influenced by the ambiance in Italy, preferred the concept of the ladder of nature. Though it first had an eschatological component in medieval versions, the Renaissance added a more contemplative–scientific twist.

NOTES

1. See Sara Heller-Willensky, "Isaac Ibn Latif—Philosopher or Kabbalist?" in *Jewish Medieval and Renaissance Studies*, ed. A. Altmann (Cambridge: Harvard University Press, 1967), p. 207.
2. See Moshe Idel, *Enchanted Chains* (forthcoming).
3. This tendency is found among the more philosophically oriented Kabbalists like Rabbi Azriel of Gerone, Rabbi Isaac ibn Latif, Rabbi David ben Abraham ha-Lavan and Rabbi Joseph ibn Waqar.
4. Alexander Altmann, "The Ladder of Ascension," in *Studies in Mysticism and Religion Presented to Gershom G. Scholem*, eds. E. E. Urbach, R. J. Z. Werblowsky, and C. Wirszubski (Jerusalem: The Magnes Press, 1967), pp. 1–32. For earlier material, see Morton Smith, *Clement of Alexandria and A Secret Gospel of Mark* (Cambridge: Harvard University Press, 1973), p. 241.
5. On this concept, see H. J. Blumenthal, "Soul, World Soul and Individual Soul in Plotinus," *Le Neoplatonisme* (Paris: Editions de Minuit, 1971), pp. 55–66; Paul E. Walker, "The Universal Soul and the Particular Soul in Isma'ili Neoplatonism," in *Neoplatonism and Islamic Thought*, ed. P. Morewedge (Albany: State University of New York Press, 1992), pp. 149–65; and Bernard McGinn, "The Role of the 'Anima Mundi' as Mediator between the Divine and Created Realms in the Twelfth Century," in *Death, Ecstasy, and Other Worldly Journeys*, eds. J. J. Collins and Michael Fishbane (Albany: State University of New York Press, 1995), pp. 289–315.
6. *Enneads* 1:1; 4. See also Arthur Lovejoy, *The Great Chain of Being: A Study in the History of an Idea* (New York: Harper Torchbooks, 1960), pp. 62–63. For the different stances regarding the descended or the undescended soul in Neoplatonism, see Gregory Shaw, *Theurgy and the Soul: The Neoplatonism of Iamblichus* (College Park: The Pennsylvania State University Press, 1995), pp. 11–12.
7. *Rasa'il Ihwan al-Safa*, epistle 22 (Cairo, 1928), II, pp. 156–57; compare to, Altmann, "Ladder of Ascension," pp. 4–5.
8. *Risa'il al-Safa* epistle 41, III, p. 370; compare to Altmann's translation, "Ladder of Ascensions," p. 6; this formula is widespread in ancient and medieval Arabic and Jewish sources.

9. Compare to the translation of Seyyed Hossein Nasr, *An Introduction to Islamic Cosmological Doctrines* (Boulder: Shambhala, 1978), p. 57.

10. For the Arabic source (unknown to Kaufmann when he printed the two Hebrew translations of Rabbi Moses ibn Tibbon and Rabbi Shmuel ibn Motot in 1880), see Miguel Asin Palacios, "Ibn al-Sid de Badajoz y su 'Libro de los cercos' [Kitab al-Hida'iq]," *Al-Andalus* 5 (1940): pp. 45–154. Georges Vajda identified a third anonymous Hebrew translation, which he described in his "Une version hebraique inconnue des 'Cercles Imaginaires' de Batalyawsi," *Semitic Studies in Memory of Immanuel Loew*, ed. Sandor Schreiber(Budapest: Alexander Kohut Foundation, 1947), pp. 202–04. For the identity of this translator, see Benjamin Richler, "The Identification of the Anonymous Translator of the Book of the Imaginary Circles" (in Hebrew), *Qiryat Sefer* 53 (1978): p. 577. For the dating of the *floruit* of this thinker to the early twelfth rather than eleventh century, as Kaufmann thought, see Hartwig Derenbourg, *Revue des Etudes Juives* 7 (1883): pp. 274–79.

11. *The Book of the Imaginary Circle* printed in David Kaufmann, *Die Spuren al-Batalyausi's in der Judischen Religionsphilosophie* (Budapest, 1880), pp. 17–18; compare to Altmann's translation, "Ladder of Ascension," pp. 6–7. For the texts of the Hebrew translations, see ibid., pp. 9–10.

12. See above, n. 4.

13. See Kaufmann, *Die Spuren al-Batalyausi*, pp. 1–2, 25, 26 and 27.

14. See Rabbi Moses de Leon, *Sheqel ha-Qodesh*, ed. Charles Mopsik (Los Angeles: Cherub Press, 1996), p. 90; Nahmanides's *Commentary on Sefer Yetzirah*, in Gershom Scholem, ed., *Studies in Kabbalah*, eds. J. ben Shlomo and M. Idel (Tel Aviv: `Am `Oved, 1998), p. 92; and Rabbi Shem Tov ibn Gaon's commentary on Nahmanides's secrets, *Keter Shem Tov*, Ms. Paris BN 774, fol. 76a. In fol. 75a, Adam, or man, is mentioned as one of the four beasts in the first chapter of Ezekiel, which corresponds to *qav shawweh*, the harmonious line that stands for the sefirah of Tiferet.

15. See the excerpt printed in Y. A. Vajda, ed., *Sefer Meshiv Devarim Nekhohim* (in Hebrew) (Jerusalem: Israeli Academy of Science and Humanities, 1969), pp. 194–95. Compare to Altmann, "Ladder of Ascension," p. 29.

16. Vajda, *Sefer Meshiv Devarim Nekhohim*, pp. 113 and 117; and Altmann, "Ladder of Ascension."

17. Isaiah Tishby, *Commentarius in Aggadot, auctores R. Azriel Geronensi* (in Hebrew) (Jerusalem: Mekize Nirdamim, 1945), p. 89. Tishby assumes that this phrase means one single sefirah, that of Hokhmah. See ibid., p. 25, n. 10; and p. 89. Altmann accepts his view ("Ladder of Ascension").

18. Rabbi Bahya ben Asher, *Commentary on the Pentateuch*, ed. C. D. Chavel (Jerusalem: Mossad ha-Rav Kook, 1968), on Genesis 2:8, 3:6 and 22, 7:23, 18:9, and Exodus 17:12, 20:7, 25:38, 26:28.

19. Ibid., on Genesis 30:23.

20. Ibid., on Exodus 20:7. This view is congruent with that of Rabbi Joseph Gikatilla.

21. Isaiah Tishby, ed., *Hiqrei Qabbalah* (Jerusalem: Magnes Press, 1982), vol. I, p. 51. I used Altmann's translation, "Ladder of Ascension," p. 27. The

"mystical meaning" refers to the Midrashic dictum, "All that happened to Jacob also happened to Joseph." The "oppressive confines" are "shells," *qelippot*, or demonic forces. The Kabbalistic symbol of the son is the linear sign. The "middle bar" refers to Exodus 26:28.

22. Altmann, "Ladder of Ascension," p. 28.

23. See also *Zohar* I, fol. 148b.

24. Genesis 28:17.

25. Nahmanides, *Kitvei ha-Ramban*, ed. C. D. Chavel (Jerusalem: Mossad ha-Rav Kook, 1963), vol. I, p. 424. The first three lines are Psalms 122: 2–3.

26. Bahya, *Commentary*, on Deuteronomy III: 24–25, vol. III, p. 255. It seems that the commentator refers here to the supernal Jerusalem, which is described by the same phrase in one of the sources of Bahya's commentary, the earlier Rabbi Jacob ben Sheshet's *Sefer ha-'Emunah ve-ha-Bitahon*, ch. XI in Chavel, *Kitvei ha-Ramban*, vol. II, pp. 377–79, and 385. See also Bahya, *Commentary*, on Deuteronomy 17:14. "See by the sense of sight" is translated from *be-hush ha-`ayin*. See the connection between sight and the line in Johann Reuchlin, "Linea *Visualis*," *On the Art of Kabbalah, De Arte Cabalistica*, trans. M. and S. Goodman (Lincoln: The Nebraska University Press, 1993). On Levanon as designating the Temple in Jerusalem, see Geza Vermes, *Scripture and Tradition in Judaism* (Leiden: Brill, 1973), pp. 28–39. For early Kabbalistic symbolism of Lebanon, see the texts translated by Alexander Altmann, "A Note on the Rabbinic Doctrine of Creation," *Journal of Jewish Studies* 6/7 (1955/1956): pp. 203–05. See also Moshe Idel, *Kabbalah: New Perspectives* (New Haven: Yale University Press, 1988), pp. 181–82. The "good mountain" refers to Deuteronomy 3:25. "Eye of the intellect" is translated from `*Ein ha-sekhel*. See Yehudah ha-Levi, *Kuzari*, discussed by Warren Zev Harvey, "Judah Halevi's Synesthetic Theory of Prophecy and a Note on the *Zohar*" (in Hebrew), in *Rivkah Shatz-Uffenheiner Memorial Volume*, eds. R. Elior and J. Dan (Jerusalem: Department of Jewish Thought, 1996), vol. I, pp. 142–47. In the vein of Nahmanides's Kabbalistic school, the importance of the performing of the commandments precisely in the land of Israel seems to be crucial to Rabbi Bahya ben Asher.

27. Bahya, *Commentary*, on Genesis 15:16, vol. I, pp. 154–55. "Path" is translated from *derekh*, and "trajectory," from *maslul*.

28. See ibid., on Genesis 49:33, pp. 394–95. "Paved path" is translated from *Derekh selulah*, an expression that occurs again in ibid., on Genesis 28:12, p. 245.

29. See ibid., Genesis 2:7, pp. 64–65, parallel to the texts printed in Kaufmann, *Spuren*, pp. 63–64.

30. Altmann, "Ladder of Ascension." For the impact of some concepts found in this book on a mid-sixteenth-century Kabbalist, see Boaz Huss, *Sockets of Fine Gold: The Kabbalah of Rabbi Shim`on Ibn Lavi* (in Hebrew) (Jerusalem: Magnes Press, Ben Tzvi Institute, 2000), pp. 37 and 96–97.

31. See also Bahya, *Commentary*, on Genesis 7:23 and 30:20, for other instances of pointing to two median lines.

32. Warren Zev Harvey, "Judah Halevi's Synesthetic Theory of Prophecy and a Note on the *Zohar*," in *Rivkah Shatz-Uffenheiner Memorial Volume* (in Hebrew), eds. R. Elior and J. Dan (Jerusalem: Department of Jewish Thought, 1996), vol. I, pp. 142–47.

33. See Altmann, "Ladder of Ascension," pp. 3–6 and 29–30.

34. See Gershom Scholem, *Origins of the Kabbalah*, trans. A. Arkush, ed. R. Z. J. Werblowsky (Philadelphia: Jewish Publishing Society and Princeton University Press, 1987), pp. 460–61.

35. This issue requires a separate analysis that cannot be done here.

36. *Sefer ha-Temunah*, fol. 30a. "By her means" is translated from `Olim we-Yordim bah*; the Hebrew is a bit ambiguous.

37. Ibid.

38. *Commentary on Sefer Ha-Temunah*, fol. 9b; and Altmann, "Ladder of Ascension," p. 28. The quote is Genesis 28:17.

39. *Commentary on Sefer ha-Temunah*, fol. 9b. The first quote is Genesis 2:19. "The righteous" is Jacob.

40. See Rabbi Shlomo Yitzhaqi's interpretation of Genesis 28:17 quoting *Genesis Rabba* 69:7.

41. I shall deal with the manner in which Mircea Eliade treated this biblical episode and its importance for his understanding of the development of Judaism in the concluding remarks to this volume.

42. See also another writing belonging to this Kabbalistic circle, the *Commentary on the Passover Haggadah*, printed anonymously together with Rabbi Moses de Leon's *Sefer ha-Nefesh ha-Hakhamah* (Basle, 1608), col. 9, fol. 4c. It should be noted that according to a reference to a Midrash that I cannot identify, the ladder of Jacob is none other than the tree of life, and Jacob has been shown the souls that ascend upon it. See the mid-thirteenth century *Commentary on the Pentateuch* by the Ashkenazi Rabbi Efrayyim ben Shimshon, ed. Joel Klugmann (Jerusalem: Orthodox Publications Co., 1992), I, p. 104, where he mentions *Midrash Tanhuma*.

43. See, for example, Haviva Pedaya, *Nahmanides: Cyclical Time and Holy Text* (in Hebrew) (Tel Aviv: Am Oved, 2003).

44. Rabbi Hayyim Vital, `Etz ha-Da`at Tov*, fol. 20c. The first quote is Isaiah 4:5. On *Wa-Yaqhel*, see *Zohar* II, fol. 211a; as well as chapter 3, n. 22 in the current study.

45. Vital, `Etz ha-Da`at Tov*, fol. 20d.

46. *BT, Niddah*, fol. 30b.

47. See Yehuda Liebes, "Myth vs. Symbol in the Zohar and in Lurianic Kabbalah," in *Essential Papers on Kabbalah*, ed. Lawrence Fine (New York: New York University Press, 1995), pp. 212–42.

48. Kaufmann, *Spuren* (German part), pp. 61–62; and Moshe Idel, "The Sources of the Circle Images in *Dialoghi d'Amore*" (in Hebrew), *Iyyun* 28 (1978): pp. 162–66.

49. See Umberto Cassuto, "Un rabino fiorentino del secolo XV," *Rivista Israelitica* 3 (1906): pp. 116–28, 224–28; and ibid., 4 (1907): pp. 33–37 and 225–29.

50. See Kaufmann, *Spuren* (German part), pp. 56–60.

51. Ms. Jerusalem NUL, Heb. 8* 598, fol. 24a. This Platonic view of the soul also is quoted in Pico's commentary on B. Benivieni's *Canzone d'Amore* III:7 in Pico della Mirandola, *Opera Omnia* (Basilia, 1557), I, p. 915.

52. Ms. Paris (BN) Heb. 849, fol. 53a. On this unnamed work by Alemanno, see Gershom Scholem, "An Unknown Work of R. Yohanan Alemanno" (in Hebrew), *Qiryat Sefer* V (1929): pp. 273–77. "Generating nature" is translated from *Teva` mehavveh*. The occurrence of the term *Teva`*—nature—in Alemanno's texts is crucial; by virtue of it, we may conclude that his perception of Jacob's ladder influenced Pico rather than other discussions of it, as shall be discussed below.

53. See Barbara Newman, *God and the Goddesses: Vision, Poetry, and Belief in the Middle Ages* (Philadelphia: University of Pennsylvania Press, 2003), pp. 51–137.

54. See Idel, "Sources of Circle Images," p. 165; and idem, "The Anthropology of Yohanan Alemanno: Sources and Influences," *Annali di storia dell'esegesi* 7:1 (1990): pp. 93–112.

55. Rabbi Yohanan ben Isaac Alemanno, *Sefer Sha`ar ha-Hesheq* (Livorno, 1790), fols. 38a–39a, corrected according to Ms. Oxford-Bodleiana 1535, fol. 103a. For more on cosmoerotism and Alemanno, see ch. 5 in Moshe Idel, *Kabbalah and Eros* (forthcoming).

56. This is the translation of E. L. Fobbes, printed in E. Cassirer, P. O. Kristeller, and J. H. Randall, Jr., eds., *The Renaissance Philosophy of Man* (Chicago: University of Chicago Press, 1956), p. 230. The Latin original is: "At nec satin hoc erit si per Jacob scalam discursantibus angelic comites esse volumus, nisi et a gradu in gradum rite promoveri et a scalarum tramite deorbitate nusquam et reciprocos obire excursus bene apti prius intructique fuerimus. Quod cum per astem sermocinalem sive rationariam erimus conse cuti, Iam cherubico spiritu animati per scalarum id est naturae, gradus phiiosophantes, a centre ad centrum omnia pervadentes, nunc unum quasi Osirim in multitudinem vi titanica discerpentes descendemus; nunc multitudimem quasi Osiridis membra in unum vi phocba colligentes ascendemus; donec in sinu Patris, qui super scales est, tandem quiescentes theologica felicitate consummabimur." Pico, *Opera Omnia* (Basileae, 1572), p. 116.

57. The term "purified souls" is used by Pico himself in a sentence immediately preceding the quoted passage: "Tum bene compositam ac expiatam animam naturalis philosophiae lumine perfundamus."

58. See Ms. Firenze, Medicea-Laurenziana Or. 493, fols. 75b–90b, which was described by Richler, "Identification of the Anonymous Translator." Interestingly enough, I identified another manuscript of this translation extant in Italy in the Vatican Library, Hebrew 290. See also, Moshe Idel, "Jewish Mystical Thought in the Florence of Lorenzo il Magnifico," in *La cultura ebraica all'epoca di Lorenzo il Magnifico*, a cura di Dora Liscia Bemporad e Ida Zatelli (Florence: Leo Olschki, 1998), pp. 36–37.

59. See Couliano, *Experiences de l'extase*, pp. 86–88. For a useful bibliography on the soul's ascent and ladder imagery, see Origen, *Contre Celse*, ed.

M. Borret (Paris: Le Cerf, 1969), vol. III, pp. 231–33; and *Contra Celsum*, ed. H. Chadwick (Cambridge: Cambridge University Press, 1980), pp. 333–35.

60. See Kaufmann, *Spuren*, pp. 56–60. Kaufmann does not discuss or identify the passage from `Einei ha-`Edah. See also Moshe Idel, "Sources of Circle Images," pp. 160–66.

61. See the sources referred to in Moshe Idel, "The Throne and the Seven-branched Candlestick: Pico Della Mirandola's Hebrew Source," *Journal of the Warburg and Courtauld Institutes* XL (1977): p. 291, n. 7.

62. Joseph Perles, "Les Savants Juifs a Florence a l'Epoque de Laurent de Medicis," *REJ* XII ((1886: p. 245.

63. See G. dell'Acqua and L. Munster, "I rapporti di Giovanni Pico della Mirandola con alcuni filosofi ebrei," *L'opera e il pensiero di Giovanni Pico della Mirandola nella storia dell'umanesimo* (Florence: Leo Olschki, 1965), vol. II, pp. 149–68.

64. See Moshe Idel, "The Study Program of R. Yohanan Alemanno" (in Hebrew), *Tarbiz* 48 (1979): pp. 304–30. Though Alemanno wrote almost all his works after 1489, he collected the pertinent materials for them at least from 1470, according to his notebook in Ms. Oxford-Bodleiana 2234. Therefore, when he first met Pico in the mid-1480s, he was already an accomplished scholar.

65. Pico enumerates the different kinds of speculations man has to pass in order to achieve the final perfection: (1) moral philosophy, (2) the art of thinking or preaching, (3) natural philosophy, and (4) theology. They form the steps of another ladder—the ladder of sciences, which also was proposed as an explanation for Jacob's ladder. Compare to the Hebrew texts adduced by Altmann, "Ladder of Ascension," pp, 11–15 and 20–21.

66. This epistemological interpretation has been forwarded by several scholars; see, for example, Henri de Lubac, *Pic de la Mirandole: Études et discussions* (Paris: Aubier-Montaigne, 1974), p. 99; and Stevie Davies, *Renaissance Views of Man* (Manchester: Manchester University Press, 1978), p. 81.

67. Altmann, "Ladder of Ascension," p. 21; the quote occurs on p. 61. Ibn Tibbon's source seems to be Al-Farabi, as pointed out by Altmann.

68. Ibid., pp. 61–62, where two Karaite versions of ibn Tibbon's view are discussed.

69. See Chaim Wiszubski, *Pico della Mirandola's Encounter with Jewish Mysticism* (Cambridge: Harvard University Press, 1988), pp. 248–50 and 262–63.

70. Pico della Mirandola, *Conclusiones cabalisticae* LIX: "Qui profunde consideraverit quadruplicem rerum statum: primo unionis et stabilitae mansionis, secundo processionis, tertio reuersionis, quarto beatificae reunionis, uidebit litteram Beth cum prima littera primum, cum media medium, cum ultimis ultimi operari."

71. Wiszubski, *Pico della Mirandola*, pp. 164–65 and 184.

72. Edgar Wind, *Pagan Mysteries in the Renaissance* (London: Farber & Farber, 1958), pp. 115 and 144–45.

73. Chaim Wirszubski, *A Christian Kabbalist Reads the Law* (in Hebrew) (Jerusalem: Mossad Bialik, 1977), pp. 16–17. This discussion on Proclus has

not been included in the English version of his book, *Pico della Mirandola*. Wind did not refer to Pico's thesis, and Chaim Wirszubski did not refer to his *Oratio*.

74. See Wind, *Pagan Mysteries*, pp. 134 and 174.

75. Macrobius, *Commentary on the Dream of Scipio*, trans. William Harris Stahl (New York: Columbia University Press, 1952), p. 136; idem, *Opera*, ed. L. Ianus (Lipsiae, 1848), I, pp. 73–74: "Ipsum autem Liberum patrem Orphaici *nous hylikon* suspicantur intellegi, Qui ab illo individuo natus in singulos ipso dividitur. Ideo in illorum sacris traditur titanio furore in membra discerptus et frustis sepultis rursus unus et integer emersisse, quia nous quem diximus mentem vocari, ex individuo praebendo se dividendum et rursus ex diviso ad individuum revertendo et mundi implet officia, et naturae suae archana non deserit."

76. On the Neoplatonic interpretations of the myth of Osiris, see Jean Pepin, "Utilisations philosophiques du myths d'Isis et Osiris dans la tradition Platonicienne," in *Sagesse et Religion* (Colloque de Strasbourg, October 1976 [Presses Universitaires de France, 1979]), pp. 51–64, especially p. 63, where Damascius's view is discussed.

77. See Bernard McGinn, *The Golden Chain* (Washington: Cisterian Studies Series, 1972).

78. I followed with few changes the translation of Martin and Sara Goodman in Reuchlin's *On the Art of the Kabbalah*, pp. 240–45; and J. Pistorius, ed., *Ars Cabalistica* (Basle, 1587), p. 687: "At illud bonum quod Deus nominatur, non plane a nobis poterit ob nostrae conditionis fragilitatem, nisi gradibus atque scalis ascendi, quae quidem ut uos loqui consueuistis instar Homericae catenae, ut uero Iudaei nos secundum divina eloquia dicimus carte ad speciem scalae Iacob patris nostri de supercoelestibus porriguntur in terram, tanquam restis quaedam aut funis aurea coelitus ad nos directa veluti linea visualis uarias penetrans naturas."

79. Pico della Mirandola, *Heptaplus, or the Discourse on the Seven Days of Creation*, Proem part V, trans. J. B. McGaw (New York: Philosophical Library, 1977), p. 70.

80. Quoted from D. P. Walker, *The Ancient Theology* (London: Duckworth, 1972), p. 57, n. 2: "Divinorum autem scientia qua veluti aurea quadam cathena in coelum trahimur pro ancilla utitur. Christiana vero theologia; qua veluti supremo schalarum Jacob gradu in coelum ascendimus pro domina atque matistra."

81. *The Works of Dionysius the Areopagite*, trans. J. Parker (Oxford, 1897), vol. I, pp. 27–28. Reuchlin knew Pseudo-Dionysius well and quoted him several times. On this passage and its impact on some Jewish thinkers, see Idel, *Enchanted Chains*, ch. 4, section 5.

82. On Pico's attempt to assimilate the doctrines of the ancient Hebrews to those of Dionysius, see F. A. Yates, *Giordano Bruno and the Hermetic Tradition* (Chicago: University of Chicago Press, 1964), pp. 121–26.

83. See Reuchlin, *On the Art of the Kabbalah*, pp. 51, 81, 115, 117, 159 and 231.

84. See Marion L. D. Kuntz, *Colloquium of the Seven about Secrets of the Sublime* (Princeton: Princeton University Press, 1975), p. 32. Kuntz does not even mention the similarity between Reuchlin's and Bodin's works. The common attribution of a Jewish interpretation of Homer's chain to a Jew is interesting evidence for the influence of Reuchlin on Bodin.

85. See the translation of A. D. Imerti, *The Expulsion of the Triumphant Beast* (New Brunswick, N.J.: Rutgers University Press, 1964), p. 236. For the original text see *Spaccio de la bestia trionfante*, dialogo terzo (G. Bruno, *Dialoghi Italiani*, ed. G. Aquilecchia (Florence, 1958), p. 777): "Sicome la divinita descende in certo modo per quanto che si comunica alla natura, cossi alla divinita s'ascende per la natura, cossi per la vita rilucente nelle cose naturali si monta alla vita che soprasiede a quelle...in fatto vedo come que sapienti con questi mezzi erano potenti a farsi familiari affabili e domestici gli dei che per voci, che mandavano da le statue, gli donavano consigli, dottrine, divinazioni ed instituzioni sopraumane; onde con magici e divini riti per la medesima scala di natura salevano a l'alto della divinita, per la quale la divinita descende sino alle cose minimo per la comunicazione di se stessa." An interesting attempt to determine Bruno's source of this passage was made by W. S. Hecksher, "Melancholia (1541)—An Essay in the Rhetoric of Description by Joachim Camerarius," in *Joachim Camerarius*, ed. Frank Baron (Munich: Fink, 1978), p. 58. According to Hecksher, Bruno was influenced by Ramon Lull's "Scala Intellectus." See Lull's *Opusculia*, III (Hildesheim, 1973), p. 16. The similarity between Lull and Bruno notwithstanding, they use different terms: *scala intellectus* versus *scala di natura*. Moreover, the Egyptian background of Pico's and Bruno's discussions of the ladder motif is missing in Lull. Nevertheless, it seems that the affinity of Lull's view to Pico and Bruno may be the result of their usage of a common source: al-Batalyawsi's *Book of Imaginary Circles*. I hope to elaborate elsewhere on the possibility of such influence. The similarity between the Andalusian Arab philosopher and Lull is ignored in the most recent and comprehensive study dedicated to Islamic influences on Lull; see Dominique Urvoy, *Penser l'Islam—Les Presupposes Islamiques de l'"Art" de Lull* (Paris: Vrin, 1980).

86. See Yates, *Giordano Bruno*, pp. 205 ff.

87. Ibid., pp. 211–16; see also pp. 216–18, where the influence of another Hermetic text, *Kore Kosmou*, is indicated, which ends with the praise of Isis and Osiris.

88. Bruno, *Dialoghi Italiani*, p. 776.

89. Compare Pico's statement on "powers scattered and sown in the world by the loving kindness of God," *Oratio* in *The Renaissance Philosophy of Man*, p. 248. For the pantheistic view of Osiris in Athanasius Kircher apparently influenced by Bruno, see Yates, *Giordano Bruno*, p. 488.

90. Bruno, *De la causa, principio e uno proemale epistola*, in *Dialoghi Italiani*, p. 186: "come ne li doi estremi, che si dicono nell'stremita de la scala della natura, noe e piu da contemplare doi principii che uno, doi enti che uno, doi contrarri che e diversi, che uno concordante e medesimo. Ivi l'altezza e

profondita, l'abisso e luce inaccessa, la tenebra e chiarezza, il magno e parvo, il confuso e distinto."

91. Ibid., p. 329: "voglio che notiate essere una e medesima scala per la quale la natura descende alla produzion de le cose, e l'intelletto ascende alla cognizion di quelle; e che l'uno e l'altra da l'unita procede all'unita, passando per la moltitudine di mezzi."

92. Ibid., p. 305. In another discussion, the ladder is clearly described as a chain of beings: "Everything that exists, beginning with the supernal and supreme entity, has a certain order and makes a dependence, a ladder by means of which there is an ascent from the compounded things to the simple ones." Ibid., p. 298: "tutto quel che e (cominciando da l'ente summo e supremo) ave un certo ordine e fa una dependenza, una scala nella quale si monta de la cose composte alle simplici." Compare to Bruno, *De Gli Eroici Furori*, in *Dialoghi Italiani*, pp. 1026–27. On the phrases "scale of nature" and "scale of beings," see also Lovejoy, *Great Chain of Being*.

93. *De magia naturali*, 6, in Bruno, *Opere magiche*, Edizione diretta da Michele Ciliberto, a cura di Simonetta Bassi, Elisabetta Scaparone, Nicoletta Tirrinazi (Milan: Adelphi, 2002), pp. 168–70. See also, in the Rumanian version of Couliano, *Eros and Magic* (Bucharest: Nemira, 1999), pp. 348–55, a discussion of this passage that was not included in the English shortened version of this book. See also the translation and notes to this passage in Giordano Bruno, *De la magie*, trans. D. Sonnier and B. Donne (Paris: Editions Allia, 2002), pp. 14–15.

Another discussion of Jacob's ladder as the ladder of nature occurs in Bruno's *De Magia*; see Lorenzo Giusso, *La Tradizione Ermetica nella filosofia italiana* (Rome, n.d.), pp. 93–94, where Bruno refers to Jacob as "cabalisticus Jacob."

94. Bruno, *Opere magiche*, p. 171, n. to ll. 16–17.

95. Ibid., pp. 160–61 and 228–29. For affinities between Bruno and Kabbalah, see Karen Silvia de Leon-Jones, *Giordano Bruno and the Kabbalah: Prophets, Magicians, and Rabbis* (New Haven: Yale University Press, 1997).

96. See Friedrich W. J. von Schelling, *Bruno, or, On the Natural and Divine Principles of Things*, trans. Michael G. Vater (Albany: State University of New York Press, 1984); idem, *Saemmtliche Werke* (Stuttgart and Augsburg, 1859), vol. l, 4, pp. 328–29. Schelling used, as Wind remarked (*Pagan Mysteries*, p. 161, n. l), F. H. Jacobi's translation of parts of Bruno's *De Cause*; see Jacobi, *Werke* (1819), vol. IV, pp. 5–46 (after his *Ueber die Lehre der Spinoza*).

97. Wind, *Pagan Mysteries*, p. 161, n. 1.

98. On this theme, see Harry A. Wolfson, *Philo* (Cambridge: Harvard University Press, 1982), vol. I, pp. 87–163.

99. The metamorphoses of the theme of Homer's *catena aurea* is traced in Lovejoy's *Great Chain of Being*. The description of the sefirot as a chain that sometimes also reaches the lowest point of the world, in the vein of the chain of being, occurs several times in medieval Kabbalistic texts, and it requires lengthy discussion. See Idel, *Enchanted Chains*.

100. *Oeuvres Completes*, ed. L. Aime-Martin (Paris, 1825), vols. 8–9.

101. Joseph Herzberg of Mohilev, *Sullam ha-Teva`* (Vilnius, 1850); Levensohn's poem is printed on pp. v–viii.

102. See Robert Bonfil, *Rabbis and Jewish Communities in Renaissance Italy*, trans. Jonathan Chipman (London: The Littman Library, 1993), pp. 295–97.

Concluding Remarks

1. PILLARS, PARADISES AND *GESTALT*-COHERENCE

The emergence of an ontic continuum between the righteous in this world, described as related to a pillar that takes him from the lower to the higher paradise, or palace, and the description of God, or one of the divine powers designated as a pillar or a median pillar, may reflect more than an attempt to create a comprehensive *axis mundi*. This cosmic continuum can be broken down into three distinct parts: the human, the path or the technique and finally the divine realm. When the righteous uses the pillar, he arrives at the divine realm, which also is conceived as a pillar.

I would like to suggest the possibility that in several important cases, some of which have been analyzed in detail elsewhere, there is an affinity among the specific nature of the technique used by a mystic, of his theology and of the experience he attains.[1] In our case, the architectural depiction of paradise, which has the pillar at the middle serving as a bridge between the lower and the higher realms, corresponds to the architecture of the divine realm, which also includes a power described as a pillar that connects different parts of this realm. This is a case of what I propose calling *Gestalt*-coherence.[2] The consonance among the three elements also is evident when we examine one of the most prominent epithetons for these three factors, the term *tzaddiq*. The mystic, the pillar and God are referred to as the righteous in rabbinic literature, and in the theosophical scheme, the ninth sefirah is described by the very same term.[3] In the Midrash, the affinity between the righteous and God is pointed out explicitly, and God describes himself as akin to the righteous.[4]

Indeed, the rabbinic use of the term righteous in connection to a cosmic pillar, and that of the Kabbalists to a pillar in order to describe the righteous, has some important parallels in the history of religion. The confluence of the pillar and the righteous constitutes a fascinating similarity to the Vedic identification of the *brahman* with the cosmic pillar, *skambha*.[5] In Manichaenism and in early Christianity, the column of light is connected to the perfect man.[6] In Islam, Muhammad is sometimes described as the pillar of light.[7] In Ismailiah, an extreme Shiite sect presumably influenced by Manicheanism, there is a strong connection between the phrases `amud al-nur, or al-`amud al-nurany, the pillar of light or the luminous pillar, and the Imam.[8] In Sufism, the perfect man is described as *qutb*, the axis of the world.[9] With the clear exception of the Hindu view, these similarities may stem from a common Semitic source.

This consonance is evident in other cases dealing with personal eschatology as well. So, for example, if for Maimonides the quintessence of man that survives his death is the intellect, then in his writings, paradise is described as an intellectual experience. Moreover, at least in some cases for Maimonides, God is conceived of as an intellect. Cultivating one's intellect is, according to this thinker, the only way to reach an eschatological experience. He does not accept the classical architectural picture of paradise from Jewish sources but rather offers a nonspatial understanding of this experience.

The same affinity also occurs in Jewish Neoplatonism. The most significant example is found in the writings of Isaac Israeli, one of the earliest Jewish philosophers, where man is described as achieving a union with "the upper soul, and the illumination by the light of the intellect and the beauty and splendor of wisdom. When attaining this rank, he becomes spiritual, and will be joined in union to the light, which is created, without mediator, by the power of God, and will become one that exalts and praises the Creator for ever and in all eternity. This then will be his paradise and the goodness of his reward, and the bliss of his rest and unsullied beauty."[10] As Alexander Altmann and Samuel Stern note, this Neoplatonic interpretation of paradise is consonant with the Talmudic view on the righteous that enjoys the splendor of the Shekhinah. As pointed out by the two scholars, the above text was paraphrased in a twelfth-century writing by Rabbi Joseph ibn Tzaddiq and served as the background for later discussions in Kabbalah. The terminology of light informs most discussions of the emanative processes in the texts of both Israeli and his disciple, Rabbi Dunash ibn Tamim, influenced by Neoplatonic sources originally in Greek as well as in their Arabic versions. Cleaving to the upper soul, or the soul of the world that is the Neoplatonic intermediary, is interpreted in biblical terms as the place the human soul enjoys. Neoplatonic spirituality, the subtle individualistic eschatology of which closely reflects mystical interests, contributed substantially to the later medieval tone of discussions on eschatological issues. Each thinker has his own description of paradise and method of reaching it.

I now turn to an understanding of paradise in the later writings of one of the Kabbalists who was very close to Zoharic literature: Rabbi Joseph Gikatilla. Man and God cooperate in their efforts to sustain an intermediary world that mediates between them; God "pushes" this structure downwards, while man "pulls" the influx, which counteracts the upward tendency to return:

> 'Eden the secret of Unity is found until the tenth *sefirah* of *Malkhut*, and from *Malkhut* downward there is the secret of separation and the secret of the "river that goes out of Eden to water the Garden, and from there it separates and becomes four heads." And from 'Eden to the Garden there is the secret of Unity and everything is done by the river that waters the garden-beds of the garden from the emanation from 'Eden. Happy is he who knows how to unify the branches of the Garden to the river, and the river to the 'Eden, then everything becomes a true and perfect union because of him, and behold he is repairing all the pipes and draws the supernal waters throughout the pipes to all the garden-beds and waters the mountains...and on this man it is said "and the righteous is the foundation of the world"...and by him the *sefirot* were unified and the supernal waters were drawn and running through the pipes of the [divine] will [*Hefetz*] through the channels and water all the garden-beds of the Garden, and all the worlds were blessed by him...and because Abraham was keeping the guard of God and drew the blessings through the pipes and the channels from the 'Eden, which is the [*sefirah* of] *Keter*, until the Garden, which is *Malkhut*, then all the worlds were nourished by all the blessings in the world.[11]

In a manner somehow reminiscent of one of the passages from the Bahir adduced above, the human righteous, rather than the divine one, is envisioned by Rabbi Gikatilla as the keeper of the garden. In another passage from this treatise we learn that:

> When a righteous who knows to unify the true unity is found in the world, and he unifies the branches with the root and waters the gar-

den-beds of the Garden, by him all the worlds are blessed and nourished... and all this is connected to the man who knows the secret of
Malkhut until *Keter*, and all that is lower than *Malkhut* is receiving
blessing and influx and maintenance each and every one according
to its species and its way. And this is the secret of [the verse] "Or let
him take hold of my strength, that he may make peace with me."[12]

The Garden and the Eden, which stand respectively for the last and the
first sefirah, symbolize the entire sefirotic realm. In other words, *Gan
`Eden* is the symbol of the whole divine pleroma. The righteous man is
considered to be a connoisseur, one who knows the structure of paradise, its pipes and channels; how to unify all its components; and, by
ensuring unity, how to create the *sine qua non* condition for the circula-
tion of energy within the divine system and from it into the lower
worlds. The repair of the divine pleroma is the quintessence of the religious obligation of the righteous, who is described both as the foundation of the world and as someone who strengthens the divine system.
As pointed out implicitly in the above quotes through the use of the
terms "righteous" and "his guard" and more explicitly elsewhere in the
same treatise, the regulation of the circuit in the intra-divine and extra-
divine realms depends upon the performance of the commandments.
They constitute the main *modus operandi* of the theurgical Kabbalist.

The phenomenological is as significant as the historical approach.
The ascent on high is just one instance in which the historical approach
might be transcended in order to determine not only which elements
are the result of historical transmission and development, but also what
the common core of the phenomena is. Pinpointing the basic phenomena that emerge from a certain literature and describing their reverberations might be considered their inner history. Here we are adopting a
specific type of phenomenological approach, which assumes that a
model that appears in Jewish mysticism may articulate its main conceptual structure, and in our case, this mystical–magical model transcends
the boundaries of various types of Jewish mystical literature. From a
more general viewpoint, the survival of shamanic imagery and perhaps
also experiences in the remnants of shamanic religions, in Yoga and in
eighteenth-century Hasidism invites new reflections on the history of
religion in general. Shamanic remnants in the Carpathian Mountains,
Hasidic practice there and elsewhere (theoretical as it may be) and the
continuous practice of Yoga in the West demonstrate that archaic im-

agery and presumably experiences have not been extinguished even in the regions and religions that Mircea Eliade believes were conquered by the "historical" penchant in religion.

2. PILLARS AND SOME SEMANTIC OBSERVATIONS

The meanings of the terms used in the above discussions require further scrutiny. Pillar, ring, firmament, male and female, or *hieros gamos*, concrete as they are in ordinary forms of discourse, may receive different types of valence in Kabbalistic discourse. In an example from one of the above passages, Moses stands on a stone and prays to the median pillar, conceived as somehow divine.[13] One way to describe the manner in which meaning is created in theosophical–theurgical Kabbalah is to assume that the authors and their readers understood specific terminology as symbolic. However, the term "symbol" itself requires more precise definition. In the introduction to this study, I addressed Gershom Scholem's view of this cardinal concept in his approach to Kabbalah. The way in which modern scholarship under the impact of Scholem, Johann Reuchlin and Franz Molitor understands symbols is informed by the German Romantic approach rather than by Kabbalah. The latter is assumed to be a transcendental theology that does not allow a precise understanding of the details and nature of the divine structure by man, thus attributing an important role to symbols. On some occasions, the assumption of scholars is that Kabbalistic symbolism is a way to overcome the ineffability of the supernal realm or of experiences of that realm. So, for example, Scholem notes that "[s]ymbols, by their very nature, are a means of expressing an experience that is in itself expressionless," and "the Kabbalist...discovers...a reflection of the true transcendence"; his view is that the symbolized realm is "a hidden and inexpressible reality."[14] Isaiah Tishby reverberates these views—though he does not mention his source—when he says that the symbol is "representative of an occult, or hidden, entity or process, that is neither revealed in itself at all nor can it be expressed in a direct manner."[15] In various studies, I have taken issue with this simplistic application of the German Romantic view of symbolism to the variegated literature of Kabbalists.[16] My basic assumption is that in many sources, the ten sefirot function as a code by means of which the Kabbalists interpreted canonical texts.

In reflecting on the topics dealt with above from this "code" perspective, the pillar rarely is used alone as a symbolic or non-symbolic object. Rather, it connects different factors, it serves as a conduit, it supports or suspends. In other words, it is part of either a natural structure or an artificial architecture. When encountering the term in Kabbalistic sources, it is impossible to impose any single meaning on the text. In some instances the pillar describes the intra-paradisiacal column, and thus a non-divine entity, while in others, it points to powers within the sefirotic structure. In some of cases, like the bulk of the Zohar, the sefirot are considered to be part of the divine essence, and thus the pillar represents a divine manifestation. In others, such as the later layers of the Zoharic literature, *Tiqqunei Zohar* and *Ra`ya' Meheimna'*, the ten sefirot are conceived as instruments of rather than part of the essence of divine activity.

Even when the same divine power is described several times in the same layer of the Zohar, the meaning of the pillar differs. Though sometimes it is identified with the sefirah of Yesod, at other times it is envisioned as the tree of life. It sometimes functions as the phallus, while in other cases it has more cosmic connotations or an eschatological function. The meaning of the pillar is Yesod in one layer of the Zohar and Tiferet according to another.[17] Yet these concepts do not exist in the extant testimonies of Kabbalists who engaged in allegedly ineffable psychanodic experiences in their efforts to reveal the nature of the distant and unknown divine power. In the vast majority of cases, Kabbalists resorted to more comprehensive modes of thought—geometrical, vegetal, architectural, organic or eschatological—known from ordinary experiences and culture. All these efforts were meant to describe the functions of a certain power within a broader net of powers that constitutes the sefirotic system. In other words, the meaning attributed to the pillar is not necessarily—if at all—derived from an experience of ineffability but from projecting conceptual schemes from this world on the structure of the supernal world.

The best way to understand discussions about the pillar in relatively late compositions, such as Zoharic literature, is to determine the comprehensive schemes in which the pillar functions and to establish the meaning of the pillar within the specific context. Understanding, for example, the approach to the center of the circle in medieval geometry helps in interpreting discussions about the pillar as a center, and medieval anatomy may provide clues to interpreting the phallic overtones of some texts. What interferes with a proper understanding of treatments of the pillar is the assumption that meanings from one set of reference automatically should be read into discussions informed by other sets. Some may intersect; for example, the geometrical scheme includes the concept that the center, sometimes referred to as the pillar, sustains the circle, just as in an architectural scheme the pillar sustains the structure. In the former case the concept of sustaining may by metaphorical, while in the latter it may function more practically. Both nuances may or may not be present in cases in which the pillar indicates the phallus.

Since Kabbalistic interpretive ingenuity is quite remarkable, even instances of the organic scheme may be loaded with other semantic valences, but such intersections do not automatically become a given and stable fact that then should be considered in other cases where the pillar is mentioned. The gist of this observation is that, when the diachronical development of a certain scheme emerges, we should not automatically assume that it can be amalgamated into a more comprehensive scheme. No doubt, such amalgamation eventually might occur, but it also might indicate a new diachronical development altogether. Both diachronical and synchronic processes should be analyzed carefully before striving to totalize the different meanings of the same symbol as if they were automatically relevant to one another.

Especially insofar as early Kabbalah is concerned, my proposal is that pillars as symbols were effective not because they pointed to one or more sefirotic powers, as imagined by Scholem and his school, but rather because they were able to describe types of relationships among sefirot. Their function was to conceptualize a web of affinities on the concrete pole, whether implicitly or explicitly, that allowed the imagining of a supernal web of affinities on the spiritual pole. The pillar connects parts of concrete reality in the manner of a house or a palace; thus it can be imagined to indicate the connectiveness of different planes of reality. It sustains and suspends here, and it may designate something similar there.

The theosophical systems presented by most Kabbalists are rarely as transcendental as some scholars claim. Though representing a reality considered to be spiritual, the early theosophical Kabbalists cultivated a few schemes that organized the order and structure of the divine powers in a relatively simple and often quite understandable manner. Comprehensive symbols like the tree, the garden and Adam organized the relationship between a set of ten divine powers. The attributes of these powers and the nature of the more comprehensive scheme were known through the study of books or with masters. Numerous symbols were not needed to describe the basics of the scheme, but rather to flesh it out and to enrich the theosophical skeleton. Then these semiotic systems "attracted" canonical linguistic material to the theosophical code and impregnated it with new meanings.[18] With time, the theosophical system became more complex, as seen in the example from Rabbi Vital's `Etz Hayyim. However, even in such cases, ineffability was hardly the name of the game. By knowing a supernal ontological paradigm that was imagined to inform all the lower processes, it became easier to load linguistic material with new valences.

Semiotically speaking, the main process that takes place in theosophical Kabbalah consists of a series of dialogues between schemes below—geometrical, vegetal or architectural—and paradigmatic schemes above, which may reflect some of the characteristics of the lower schemes. When the two correspond, we may speak about isomorphism and detailed correspondences. In cases in which they do not, the higher scheme or the theosophical code is enriched by adopting details of the lower scheme.

Despite the recurrence of the pillar theme in many Kabbalistic discussions, there is little of *realia* that transpires from them. The pillar as an eschatological path obviously could not be represented in the immediate reality of anyone in Spain or elsewhere; no specifically tangible pillar seems to have existed beyond the Kabbalistic discussions. The affinities between the pillar and the supernal Jerusalem and Zion do not encourage the possibility that a specific place in Spain, where most of the quotes analyzed above were written, is being described. Neither did the sixteenth-century Kabbalists living in the land of Israel elaborate on a specific locale connected with the different pillars.

What is more salient for our discussion is the fact that little about the detailed nature of the pillars can be extracted from Kabbalistic treatments. This literature, based on *imaginaire* of other worlds, fails to flesh out a more elaborated image of the pillars. No specific details— length, breadth or specific form—are mentioned. It is the word, `amud or *samkha'*, more than any imagined object that draws the attention of the Kabbalists. Or, to put it differently, the type of imagination that is representative of the Kabbalists is connected more to words, their contexts and the conceptual schemes in which they appear than to what they represent in external reality as objects. From this point of view, the Kabbalists differ dramatically from the experience of the archaic specialists of the sacred as described by Eliade. These experts were less concerned with texts and words and emphasized the importance of objects, understood to have some privileged status, which allow, in some cases, extraordinary experiences for elites. To take one example, the median pillar is described in some sources as related to the letter *Waw* in the Hebrew alphabet, especially in the divine name.[19] However, in Zoharic literature, the letter *Waw* is described as the pillar that comprises six other sefirot. What is new is the addition of the concept of median pillar to discussions that previously preferred the term median line.[20]

As described by Eliade, archaic mentalities were much more concrete, though they too dealt not only with the simple objective valences of their immediate reality but also with imaginary constructs that had special qualities attributed to them. From this point of view, Eliade's religious categories of center and *axis mundi* represent not the inherent qualities of a certain place but the manner in which that place was seen by archaists. However—and this needs to be emphasized—the Kabbalists did not believe, as the archaists did, that they were living in but outside of the immediate vicinity of what they considered to be the center of the world. Exile was a complex concept that assumed displacement of an individual not just from a political establishment or a geographical area fraught with nostalgic values—as in the case of Ovidius Naso's exile from Rome to Tomis, for example—but also from the very center of reality. The Roman poet did not want to recreate Rome in his imagination and lived with an acute feeling that he was missing important events taking place in the remote Rome. He did not attempt to build a spiritual architecture that would allow a form of access to *axis mundi*, even post-mortem. His worldview was basically a secular one.

Terms, however, that in some Kabbalistic writings point to distinct entities may be identified in other Kabbalistic works as closely related to one another. So, for example, in many of the discussions above, the pillar is conceived of as distinct from the firmament, while in a certain case in *Tiqqunei Zohar*, the two are explicitly conflated.[21] Following from the discussions above, I conclude that the examination of the details of the treatments of different pillars does not allow an understanding of their function as envisioned by Scholem and his disciples. The pillar is indeed a symbol in many cases, but it must be considered within its particular framework, which may be understood from ordinary human experiences that were projected on high. If this approach is accepted, there is no reason to assume that the supernal world cannot be understood in principle, since its very structure stems from experiences below that were projected on high. German Romantic ineffability does not help us understand the manner in which the pillar functioned but rather the semantic transformations of the term within different conceptual frameworks. These schemes were transmitted over centuries because they were understood and could provide worldviews and meaning, not because they reflected entities beyond human perception. This does not mean that theosophical–theurgical Kabbalah was a sort of casuistics—a second claim of Scholem's school, which in fact neutralizes the first.[22] I propose that an experiential dimension should be assumed in the main layers of the Zohar but less so in its later layers. The emphasis placed in this literature on the posthumous ascent of the soul, rather than living ascensions, may serve as an indication of the attenuation of this ancient ideal among Spanish Jewish mystics, some of whom preferred nousanodia to psychanodia.

3. BETWEEN LITERATURE AND EXPERIENCE

Many of the descriptions dealt with in this study describe posthumous experiences. This is the case in almost all the passages addressed in chapter three and some of the quotes in chapter five. A remaining question concerns the status of these descriptions in comparison to the Besht's discussion of ascents he performed while alive and to other forms of Kabbalah in which experiences of adherence and union with the divine sphere are considered attainable while alive through nousanodia or otherwise. This is important because it deals with the type of mysticism that is characteristic of the main layer of Zoharic literature.

As exemplified in most of the quotes from this literature, there is a certain reticence in admitting a full-fledged mystical union with the divinity, even in the case of the select righteous souls. The pillar is described as a vehicle for both the ascent and descent of these souls, so we must assume that the anonymous Kabbalist did not envisage a total absorption of them. Only in one case do we witness absorption into the "body of the king," namely the sefirah of Tiferet. As noted above, this is not the view of Rabbi Moses de Leon or of Rabbi Joseph Gikatilla, who assume that it is possible to attain the experience of Keter. I propose that emphasis on the architectural image of the sefirot, with the pillar at the center, represents something deeper than a form of *imaginaire*. It is assumed that Rabbi Gikatilla, in a manner similar to other Kabbalists, such as the anonymous author of *Sefer Ma`arekhet ha-'Elohut*, worked with strong architectural images. The sefirotic realm is understood to function as a space within which it is possible to ascend and descend, to integrate for a while and to exit, as discussed in chapter one. Or, to put it in other terms, just as the seven palaces of the paradises were projected on high, so too the pillar as the center of the palaces is projected on the seven lower sefirot. A similar pattern reverberates three times: the seven palaces of the lower paradise and the pillar, the seven higher palaces to which the pillar arrives and the seven lower sefirot. This pattern is reminiscent of the importance of the number seven in time.

The question of time is quintessential. One expects a trans-temporal existence in paradise. However, it is quite obvious that the souls of the righteous follow the same type of order they pursued in this world, dictated by the lunar calendar, gravitating around the seven days of the week and the lunar month. The space and time of the various worlds is dominated by similar patterns. However, time is not just a matter of rhythm. The eve of Sabbath and the head of the month are moments for special forms of rituals that differ from those of the weekdays. This special liturgy is not mentioned explicitly. In at least two cases, however, it is clear that practices below are projected on high: the sacrifices of the souls of the righteous and the copulation of the spirits of the deceased righteous that generates the spirits of the converts. This rhythm also is found in the Hasidic reference to the New Year as a propitious moment for the ascent of the soul. Like space, represented by the special status of the central pillar, time is not homogenous. In other words, the ritualistic structure of Judaism as practiced in the mundane world is reflected by the special mode of existence of the souls of the righteous in paradise. Eschatology is not escapism, an attempt to free oneself from the impositions of rituals in order to attain a beatific vision, which often is a reverberation of the Halakhic way of life on a more sublime plane of being. We learn about the manner in which the Kabbalists envisioned religious perfection while alive from the manner in which the paradisiacal experience is imagined. The historicistic reduction of both eschatology and messianism to an attempt to avoid the pain of the present is too simplistic an approach.

In many descriptions, the afterworld is strongly related to this world. Are the Zoharic descriptions dealt with in earlier chapters "mere" literature? This question recurs in the scholarship of pseudoepigraphical books. It is well known in the study of Jewish ancient apocalypticism, where literary and visionary approaches confront one another.[23] In my opinion, this issue remains an open one in the case of Zoharic literature. It is difficult to find examples of mystical union or ecstatic experiences in the discussions above and in others found in this literature. This does not mean that there is nothing mystical in the ways in which the book portrays the emotional arousal of its heroes. The sharp presence of the divine is presupposed in the homiletic elaboration that permeates this literature. However, their ontology assumes a much more mythical stance for the mystic here below, one in which the continuum between his soul—and sometimes even his body—and the divine is rather strong. In many theosophical–theurgical writings, the most essential human faculty is a prolongation of the divine. In a way, the highest parts of the soul are the lowest extremity of a continuum that includes the divine median line or pillar.

4. On the Pillar and Mircea Eliade's Views on Judaism

The centrality of the views described in the Zohar, a canonical book for many Jewish circles, should qualify any simple description of Judaism. The presence of a strong mythical component in the different stages of this religion is accepted in scholarship now more than ever before, and discussions about the divine pillar in the Zohar, are part of this mythical approach. This relatively new trend should take into consideration not only forms of Kabbalah, but also biblical and rabbinic literature.[24] Such a variegated and complex approach is slowly but steadily making its way into Jewish study.[25] This different understanding of Judaism, which is corroborated by the discussions in this book, proposes a revision to the way that Mircea Eliade understood this religion in most of his writings. If the presence of a pillar is important to "archaic" religiosity, references to pillars are found in abundance in the texts analyzed above.

It is quite obvious that Eliade was acquainted with the importance of the geographical center in rabbinic literature, as several references to its sources are found in his discussions on the center.[26] But in other cases, this rather adequate awareness apparently dissipates. Analyzing Eliade's first sustained efforts to explore the manner in which Judaism developed reveals important pieces of evidence in the evolution of his approach to Judaism and western religions in general. Since they were written in Rumanian in weekly journals, these studies have escaped the attention of scholars dealing with Eliade's thought and its evolution.

In 1937, Eliade expressed particular interest in archeology, architecture and religion. In this year, he delivered some Rumanian radio broadcasts; the first, "New Research on the Most Ancient Civilizations," discussed excavations in Mohenjo-Daro and Ras Amarna, and the second, "Archeological Excavations in the Holy Land."[27] Though related to exceptional building rather than archeology, Eliade also wrote a review in this year of Paul Mus's voluminous *Barabudur*, itself a book review.[28] In a passage printed early in 1937 as part of a chronicle entitled "Before and After the Biblical Miracle," Eliade wrote that:

> The "biblical miracle" remains a question mark; while in Egypt and Babylonia there were perfect moral and religious ideas, the Jewish people transformed those ideas into a religious experience, which was excessively fertile. As Charles Jean has noted, nothing compelled the Jews to be monotheists, prophets, or messianics. An explanation by the dint of race, by the background, by social circumstances, by external influences is insufficient. Some of the biblical ideas have been discovered. Only the Jewish people lived a religious life of the tenacity and density of biblical life.[29]

This passage is the beginning of a long elaboration that gradually shaped Eliade's entire vision of the biblical contribution to religion. The "miracle" refers to not only extraordinary but also unnatural, supernatural development. The three nouns "monotheists, prophets, or messianics"—which stem from Charles Jean—recur in different forms as the quintessence of Jewish religious groups, which revolutionized the history of religion.

More pertinent to our topic, however, is a review that Eliade wrote in 1937 on the results of another excavation made some decades earlier in southern Egypt. Elephantine documents written in Aramaic were discovered that contain a series of testimonies about a colony of Israelites who lived for several decades of the fifth century BC on an island in the Nile. In these documents is evidence of the existence of a temple and the worship of gods like Bethel or Anath, which had been eliminated from official worship in Jerusalem. A French scholar, Albert Vincent, dedicated a voluminous study, *La Religion des Judeo-Arameens d'Elephantine*, to this major finding on the ancient Israelites.[30] The review, entitled "Between Elephantine and Jerusalem,"[31] was printed in the same year and promoted the theory—not embraced by Vincent, but by another scholar, Adolphe Lods—that the Elephantine colony's worship reflected a form of religion shared by the population of Israelites in the seventh and sixth centuries BC and the emigrées who accompanied them when they left their land in the fifth century, the cult of their Israelite contemporaries.[32]

Eliade's major point is that the dream of Jacob in Genesis 28:11–13, which took place in Bethel, is strongly related to the concept of *axis mundi* on the one hand and to a cult of the stone or the column—in Hebrew, *matzevah*—on the other. This natural form of religion was affected by the activity of Jerusalem's elite, who preserved the monotheism of Moses and imposed their ideals by force, destroying the expected development of this religion, which otherwise would have been similar to that of the Elephantine Jews:

> Nothing compelled the people of Israel to become monotheistic. The religious evolution of the Semitic race has nothing exceptional in its structure. An elite revealed monotheism to the Jewish people. The Jews were *converted to* monotheism after long and hard resistance. If left to "evolve" in a natural fashion, the Jews would have obtained a pantheon as large as that which is displayed to us by the Elephantine papyri: with a Great Goddess (like all the other people that participate in the afroasiatic protohistorical cults), with a God of vegetation (so "popular" on the Mediterranean shores and in Asia Minor), and with some other minor gods.[33]

The first sentence constitutes a precise repetition of Charles Jean's view mentioned some months earlier in the same journal but uncited here. An analysis of this dense passage and others discussed below reveals the kernel of Eliade's vision of religion not only in the 1930s, but also later: on the positive side are polytheism, nature, vegetation, stasis, inertia, universality and populace, and on the other, monotheism, elites, miracles and rupture. Therefore, religion is not a variety of approaches that are phenomenologically different from one another but rather exists in two major forms: the first, primordial and natural; the second, unnatural and historical resulting from a deep shift in history.

Who are the elite that, according to Eliade, were responsible for converting the population and changing the "natural" course of development? The answer emerges some lines later: "in Jerusalem the 'monotheistic' elites were watching," the keepers of Moses's message,[34] and, according to another formulation, those who dealt with the "mosaic message":

> But the intervention and history of this message belongs to "the miraculous." A firm will for proselytism makes room for the first time in the history of mankind (IX–VIII centuries). When Moses's message was taken over by the Jerusalemite elites, the history of the Orient starts to change its face. The natural "evolution" would have brought about a religion similar to that at Elephantine. The violence, the pathos, the genius, and the tears of an elite caused an absolute monotheism, prophetism, messianism...[35]

At the end of this quote, we find the trio that emerge in the early 1937 chronicle quoted above, again without reference to Charles Jean. Elsewhere, Eliade describes the "Jerusalem elite" as "intolerant and fanatical." He also uses the phrase "natural evolution," as well as the "monotheistic elite of Jerusalem."[36] This terminology of organicity and naturality appears in the most essential question Eliade attempts to deal with in this review:

> [T]he fundamental problem of Judaism is this: *Is monotheism a category specific to the Judaic spirit or not?* Did the Jew (or the Semite in general) discover it in a natural fashion, in an *organic* [manner], because he had to discover it, because *he could not do otherwise*, because monotheism alone conformed to his mental structure? Or was monotheism the experience of an elite very restrained in the times that immediately followed Moses, very active during the period of the exile, intolerant and fanatical in the postexilic centuries?[37]

What is the basic difference between the elite and the masses? Eliade is quite explicit: "While Jacob (namely the tradition of the mosaic elites, which are monotheistic) receives that primeval symbol with all its metaphysical juice, giving to it a theistic nuance, the Palestinian populations transformed that symbolic formula in a 'concrete religious experience,' living and personifying it."[38]

This is an interesting point of speculation concerning the original vision of the elite and its transformation. Indeed, Eliade elsewhere speculates that:

> The example of Bethel seems to us to be significant. Indubitably, the Palestinian *populations* were acquainted with a god Bethel, just as we found in the pantheon of the Jews from Elephantine. But the "monotheistic" elites in Jerusalem were watching, who faithfully preserved Moses' message. And in the Ancient testament there are sufficient indications that there were true religious fights against the sanctuary of Bethel, where tradition made Jacob see the ladder of the angels and the house of God, while the Palestinian peasants were seeing just the god Bethel.[39]

This distinction between the more abstractly-oriented elite and the more concrete and experiential life of the population occurs earlier on the same page and becomes more explicit some lines later: "This tendency for the concrete, for the personal, for the organic is almost 'physiological'; this 'experience' has deep roots in the soil of all of Asia and has as its flowers the popular orgies."[40]

We may safely assume that, for Eliade, the concreteness of the religious experience of the Israelite population or peasants is similar to or has been preserved by the Elephantine Israelites. This emphasis on the population stems, indubitably, from Vincent, whom he quotes quite explicitly to this effect.[41] In the same period, a major religious revolution took place by force in the land of Israel, or as he puts it elsewhere, "the appearance of the mosaic message means a great rupture of level, which almost changed the mental evolution of mankind."[42]

In pondering the possible identity of the unidentified Jerusalemite elites, one must consider that a small town like the ancient Jerusalem did not have a plethora of social or political layers. Since messianism was not a pressing issue during the period of the first temple, and since there also was no elite dedicated to "monotheism" as its function, what remains from Eliade's short list by dint of elimination is prophetism— the prophets are the elite he had in mind. It was they (I propose Eliade imagined) who did the repressive job. They did indeed criticize the cult's concrete elements of worship and sacrifices.[43] However, this vision of the Jerusalemite elite as prophets is highly problematic, to put it mildly, from the social point of view. Prophets were almost invariably part of the opposition to not only popular or any other type of idolatry but also to the highest elites active in Jerusalem—the king and the priests. And the only influential Jerusalemite elite that indeed could count was the priestly elite, who were quite immersed in performing rituals at the center of the world, considered to be the temple in Jerusalem, which corresponded to the heavenly city. The rupture allegedly introduced by the Jerusalemite elites, about which Eliade is so insistent, is a matter of speculation. I am not going to debate this complex question here, but what seems edifying to me is the fact that Eliade's presentation conflicts with another of his stances expressed earlier in the very same year. In the monograph entitled *Babylonian Cosmology and Alchemy*, Eliade deals with the importance of the geographical center, *axis mundi*, or homologies between heaven and earth, adducing Jewish material to support his view.[44] In this book, however, there is no mention of a mosaic revolution, or of Jerusalemite elites for that matter. He quotes Jewish material dealing with issues central to his vision of cosmic religion without hesitation and without differentiating it from the plethora of testimonies he used from many other religions.

We have, therefore, in the very same year, two different views expressed by Eliade. On the one hand, the mosaic revolution removed the concrete, the affinity between heaven and earth, the omphalic vision of sacred geography, and on the other hand, these religious elements remained for some centuries in rabbinic literature and, as we have seen above, in later Jewish literatures—all of them elite literatures of Judaism. The piece on Vincent's book was printed in November 1937, and in this essay is a reference to the monograph on Babylonia, which hence was in print at the time and must have been accomplished in late 1936 or very early 1937.

What happened in the interval between the printing of these two diverging approaches? The most interesting testimony for the change in Eliade's attitude to Jews and Judaism is given in the autobiography of his friend, the Jewish Romanian writer Mihail Sebastian. On February 25, 1937, he noted in his journal that Eliade converted to the Iron Guard: "Mircea Eliade's more recent stories in *Vremea* were more and more 'legionnaire.'"[45] Eliade's adherence to the right-wing Rumanian political scene no doubt left traces on his attitude to Judaism, and I believe that Sebastian's testimony is reliable as corroborated by the analysis suggested above.

It would be simplistic, though, to reduce Eliade's dichotomy between the Jerusalemite elites and the rural population of the land of Israel during the first temple period to an unfortunate anti-Semitic slide toward the right. I believe that something much deeper in Eliade's worldview, originating several years before he adopted the ideology of the Iron Guard, should also be taken into consideration. In the summer of 1931, while waiting to leave India, he wrote: "It was precisely the peasant roots of a good part of our Romanian culture that compelled us to transcend nationalism and cultural provincialism and to aim for 'universalism.' The common elements of Indian, Balkan, and Mediterranean folk cultures prove to me that it is here that organic universalism exists, that it is the result of a common history (the history of peasant cultures) and not an abstract construct."[46]

This modest international peasant religion was conceived of not just as a culture in itself, but also as a superior and somehow more universal culture, which became a leitmotif in Eliade's academic activity. In many ways, it remained the top priority on his agenda and guided much of what he wrote afterwards. Sometimes it amounted to an attempt to establish, at least obliquely, the superiority of Rumanian agrarian culture. This statement is corroborated by two stories printed in 1932 after his return from India to Rumania in *Cuvîntul*, the Bucharest-based newspaper on which he collaborated. In a dispute on the need of alphabetization of Rumanian peasants, Eliade took an interesting position: he did not oppose it, but claimed that peasants have their own cultural style and assumes that Rumania is at a point of no return with the project of alphabetization. However, the tone in which he describes the process is almost elegiatic: "It [d]oes not matter how much we may regret, we cannot return to the organic rural culture."[47] He repeatedly resorts to the "centauric nature" of any important culture, which is rooted in life and earth.[48] He insists that: "The rural Rumanians, for example, have known a culture of an organicity yet unattained by any official 'culture,' leaning to the Occident."[49] He recurrently emphasizes that culture implies a return to nature. In 1935, Eliade envisions only two layers in Rumania that are indispensable: the peasants and the creative elites.[50] These and similar views expressed in the first half of the 1930s demonstrate that the concept of elite versus popular culture, the latter of which is conceived of as rural *par excellence*, is a problematic that antedates the review of Vincent's book in late 1937. This mission of documenting, describing and disseminating the importance of cosmic Christianity of the Rumanian peasant remained a leitmotif in Eliade's thought. So, for example, we read in a note from July 1960 a statement quite reminiscent of that quoted from his description of his mission while in India: "I think I can count myself among the rare Europeans who have succeeded in revaluing nature by discovering the dialectics of hierophanies and the structure of the cosmic religiosity...I arrived at cosmic sacralities by reflecting on the daily experience of Rumanian and Bengali peasants."[51]

Eliade projects this type of distinction upon an ancient society whose social structure was even more obscure than the Rumanian situation in the 1930s. In his most famous books, he reiterates his problematic presentation of Judaism as both changing the course of religious history of mankind and possessing the same ideas that reflect the concrete attitude to sacred places. In fact, the kernel of the *Myth of Eternal Return* is no more than a representation of these two diverging approaches without attempting to resolve the quandary they present. Given the role this book played in the dissemination of Eliade's view, let me attempt to substantiate this claim. Eliade reiterates his views about the possible natural development of ancient Judaism in the direction represented by the Elephantine papyri, this time referring explicitly to Vincent's book.[52] Here, however, the elites are no more "violent and fanatical" as they were in the Rumanian essay, and they are identified as the "prophets."[53] This elite is presented as involved in religious education, which is now much more concerned with the introduction of the new value of history rather than with shaping a less concrete religion; it appears that a fascinating and miraculous transformation took place between 1937 and 1946 in the ancient Jewish elites.[54] However, at the same time, Eliade presents much of the same evidence on centers, omphalologies, parallel cities, sacred trees, et cetera, that he adduced in *Babylonian Cosmology and Alchemy* and resorts to roughly the same scholarly bibliography.[55]

With time, the range of the Jewish elite, which allegedly eliminated the concrete aspects of religion, expanded in Eliade's writing. In his memoirs of 1965, Eliade wrote when reading Gershom Scholem's *On the Kabbalah and Its Symbolism*: "In Kabbalah we have to do with a new, real creation of the Judaic religious genius, due to the need to recover a part of the cosmic religiosity smothered and persecuted as much by the prophets as by the later Talmudic rigorists."[56] The addition of the rigorist Talmudists to the repressive Jewish elites has much to do with Scholem's theory about the repression of myths in rabbinic thought, expressed in its starkest manner in the book that Eliade was reading.[57] The violence of the elite is eliminated, but they are still described as persecutors who suffocated the "true" natural religion. However, late in their history, the Jews who invented and accepted

Kabbalah return to normality. The medieval recuperation of the repressed elements restores the forgotten and forlorn cosmicity. Finally, the Jews return to the common denominator. Indeed, while reading Scholem's book, Eliade reacted positively to Kabbalah because "it will be interesting to compare cosmic Christianity, that is the belief of the rural populations of southeastern Europe and of the Mediterranean, with these medieval and postmedieval Judaic religious creations."[58]

It is therefore neither the uniqueness of Kabbalah nor its exceptional nature that attracted Eliade's attention but its alleged conformity with the ubiquitous cosmic religion, the possibility that it could be inserted into his general scheme of cosmic religiosity. To be sure, on numerous occasions Eliade judges texts only on the basis of secondary literature, dealing with material that is extremely complex and the meaning of which may remain a matter of debate forever. In its vast majority, Eliade's *oeuvre* is an interpretation of interpretations—a reading of secondary literature that in itself is an interpretation. Such reading is guided by essentialistic presuppositions that are highly selective. He believed in some form of primordial universalism that embraces all archaic religions. This is a true alternative for the fall of later religions and of modern man, a modern form of *prisca theologia* or of a *philosophia perennis*. The paradisiacal state in which the first couple safely lived in the shadow of the two trees in the bliss of nature was discontinued by a sin that caused the fall, and this nostalgia for paradise is recurrent in Eliade's approach to religion. So Eliade was certainly influenced by the manner in which Scholem described Rabbinism as "rigorist," as the:

> hypertrophy of ritual, which became all-pervasive... accompanied by no magical action. The rites of remembrance produce no effect... and what they conjure up without the slightest gesture of conjuration is the memory, the community of generations, and the identification of the pious with the experience of the founding generation that received the Revelation. The ritual of rabbinic Judaism makes nothing happen and transforms nothing...there is something strangely sober and dry about the rites of remembrance with which the Jew calls to mind his unique historical identity."[59]

Eliade and Scholem are both towering figures in the modern study of religion. Nevertheless, their areas of research were very different. Eliade, an admirer of Hindu religiosity, focused his academic studies on the mythical side of religion in general, whereas the mystical was addressed only rarely and tangentially. Scholem focused his academic writings on the mysticism of Judaism; the problem of the myth *per se* was only a secondary issue. Though he used the term frequently in his writings, Scholem did not attempt to construct an independent theory of myth or of Jewish mythical thought. His assumption was that we all understand the nature of the mythical phenomenon.

The first time Scholem directly and elaborately addressed the question of myth was the result of an invitation to a conference in Ascona, where this topic was predetermined. In his essay on "Kabbalah and Myth," mythical rituals were not addressed; this occurred only in 1950, when for the first time Scholem explored the distinction between rabbinic ritual and mythical ritual. The introduction of the criterion of orgiastic elements in the definition of the real mythical ritual is strange and superfluous in this specific context of Jewish tradition. It is reasonable that Scholem attempted to adopt categories proposed by Eliade in order to formulate better the difference between the two versions of Judaism. Eliade, for reasons of his own, embraced views connecting ancient Hindu and Balkan religions. A conspicuously negative attitude toward Rabbinism becomes especially evident in the article Scholem read at Ascona rather than in earlier or even later discussions on this issue. Hence, it seems that he adopted Eliade's criterion for "authentic" religion in order to apply it to Kabbalism or to define Rabbinism in a negative way.

To what extent Eliade's reticent attitude toward the Judeo-Christian tradition influenced Scholem's presentation of Rabbinism—which, to be sure, also had other sources—is a psychological matter that I cannot address here. However, it is noteworthy that the two scholars did indeed revolt separately against the common versions of the religions within which they were born. If for Eliade real Christianity was a cosmic religion to be found only in India in his generation, it seems that for Scholem, "the heart of Judaism"—as he described Kabbalah from time to time—was deeply structured by Gnosticism. In both cases, the attempt to revolutionize the understanding of religions in general and the understanding of specific religions in particular was motivated by an initial alienation from the institutionalized forms of the religions these scholars encountered. Eliade was much more fascinated by the archaic peasant religions of the Balkans than with official Orthodox Christianity. The peasant religiosity was reminiscent, in his opinion, of the Hindu cosmic and mythical religion. Scholem was attracted by the anarchic elements of Gnosticism, which allegedly served as the main fountain whence the "dry" rabbinic religion drank in order to become fertile. Though these two scholars considered their academic work to express the religious genius of their specific religions and culture, they imported conceptions from outside in order to elucidate the essence of the respective religions.

Revolt against or antagonism toward modern religiosity motivated the iconoclastic approaches of these two scholars. They were concerned not only with the past but also with the implications of their scholarly activity for the future. Eliade addressed what he considered to be the universals of archaic religion as they surfaced in tens of religions; nevertheless, his main enthrallment was mythical archaic religiosity. Scholem directed his efforts to describe only one type of mysticism, mostly medieval and post-medieval, but he repeated time and again the importance of gnostic, namely mythical, substrata of the later developments. It seems that the ambiance of Ascona, both because of the issues discussed there and because of the spiritual concerns of the participants, contributed to Scholem's decision to explore the issue of myth and mythical ritual in a phenomenological manner. The attempt to reevaluate the archaic in order to reinstitute the "lost" soul to modern man was an implicit though integral part of the agenda of the group meeting at Ascona; Scholem and Eliade perfectly integrated themselves into this endeavor. The revisionist approaches of the two scholars were more radical in comparison to those of most of the other participants. Though they cannot be defined as followers of Jung in the restricted sense of the word, the activity of Scholem and Eliade fell into the orbit of the Jungian agenda calling for a reevaluation of the role of the irrational as an essential task for modern approaches.

We turn now to another description of rabbinic ritual, which Scholem contrasted with the Kabbalistic. As quoted above, he criticized the former as making nothing happen and as transforming nothing. Indeed, I cannot comment on whether or not either Kabbalistic or rabbinic ritual really transforms anything. I assume that Scholem intended to indicate the different types of awareness that characterize the observant of the commandments. In this case, the Kabbalists indeed strove to influence the divine pleroma through the peculiar manner in which they performed the Jewish rites. But if the self-awareness of the performer is a major criterion for a different conception of historical versus mythical ritual, then I introduce a well-known rabbinic ritual that may contest Scholem's assertion as I understand it.

According to an ancient tradition stemming from the Mishnah period, it was incumbent upon groups of Israelites to recite the account of creation concomitant with the performance of sacrifices in the temple. The rationale offered for this practice, as explained by a fourth-century Palestinian Ammora, Rabbi Jacob bar Aha, is that "without the [practice of] *Ma`amadot*, neither heaven nor earth could remain in existence."[60] Therefore, an important—perhaps the most important—Jewish ritual, sacrifice, was understood in late antiquity as being crucial to maintaining the universe. Interestingly enough, this ritual was accompanied by the recitation of the first chapter of Genesis, which has some commemorative implications that, nevertheless, do not attenuate the mythical consciousness of the performers.

The conception inherent in this issue can be compared to another characterization of the rabbinic ritual in Scholem: "What in rabbinical Judaism separated the law from myth? The answer is clear: the dissociation of the law from cosmic events."[61] This alleged dissociation is very precarious, as the above example testifies. Its task was to stress the importance of the law and of Jewish practices in certain ancient and medieval Jewish circles and attribute a universe-maintaining role to their performance. As mentioned earlier, according to the ancient conception of the *Ma`amadot*, the welfare of the universe depended upon the performance of sacrifices and the recitation of the first chapter of Genesis. Therefore, a significant relationship between the commandments and a cosmic process is indeed found in rabbinic Judaism. History seems to be entirely absent from this instance of mythical ritual. The performance of the recitation is not connected to the exact moment of the New Year, so envisioning the role of the *Ma`amadot* as enacting the precise moment of the creation is strange. It has much more to do with the maintenance of creation than with a return to the *illud tempus*. What is nevertheless important in this case of the *Ma`amadot* is the fact that rabbinic Judaism found theological motivation for a ritual, a rationale that has some cosmic implications. Therefore, the assumption that the rabbinic form of religion is totally devoid of cosmic dimensions is somehow surprising, even more so when we remember the connections between the righteous as the pillar of the world and as the person who maintains it, as seen in chapters two and three above. Eighteenth-century Hasidism, in my opinion, may be portrayed as closer to nature and to the concrete than Kabbalah. It celebrated worship in corporeality, `avodah be-gashmiyyut; a certain form of immanentism is much more evident.

5. ORGANISM, ORGANIZATION AND THE SPECTRUM BETWEEN THEM

In his newspaper story "Between Culture and Alphabet," Eliade draws a stark dichotomy between the organic culture and artificial organization related to semi-literates—which he calls *semidocts* and which he utterly detested. In Rumanian, this dichotomy was expressed in a fascinating aliteration: "*organismul (nu organizaţia)*."[62] This antagonism differentiates Eliade's approach from that of the late Ioan P. Culianu, and also from my own. What is characteristic of the organism is its congenital connectiveness. It is not a free combination of components, brought together after they already exist, or an artifact that assembles disparate elements in new manners of integration. For Eliade, religion is an organic original given, the evolution of which is basically a negative change. Moreover, he sees a deep affinity among various religions and depicts the differences between them as a matter of nuance. So, for example, he confesses: "continuous reading reveals above all the *fundamental unity* of religious phenomena and at the same time the inexhaustible newness of their expressions."[63] This is but another formulation of the notion of "organic universalism" that he conceived in 1931, as seen in the quote adduced above from his journal. In other words, we may call Eliade's approach a basically rural one that emerged during his encounter with India and as a result of the more general movement of some Rumanian intellectuals toward the village as the quintessence of Rumanian culture in the early 1930s.

Culianu, on the other hand, was an urban type of intellectual. For him, the entire realm of religion and of human creativity is a matter of different combinations of some basic elements that return in various forms of interaction or systems. In other words, evolution in his thought is not the manner in which an organism develops over time, but rather the arrangement of the same elements in new and different forms of interaction. The concepts natural and organic that played so central a role in Eliade's Romanticized vision of the cosmic religion have no role in Culianu's writing from the very beginning. He is concerned much more with differences—their importance and their histories—than with common denominators. The question is how, according to Culianu, did systems emerge from these basic elements? Do these combinations occur due to a latent possibility that is actualized systemically? Are they the result of social, political or spiritual circumstances, independent of any individual or group? Or are they the result of human choices that bring some elements together and project them in history? To the best of my knowledge, Culianu did not explicitly address these three possibilities; specific reasons for the emergence of one combination or another did not attract too much of his attention. But the third possibility is least congruent with Culianu's views, since for him the system is much stronger than the individual. In a manner reminiscent of Foucault and Derrida, Culianu gives priority to the system as a more comprehensive power that determines much of human creativity. On the other hand, Culianu is less concerned with social, economic or political determinism, though he recurrently asserts that the materialization of one combination or another is found throughout history. To a great degree, circumstances factor as places in which spiritual developments are embodied rather than as their shaper. By this process of elimination, therefore, the first alternative emerges as the most probable: the assumption that there is some immanent force within the basic elements and their interactions. Since these interactions are rather mathematical, and ideally all combinations of them are possible, organicity hardly can be considered an inherent dimension of such combinations.

In lieu of offering a methodological compromise between organism and organization, I assume that religion changes, that such change follows the laws of the growing organism and that these changes do not automatically imply the destruction of organicity. However, organization may start with a more technical bringing together of elements stemming from diverse systems and thus may assume some form of artificial cohesion. With time, the religious imagination may cement the affinities among these diverse elements and create something that is presented as organic. This elaboration is mainly the result of the speculative efforts of elites. Therefore, the methodological alternatives are not limited to the two extremes of artificial organization versus congenial organicity but include a wide spectrum of different compromises, syntheses and attempts to reduce tensions and create new linkages among disparate conceptual and spiritual modes of thought. Neither the congenital organicity of a system nor the artificiality of the *combinatoria* may account for the diversity of variants found within one type of religion or even within one of its major phases.

What I propose, in general terms, is the exploration of transitions between the relatively artificial stage of a nascent religion and its more organic—though never a closed organism—more mature stage of development.

I do not pass judgment on the superiority or inferiority of any of these stages; they simply represent, in my opinion, different stages in the organization of religious knowledge. Neither do I refer to progress when I describe the later stage as more mature. Rather, I assume that for the believer, the various forms of organization, initial and mature, are as coherent as any other system, a coherence that is not the result of systemic cohesion but of the deep conviction of that believer. It does not matter how frequently scholars point out the divergences among the various parts of the Hebrew Bible; the Jewish or Christian believer will adopt some form of harmonization that will "solve" the problem. This is also the case with the Greek Bible; the divergences between Judaism and Hellenism, deep as they indeed may be, are more a matter of scholarly awareness than a problem with which believers are preoccupied. The deep discrepancies between biblical sources and different forms of Greek and Hellenistic philosophical systems did not deter first-rank thinkers like Philo and Maimonides from offering syntheses of the two conceptual corpora. My assumption as a scholar is that these syntheses are artificial, but they remain part and parcel of some influential Jewish and Christian ways of thinking.

In our case, let us draw attention to the conjugation of the concept of the eschatological pillar with that of two paradises. It goes without saying that the theme of paradise existed and still exists in numerous documents without reference to the concept of the pillar or the eschatological. The same is true in Manichaeanism, where the eschatological pillar is found together with the wheel of souls but not with the two paradises. However, at a certain moment in time, the two concepts are combined in Zoharic literature, elaborated upon, and finally put in the service of the personal journey by the Besht. Artificial combination is also obvious in the case of the association among Jacob's ladder, the Homeric *aurea catena* and its Platonic interpretation in the writings of Renaissance Christian Kabbalists. These are cases of what I call intercorporal readings—the intersection of one conceptual system with another—that played a cardinal role in the history of Jewish speculative literatures.[64] Interestingly enough, his emphasis on organicity notwithstanding, Eliade was aware of the possible fertility of syncretism, though he limits its discussion solely to Christianity.[65] I am not aware of any effort by him to account for the potential tension between organicity and syncretism as two dimensions of religion.

Reverting to organicity-organization alternatives, I believe that they are not extremes only in the realm of religion. They do not account for the fuller forms of most religions, which developed and created new nets of meaning by integrating "alien" forms of thought. The very development of religions from initial revelations, with relatively simple concepts and ethics, to much more complex ways of thought seems to me evident. After absorbing these revelations, the tensions and the affinities among its different elements, whether true or imaginary, gradually emerge. A great part of the fabric of religious literature is the result of attempts to overcome tensions, strengthen affinities and add more, tenuous as they are for a scholar acquainted with the history of ideas.

Eliade's attempt to operate on the simple assumption that the stasis of the primordial is preferable to developments introduced by other understandings of religion ignores the obvious. Change is inevitable. This does not mean that change is good or bad; I embrace no form of evolutionary assumption regarding progress. Eliade's lamenting tone regarding the deterioration of religion as the result of change introduced by one elite or another is, from a scholarly perspective, deplorable. Artificiality is not by definition good or bad. Neither are "original religions." Such epithets reflect only the vantage point of the scholar or his predilections.

6. Time, Ritual, Technique

The restriction of the ascent to specific privileged places—Jerusalem—or to pillars, ladders, bridges or lines is sometimes related to specific moments in time that recur and that sometimes are cyclical, such as the New Year in the case of the Besht.[66] Such moments may be described as *microchronoi*.[67] Techniques related to the ascents of the soul, such as the incantations in the *Epistle of the Besht*, are not part of regular communal ritual but tend to be related to special openings in time and space that facilitate the ascent. The linkage of time, technique and revelation is found as early as the thirteenth century.[68] Thus, the description of Judaism as a religion that represents a unilinear vision of time found so often in Eliade's writings is flawed. This is true not only in modest cases of shamanic understandings of the activities of the major figures in Jewish mysticism, but also in the importance of cyclical time characteristic of so many Jewish rituals. Both cyclical visions of time and discussions of the pillar reflect religious attitudes that differ sharply from the simplistic descriptions of this religion that still linger in scholarship.

Though I hesitate to create too strong a connection between restrictions on place and restrictions on time, it seems to me that such a linkage is nevertheless quite meaningful in many cases. Suspicious as I am of automatic or organic affinities between different aspects of a religious outlook, the concept of *Gestalt*-coherence as discussed above may allow for a better understanding of the emergence of some structures over the passage of time after two different elements have been brought together within a certain religious school.

I finish with a general though important observation made while dealing with the material analyzed here. The pillars referred to in these texts are not tangible pieces of architecture, as is often the case in popular religions in Europe or the *stupa* in Buddhism.[69] The term "pillar" recurs in other contexts in Judaism, like the "pillar of prayer." In the context of our discussions, however, the pillar is understood in two ways. It is either projected in transcendental realms, like paradise, and sensed in some form of imaginary homiletic experience or identified with the righteous, the body of the person who performs the rites or techniques that transform him into a pontific figure. Whether imaginary or concrete, these pillars inspired the lives, dreams and aspirations of many Jews, and a sense of personal transcendence, of touching higher worlds, informed their experiences and their performance of religious deeds. Were these experiences less concrete, meaningful or formative than those of worshippers of "real" pillars? This is a question that stands at the very basis of the understanding—or, in my opinion, the misunderstanding—of religion as proposed by Eliade. He implies that human feelings were triggered by the natural and concrete stimuli that impacted the lives of the archaic believers. He was a metaphysician of the sacred in search of its manifestations. This is quite a one-sided way to see the nature of man, and maybe also of reality. Under the linguistic influence in recent decades of Derrida, Eco or Rorty, words are regarded as formative if not more so than anything else in "reality." What was once conceived as casuism and legalism in Jewish mysticism may turn into a way to conjure imaginary universes that produced meaning. The discussions above did not involve the mere copying of terms from one book to another by a learned scholar. Rather, they created worldviews that conferred forms of meaning upon a certain way of life, influenced by strength of belief rather than solely concrete artifacts. Meaning wells not only from the external world, as Eliade implies, but even more so from the strength of one's conviction, from the powers of one's imagination, from the will of the community to allow these types of religious *imaginaire* to flourish. Religious man is someone shaped not just by natural factors and the triggers that bombard him but also, and in my opinion eminently, by the *imaginaire* adopted by a certain individual or school. As such, I do not assume religious man may be spoken of simply and neatly, since different forms of religiosities are shaped by different elites. Here, rather, my concern is with some of those elites who shared some elements in common with archaic religions. These common denominators are sometimes related to earlier elements in the history of Judaism, as exemplified by the Hagigah dictum and Kabbalistic elaborations on it; sometimes the result of Manichaean influence; and sometimes various combinations of the two.

NOTES

1. See Moshe Idel, *Enchanted Chains* (forthcoming).
2. See Aron Gurwitsch, "Phenomenology of Perception: Perceptual Implications," in *An Invitation to Phenomenology*, ed. James M. Edie (Chicago: Quadrangle Books, 1965), p. 21; and Moshe Idel, *Hasidism: Between Ecstasy and Magic* (Albany: State University of New York Press, 1995), pp. 49–50.
3. See the sources adduced in R. Mach, *Der Zaddik in Talmud und Midrasch* (Leiden: Brill, 1957), p. 4, n. 4.
4. *Sifra'*, Be-Huqotai, III, fol. 111b; and Mach, *Der Zaddik*, pp. 209–10.
5. Mircea Eliade, *Yoga, Immortality and Freedom* (Princeton: Princeton University Press, 1971), pp. 115–17.
6. See Gedaliahu G. Stroumsa, *Savoir et Salut* (Paris: Le Cerf, 1992), pp. 267–68.
7. See Cyril Glasse, "Crypto-Manicheism in the Abbasid Empire," in *Manicheismo e oriente christiano antico*, eds. Luigi Cirillo and Alois van Tongerloo (Lovanii-Neapoli: Brepols, 1997), pp. 119–20.
8. Henry Corbin, *Cyclical Time and Ismaili Gnosis* (London: Kegan Paul International, 1983), pp. 111–13.
9. Henry Corbin, *The Man of Light in Iranian Sufism*, trans. Nancy Pearson (Boulder, Colo. and London: Shambala, 1978), pp. 48, 52, 54, 56 and 134–35.
10. See *Sefer ha-Gedarim*, "The Book of Definitions," originally written in Arabic but preserved in full Latin and Hebrew translations and in another,

partial Hebrew, one. See Alexander Altmann and Samuel M. Stern, *Isaac Israeli: A Neoplatonic Philosopher of the Early Tenth Century* (Oxford: Oxford University Press, 1958), pp. 25–26 and p. 192. According to the complete Hebrew version printed by H. Hirschfeld in *Festschrift zum achtzigsten Geburtstag Moritz Steinschneider* (Leipzig, 1896), p. 133, it is also possible to translate "created by" as "created from" the power of God. This passage does not occur in the fragments published by Alexander Altmann, "Isaac Israeli's Book of Definitions: Some Fragments of a Second Hebrew Translation," *Journal of Semitic Studies* II (1957): pp. 232–42. "His paradise" is translated from *Gan `Edno*. In the Hebrew version of Ibn Tzaddiq's *Microcosmos*, influenced as it was by Israeli's text, it is written as *Ginah*, "Her Garden," which may reflect the Arabic term for paradise, *Jannah*. Another identification of paradise and light is found in Rabbi Abraham bar Hiyya's *Megilat ha-Megalleh* (in Hebrew), ed. Adolf Poznanski (Berlin: Mekize Nirdamim, 1924), pp. 16–17. The vision of paradise as light occurs previously in the hymns of Ephrem the Syrian; see Nicholas Sed, "Les hymnes sur le paradis," *Le Museon* 81 (1968): pp. 482–87.

11. *Sod ha-Keruvim*, Ms. Parma, de Rossi 1230, fols. 108b–109a; Ms. Paris BN 823, fol. 823, fol. 54a. The first quote is Genesis 2:10; the second, Proverbs 10:25.

12. *Sod ha-Keruvim*, Ms. Parma, de Rossi 1230, fol. 109b. "By" him also means "because of." The verse is Isaiah 27:5.

13. See above the text from *Tiqqunei Zohar*.

14. See Gershom Scholem, *On the Kabbalah and Its Symbolism*, trans. R. Manheim (New York: Schocken Books, 1969), pp. 22 and 36; idem, *On Jews and Judaism in Crisis*, ed. Werner J. Dannhauser (New York: Schocken Books, 1976), p. 48. The second quote is from idem, *Major Trends in Jewish Mysticism* (New York: Schocken Books, 1967), pp. 27 and 28. This approach has been accepted by Joseph Dan, *The Early Kabbalah* (New York: Paulist Press, 1986), pp. 9–13 and permeates his collection of articles, *On Sanctity* (in Hebrew)(Jerusalem, The Magnes Press, 1987).

15. Isaiah Tishby, *Paths of Faith and Heresy* (in Hebrew)(Ramat Gan: Masadah, 1964), p. 13; and idem, *The Wisdom of the Zohar: An Anthology of Texts*, trans. D. Goldstein (London and Washington: Littman Library, 1991), vol. I, p. 284.

16. See, especially, Moshe Idel, *Absorbing Perfections: Kabbalah and Interpretation* (New Haven: Yale University Press, 2002), pp. 272–313; and idem, "The Function of Symbols in G. G. Scholem" (in Hebrew), *Jewish Studies* 38 (1998): pp. 43–72.

17. See, for example, the clear distinction in *Tiqqunei Zohar*, fol. 14b.

18. See Idel, *Absorbing Perfections*, pp. 221–49.

19. See *Zohar* II, fol. 266a; III, fols. 227a, 228a, all texts from *Ra`ya' Meheimna'*. See also chapter 2 in the current study.

20. Compare to Rabbi Moshe de Leon, *Sheqel ha-Qodesh*, ed. Charles Mopsik (Los Angeles: Cherub Press, 1996), p. 90.

21. See *Tiqqunei Zohar*, fol. 7a; Tiqqun 30, fol. 74ab.

22. Gershom Scholem, *Kabbalah* (Jerusalem: Keter Publishing House, 1974), p. 4; and R. J. Z. Werblowsky, *Joseph Karo: Lawyer and Mystic* (Oxford: Oxford University Press, 1962), pp. 40 and 158–59.

23. See, for example, the basic approach of Martha Himmelfarb, *Ascent to Heaven in Jewish and Christian Apocalypses* (New York: Oxford University Press, 1993) versus Michael Stone, "A Reconsideration of Apocalyptic Visions," *HTR* 96:2 (2003): pp. 167–80; and Daniel Merkur, "The Visionary Practices of Jewish Apocalyptists," in *The Psychoanalytical Study of Society*, eds. L. Bryce Boyer and S. A. Grolnik (Hillsdale, N.J., 1989), pp. 119–48.

24. See Michael Fishbane, *Biblical Myth and Rabbinic Mythmaking* (Oxford: Oxford University Press, 2003).

25. See, most recently, Yair Lorberbaum, *The Image of God: Halakhah and Aggadah* (in Hebrew) (Jerusalem and Tel Aviv: Schocken, 2004); Jonathan Garb, "Power, Ritual, and Myth—A Comparative Methodological Proposal," in *Myth in Judaism* (in Hebrew), eds. M. Idel and I. Gruenwald (Jerusalem: Shazar Center, 2004), pp. 53–71; and Moshe Idel, "Leviathan and its Consort: From Talmudic to Kabbalistic Myth" (in Hebrew), in ibid., pp. 145–86.

26. See, for example, Mircea Eliade, *Images and Symbols: Studies in Religious Symbolism* (Princeton: Princeton University Press Bollingen Series, 1991), pp. 43–45; and idem, *Cosmos and History: The Myth of the Eternal Return* (New York: Harper Torchbooks, 1959), pp. 13–17.

27. See Mircea Eliade, *50 de Conferințe Radiofonice 1932–1938* (Bucharest: Humanitas, 2001), pp. 248–52 and pp. 263–67.

28. Paul Mus, *Barabudur* (Paris: Geuthner, 1935), reprinted in *Drumul spre centru*, eds. G. Liiceanu and A. Pleşu (Bucharest: Univers, 1991), pp. 184–97.

29. Mircea Eliade, "Before and After the Biblical Miracle" (in Romanian), in *Revista Fundațiilor Regale*, vol. IV, no. 3 (Bucharest, 1937), pp. 657–61. The quote is on p. 661.

30. Albert Vincent, *La Religion des Judeo-Arameens d'Elephantine* (Paris: Geuthner, 1937).

31. Mircea Eliade, "Between Elephantine and Jerusalem" (in Romanian), printed originally in *Revista Fundațiilor regale* IV (November 1937): pp. 421–26; and reprinted in Liiceanu and Pleşu, *Drumul spre centru*, pp. 225–31.

32. Liiceanu and Pleşu, *Drumul spre centru*, p. 228.

33. Ibid., p. 229. Emphases in the original.

34. Ibid., p. 229.

35. Ibid., p. 231.

36. Ibid., pp. 228, 229 and 231.

37. Ibid., p. 229. Emphases in the original.

38. Ibid., p. 230. Emphases in the original.

39. Ibid., p. 229. Emphases in the original.

40. Ibid., p. 230.

41. Ibid., p. 229.

42. Ibid., p. 231. The Rumanian formulations in this passage are a little obscure. "Rupture of level" is translated from *rupere de nivel*. Elsewhere in this essay (p. 230), Eliade uses this phrase in a positive manner to describe the revelation of God. See also his commentary in Magda and Petru Ursache, eds., *Meşterul Manole* (Iasi: Editura Junimea, 1992), pp. 103–04.

43. See also Mircea Eliade, *Patterns in Comparative Religion*, trans. Rosemary Sheed (New York: Meridian, 1972), pp. 4 and 74.

44. Ibid., pp. 495–96, 500–03 and 505–07.

45. Mihail Sebastian, *Journal: 1935–1944*, eds. Gabriela Omăt and Leon Volovici (Bucharest: Humanitas, 1996), p. 114. Though I am aware that there were some Romanian intellectuals who doubted the authenticity of the passage quoted, I see no reason to agree with their skepticism since my analysis of the book reviews confirms the content from an independent angle. *Vremea* is a rightist newspaper, and the articles by Eliade published there constitute his most anti-Jewish texts, though he later claimed that they did not reflect his own opinion but rather responses to questions he was asked. I hope to deal with this issue in a separate study.

46. Mircea Eliade, *Autobiography, Volume I, 1907–1937: Journey East, Journey West*, trans. Mac Linscott Ricketts (San Francisco: Harper and Row, 1981), p. 204. The French original is:

"Le vieux fonds payan d'ou la culture roumaine tirait le meilleur d'elle-meme etait justement ce qui devait nous inciter a depasser le nationalisme et le provincialisme culturels, et a tendre vers l'universalite. L'existence d'elements communs aux cultures populaires indienne, mediteraneene et balkanique prouvait a mes yeux que c'etait ici, chez nous, qu'existait ce sentiment instinctif d'universalite qui, loin d'etre concu de facon abstraite, etait au contraire le fruit d'une longue histoire commune, celle des civilisations payennes." Mircea Eliade, *Memoire I 1907–1937*, (Paris: Gallimard, 1980), p. 288. See also pp. 202–04.

47. Mircea Eliade, "Between Culture and Alphabet," in Ursache and Ursache, *Meşterul Manole*, p. 201.

48. See Eliade, "Culture," ibid., pp. 198–99; and ibid., "Between Culture and Alphabet," p. 202. I assume that the emergence of this epitheton has to do with Georges Dumezil, the editor who sent books to Eliade to be reviewed and who printed an essay in 1929 on Centaurs at Geuthner in Paris.

49. Ibid., p. 199.

50. Mircea Eliade, "Rumanian Realities," reprinted in Ursache and Ursache, *Mesterul Manole*, pp. 272–73.

51. Mircea Eliade, *No Souvenirs: Journal, 1957–1969*, trans. Fred H. Johnson Jr. (San Francisco: Harper and Row, 1977), p. 101.

52. Mircea Eliade, *Cosmos and History: The Myth of the Eternal Return*, trans. Willard R. Trask (New York: Harper Torchbooks, 1959), p. 108, n. 5.

53. Ibid., pp. 103–04, and p. 108, n. 5.

54. Ibid., p. 107.

55. See ibid. The question is not so much the repetition of the same ideas and bibliography, but the lack of updating and rethinking that should be natural in such instances.

56. Eliade, *No Souvenirs*, p. 266.
57. See, especially, Scholem, *On the Kabbalah*, pp. 98 and 121.
58. Eliade, *No Souvenirs*, p. 267. Compare to Scholem, *On the Kabbalah*, p. 189. For Eliade's review of this book, see his "Cosmic Religion," *Commentary* 41:3 (March 1966): pp. 95–98.
59. Scholem, *On the Kabbalah*, pp. 120–21. On the paradoxical character of this passage, see Harold Bloom, "Scholem: Unhistorical or Jewish Gnosticism," in *Gershom Scholem*, ed. Harold Bloom (New York: Chelsea, 1987), pp. 212–13.
60. *BT, Ta`anit*, fol. 27b. *Ma`amad*, whose plural is *ma`amadot*, is related to sustaining the world, and stems from the same root as `amud, pillar.
61. Scholem, *On the Kabbalah*, p. 94.
62. "Between Culture and Alphabet," in Ursache and Ursache, *Mesterul Manole*, p. 201.
63. Mircea Eliade, *A History of Religious Ideas*, trans. W. R. Task (Chicago: Chicago University Press, 1978), vol. I, p. xv; emphasis in the original.
64. Idel, *Absorbing Perfections*, pp. 251–52, 340–42 and 415–16.
65. Eliade, *A History of Religious Ideas*, vol. II, p. 274.
66. See chapter 4.
67. On microchronos, a category I suggested in the context of a more complex distinction between different categories of time in Judaism, see Moshe Idel, "Some Concepts of Time and History in Kabbalah," *Jewish History and Jewish Memory: Essays in Honor of Yosef Hayim Yerushalmi*, eds. E. Carlebach, J. M. Efron, and D. N. Myers (Hanover and London: Brandeis University Press, 1998), pp. 153–88. The gist of this article is to distinguish between various visions of time in order to qualify the simplistic assumption that "Judaism" adopted just one type of time.
68. See Scholem, *Origins of the Kabbalah*, pp. 241–42; and idem, "*Sidrei Shimmusha' Rabba*'" (in Hebrew), in *Devils, Demons, and Souls: Essays in Demonology*, ed. Esther Liebes (Jerusalem: Makhon be-Tzvi, 2004), pp. 116–44.
69. See the lavish illustrations found in Romulus Vulcanescu, *Coloana Cerului* (Bucharest: Editura Academiei, 1972); and Anna Libera Dallapicola, ed., *The Stupa: Its Religious, Historical and Architectural Significance*, in collaboration with Stephanie Zinge-Ave Lallemant (Wiesbaden: Franz Steiner Verlag, 1980).

Name Index

Subject Index